Abstracts of the

DEBT BOOKS

of the

PROVINCIAL LAND OFFICE OF MARYLAND

Talbot County

Volume I

Liber 46: 1733
Liber 54: 1734-1759
Liber 47: 1738, 1739
Liber 46: 1744
Liber 48: 1748
Liber 49: 1756, 1757-1758

By
V. L. Skinner, Jr.

CLEARFIELD

Printed for Clearfield Company by
Genealogical Publishing Company
Baltimore, Maryland
2016

ISBN 978-0-8063-5823-9

Made in the United States of America

Introduction

The Provincial Land Office of Maryland was responsible for the dispensing of land from 1634 to 1777. Land was initially acquired by a warrant and was then patented. Information concerning these documents are found in the Warrants and Patents series of the Provincial Land Office located at the Maryland State Archives and are indexed by Peter Wilson Coldham in his five-volume series *Settlers of Maryland*, published by Genealogical Publishing Company.

Land was patented according to the desires of the patentee, and the name given to a patent was not necessarily unique within any particular jurisdiction.

The Lord Proprietor's personal hold on land affairs was much weakened during the royal period from 1689 to 1715. However, it was immediately revived when his proprietary rights were restored in 1715 (Hartsook and Skordas, *Land Office and Prerogative Court Records*). Both the Rent Rolls and the Debt Books date from this restoration period.

The Rent Rolls and the Debt Books are the means by which the Lord Proprietor kept track of the rents due him. Each piece of land granted to a person was subject to a yearly rent according to the terms of the patent.

A Rent Roll consists of entries for each tract of land patented, plus the name of the person for whom it was originally surveyed, the present owner, the acreage, and the rent. Alienations, or subsequent sales and leases of the piece of land, are also included.

A Debt Book consists of a list of persons owning land with the names and rents of each tract that he or she owned, all listed in one place under his or her name.

The Debt Books

The Debt Books are arranged by county, by year, and then by the name of the person paying the rent. There are a total of 54 libers, covering all of the counties. The extant Debt Books for the Western Shore counties are essentially annual, dating from 1753 to 1774. (The Debt Books for 1750 for five Western Shore counties–Anne Arundel, Baltimore, Charles, Prince George's, Frederick–are found in the Calvert Papers, located at the Maryland State Archives.) The extant Debt Books for the Eastern Shore counties are also essentially annual, dating from 1733 to 1775.

Each liber contains information for only one county, but for multiple years. For purposes of identification, each section (i.e., year) of any particular liber is given the denotation of the specific year.

Tracking land ownership over various years is particularly important for intestate estates, land inherited by women, and land that is not specified in a will.

The information in this series is presented in a tabular form:

- liber and folio citation, with any pertinent date.
- name of the person paying the taxes.
- name of the tract of land.
- acreage.

Notes to Reader

The following conventions are used in this book:

1. "The" and "A" at the beginning of any tract name has been omitted.
2. The index contains both tract names and surnames, sorted together.

3. "Crossed out" entries in the original libers have been included. as such.
4. Names have been transcribed as they are written; no attempt has been made to standardize any spelling.
5. Introduction and index pages of the original libers have been omitted.

Abbreviations

AA	Anne Arundel County
ACC	Accomac County
a/s	alias
BA	Baltimore County
CE	Cecil County
CH	Charles County
cnp	name continued on next page
c/o	child/children of
CR	Caroline County
CV	Calvert County
DE	Delaware
DO	Dorchester County
d/o	daughter of
FR	Frederick County
h/o	heir(s) of
KE	Kent County MD
KEDE	Kent County DE
KI	Kent Island
n/a	not available
NE	New England
n/g	not given
o/c	overcharged
o/o	orphans of
PA	Pennsylvania
PG	Prince George's County
PW	Prince William County
pt	part of
QA	Queen Anne's County
RI	Rhode Island
SM	St. Mary's County
SO	Somerset County
s.p.	square poles
SU	Sussex County
s/o	son of
<t>	torn
TA	Talbot County
tbc	to be charged to
unr	unreadable
VA	Virginia
w/o	widow of
WO	Worcester County

Contents of this volume

This book is the first of two volumes for Talbot County. The debt books for Talbot County cover the following years: 1733, 1734-1759, 1738, 1739, 1744, 1748, 1756, 1757-8, 1759, 1761, 1766, 1768, 1769, 1770, 1771, 1772.

From the Debt Books entries, several interesting facts are evident: (1) Talbot County had a Free School and a Charity School established by 1744; and, (2) Oxford was an established community, with several lots occupied. The leading landowners were: Samuel Chamberlain, Samuel Dickinson, the Goldsborough family, the Lloyd family. In 1738, the entries are organized by hundred. In 1770, five families were cited as "papist". Some Talbot County landowners were cited as inhabiting the following jurisdictions: Anne Arundel County, Calvert County, Cecil County, Dorchester County, Prince George's County, Queen Anne's County, Somerset County, St. Mary's County, Annapolis, Kent Island, Patuxent, Dover, Kent County Delaware, Carolina, Jersey, Long Island, New England, North Carolina, Pennsylvania, Rhode Island, Virginia, Liverpool, London, England.

46:1733:1 ...		**Acres**
William Clayton	pt. "Winterton"	290
	"Wisbich"	100
	"Poplar Hill"	200
	pt. "Normanton" – from (N) Sewell	767
	pt. "Bettys Dowrey" – from (N) King	<n/g>
	pt. "Kings Neglect" – from (N) King	<n/g>
	"Addition" – from (N) King	200
	"Colesbanck" – from (N) Troth	300
	"Colesbank Addition" – from (N) Troth	160
William Finney	"Finneys Range"	225
	pt. "Waterton"	170
Thomas Emerson	½ "Widows Choice"	320
	"Harwoods Lyon"	600
	pt. "Whettstone"	100
	"Hamiltons Park"	263
	"Keilding" & "Buckingham Addition"	393
Absolom Thrift	pt. "Hemsleys Arcadia"	50
46:1733:2 ...		
h/o John Emerson	"Vincents Lott"	43
w/o John Blackwell	pt. "Bedworth"	100
	"Rich Farme Addition"	200
Charles Stevens	"Nobles Ridge"	150
	½ "Nunams Lott"	100
	½ "Planters Delight"	100
	pt. "Nobles Chance"	100
	"Stevens Lott"	19
	"Stevens Addition"	75
John Pooley	pt. "Nobles Chance"	200
	"Tallys Addition"	300
Robert Noble	pt. "Nunams Lott"	100
	pt. "Planters Delight"	150
Daniell Baker	pt. "Betts Chance"	100
	pt. "Stevens Plains"	50
46:1733:3 ...		

Oliver Millington	pt. "Betts Chance"	100
	"Nobles Meadows"	150
Thomas Beswick	"Christophers Lott"	200
	½ "Stevens Plains"	100
	pt. "Harris Lott"	111
William Warner, Jr.	"Pooleys Discovery"	168
Mary Harris	"Skipton" – for Mos. Harris	300
	pt. "Rumneys Forrest" for Mos. Harris	43
	"Finneys Hermitage" for Mos. Harris	200
	"Harris Range" for Mos. Harris	400
James, William, & John Benny	pt. "Rumney Forrest"	150
	"Bennys Addition"	60
	"Bennys Thickett"	<n/g>
widow Haddin	pt. "Rumney Forrest"	107
	"Inclosure"	150
46:1733:4 ...		
John Morgan	pt. "Morgans Neglect"	30
John Storey	"Storeys Park" – ~~tbe Mathias Docwra (f. 107)~~	100
William Turner – ~~David Kirby for William Turner & wife; June 3 1729~~	pt. "Turners Ridge"	10
	"Moore Fields"	200
	"Moore Fields Addition"	65
	"Marys Dowry" – from (N) Rogers	200
w/o Thomas Faulknor	"Falkners Levell"	150
h/o Col. Robert Finley	pt. "Rich Farme"	200
	½ "Dixons Lott"	50
	pt. "Mount Hope" – from (N) Edmondson	200
Francis Storey	"Storeys Lott"	56
h/o Nicholas Kelly	"Virgins Inn"	200
	"Virgins Inn Addition"	100
h/o Vincent Hemsly	~~"Long Point"~~	~~50~~
	"Carter's Inheritance" – from Jonathan Davis	220
46:1733:5 ...		

Mr. William Hemsley	~~"Old Mill" – included in resurvey called "Hemsley on Wye"~~	~~250~~
	"Piccadella"	200
	~~"Yorkfield" – included in resurvey called "Hemsley on Wye"~~	~~466~~
	~~"Hemsleys Addition" – 470 a. received from widow Hemsley 8 September 1729; pt. (150 a.) included in resurvey called "Hemsley on Wye"~~	~~520~~
	"Outrange"	620
	"Addition"	63
	pt. "Brittannia"	230
	"Tryangle" – received from widow Hemsley 8 September 1729	55
	~~"Hopton William Hemsley" – from (N) Banberry; included in resurvey called "Hemsley on Wye"~~	~~320~~
	"Hemsleys Reserve" – in QA	231
	"Hemsly upon Wye"	1160
w/o Capt. John Davis	"Hope Chance"	50
	"Knave Keep Out"	50
	"Parsonage"	100
	"Batchelors Point"	100
	pt. "Ashby"	147
	½ "Widows Chance"	320
	pt. "Bettys Cove"	20
	"Addition"	350
	"Davis Outlett"	50
Richard Woolman	pt. "Woolman's Hermitage"	158
	pt. of a tract nameless	
Sarah Woolman	"Sarahs Lott"	50
	pt. "Carter's Inheritance"	100
46:1733:6 ...		
Peter Blake	"Chance" – for h/o (N) St. Tee	100
	"Knave Stand Off" – for h/o (N) St. Tee	50
Richard Bruffe (cnp)	"Daniells Addition" – from (N) Hall	70
	"Millington"	50
	"Walkers Tooth"	147
	"Daniells Rest"	50

	"Partnership"	106
	"Walkers Corner"	18
James Hollyday, Esq. for h/o Col. Edward Lloyd	"Meersgate" – E. Lloyd	300
	"Thrimby Grange" – E. Lloyd	500
	"Natts Point" – E. Lloyd	50
	"New Designe Bettys Branch" – J. Hollyday	325
	"Lynton"– E. Lloyd	600
	"Grange" – E. Lloyd	150
	"Salters Marsh" – E. Lloyd	100
	"Long Neglect" – E. Lloyd	133
	"Meersgate Addition" – E. Lloyd	267
	"Stock Range" – J. Hollyday	400
	"Granny" – E. Lloyd	100
	another tract against (N) Woolman – E. Lloyd	150
	pt. "Crouches Choyce" – E. Lloyd	50
	"Inlett" – E. Lloyd	88
	"Broadway" – E. LLoyd	50
	"Addition to <unr>" – J. Hollyday	100
	~~"Long Neglect" – charged as above~~	~~133~~
	"Scotts Close" – from (N) Start; E. Lloyd	200
	"Woolman <unr>" – E. Lloyd	150
	~~"Brittania" – for your wife from (N) Clayland; E. Lloyd~~	~~200~~
	"Falconar's Folly" – for self; from James Hollyday & wife 23 November 1731	100
46:1733:7 ...		
George Grason	"Tanners Helpe"	50
	"Skinners Outlett"	50
	"Infancy" – for R. Grason	65
h/o Mr. James Lloyd (cnp)	"Pickburne"	200
	"Elliotts Discovery"	100
	"Adjunction"	50
	"Scottland"	50
	"Lloyds Discovery"	96
	"Hope" – from (N) Collins	100
	pt. "Turner's Point" – from (N) Turner	200

	pt. "Partnership"	1020
Andrew Skinner	"Tanners Choice"	340
	"Skinners Borders"	100
	"Skinner's Vineyard"	75
	"Skinners Addition"	150
	"Skinners Security"	103
	~~"Tanners Choice"~~	~~120~~
	~~"Huntington"~~	~~300~~
	pt. "Nether Foster"	150
	"Hopewell"	100
~~John~~ Lewis Jones, ~~Sr.~~	"Tryangle" – from John Jones & wife 1 November 1729	100
46:1733:8 ...		
w/o John Jones	"Jones Armour" – by Jones Armour sold to Richard Bennett & charged in f. 84	180
Jacob Gibson	"Rebeccahs Garden"	150
	"Bishops Fields"	170
	"Champenham" & "Bendon Reserve"	550
	"Todd on Dirsan" – from (N) Evans	17
	"Todd on Dirsan" – from (N) Thirrold	400
Elizabeth Evans	pt. "Bendon" – from (N) Gibson	17
Andrew Kininmont	~~"Addition" – from John Kininmont & wife 11 December 1728~~	~~50~~
	~~pt. "Bartram" – from John Kininmont & wife 11 December 1728~~	~~50~~
	"Kininmonts Delight"	244
Robert Hall	"Parkers Thickett"	100
	"Limrick"	70
46:1733:9 ...		
Perry Benson	"Addition to Huntington" – for h/o Michael Russell	80
	"Huntington" – for h/o Michael Russell	510
	"Huntington Grange" – for h/o Michael Russell	100
	pt. "Cornelius Coll Spring" – for h/o Michael Russell	50
Thomas Hopkins	~~"Addition"~~	~~150~~
	"Addition & James"	33

Thomas Hopkins	~~"Batchelors Branch" – for h/o Alexander Ray~~	~~100~~
	~~"Addition to Batchelors Branch" – for h/o Alexander Ray~~	~~100~~
	~~pt. "Dundee" – for h/o Alexander Ray~~	~~100~~
	"Addition" – for h/o (N) Horney	100
w/o Ambrose Kininmont	"Limbeth"	200
Christopher Higges	"Pattingham"	100
Vestry of St. Michaels Parish	"Forked Neck"	50
	"Widdows Chance"	50
	"Taly Farme"	100
Joseph Kininmont	pt. "Dundee"	300
46:1733:10 ...		
William Clayland	"Stevens Plains" – from (N) Ross	50
	pt. "Cottingham" – from (N) Abrams	140
George Garey	~~"Soldiers Delight"~~	~~100~~
	~~"Knightly"~~	~~100~~
	~~"Gareys Delight"~~	~~50~~
	~~pt. "Hemsleys Arcadia"~~	~~249~~
	"Dirty Wooden"	100
	"Fortunes Addition"	52
	"Dirty Wooden Addition"	100
	"Brafferton"	100
	"Fortune"	150
	"Little Brittaine"	150
	"Tod Upon Dirven" – from (N) Thorold	80
John Pitts	pt. "White Marsh"	760
	pt. "Rich Farme"	100
	"Milland"	130
	~~pt. "Partnership"~~	~~750~~
Michaell Kerwick	"Strawberry Fields"	100
	"Kerwicks Addition"	49
	"Limrick"	60
46:1733:11 ...		
h/o John Stacey	pt. "Turkey Neck"	100
	pt. "Turkey Neck" – another part from (N) Taylor	25

James Willson	"Kingsberry"	200
	"White Oak Swamp" – from (N) Parrott	100
	pt. "Middle Spring" – from (N) Parrott	50
John Parrott	pt. "Middle Spring"	50
Edward Turner	"Johns Hill"	220
	"Hasco Green" – from (N) Parvis	160
	"Sought Out" – from (N) Laswell	100
	"Turners Discovery"	97
Stephen Darden	"John's Neck"	700
Robert Frampton	"Collins Pasture"	50
46:1733:12 ...		
~~w/o John Cook~~	~~"Hagsley"~~	~~200~~
Thomas Dudley	pt. "Broad Lane"	53
	pt. "Bever Neck"	150
	pt. "Broad Lane"	
Richard Dudley	"Dudleys Inclosure"	104
	pt. "Kingstone" – from (N) Pratt	100
	"Dudlys Addition"	37
William Dudley	"Dudleys Demeasne"	115
	pt. "Bugby" – from (N) Bradbury	50
	pt. "Smiths Clifts" – from (N) Loveday	138
	"Coallin" – from (N) Ball	300
~~John Willson~~	~~"Highfields Addition"~~	~~150~~
46:1733:13 ...		
Edward Russam	"Russams Inclosure"	65
widow Alcock	pt. "Strawbridge"	163
	~~"Dudleys Choice"~~	~~100~~
	~~pt. "Advantage"~~	~~440~~
	~~"New Town"~~	~~100~~
Thomas Berry	pt. "Roadly" – from (N) Boram	300
	~~"Borams Range"~~	~~517~~
Thomas Buckingham	pt. "Middle Spring"	100
John Needles	pt. "Roecliffe"	150
	⅓ pt. "Pitts Range"	200
	⅓ pt. "Killam"	369
	"Killam" – from (N) Sherwood	140

46:1733:14 ...		
Anne Darbye	"Pitts Choyce"	400
Roger Bradbury	"Westmoreland"	100
	pt. "Killam"	269
	⅓ "Pitts Range"	200
Jacob Bradbury	pt. "Bugby"	100
	pt. "Bugby" – from (N) Turner	50
George Bowes	~~"Sybland"~~	~~200~~
	~~"Maxfield"~~	~~152~~
	~~"Syblands Addition"~~	~~110~~
	"Kendall"	273
	"Bowes Range"	227
	~~pt. "Callyn"~~	~~100~~
	"Moorfields"	280
46:1733:15 ...		
Benjamin Parrott	pt. "Parrotts Reserve"	50
	"Salop"	200
	"Oaken"	100
	pt. "Kingstone"	100
Richard Cribb	pt. "Kingstone"	49
	"Middle Spring" – from Thomas Pratt	100
Richard Purnell	pt. "Rich Range"	50
	"Dudleys Choice"	100
David Airey	pt. "Worgons Reserve"	300
	"Parkers Park"	500
	"Davids Ridge"	125
	"Newnams Lott"	200
~~h/o George Pratt~~	~~"Green Hill"~~	~~100~~
46:1733:16 ...		
w/o William Nedls	pt. "Adventure"	100
George Parrott	"Ottwell"	100
	"Thawney Close"	50
h/o James Ridley	"Poplar Neck"	400
John Willds	pt. "Hiccory Ridge"	75
	"Bently Hay"	50
Richard Hill	pt. "Smiths Clifts"	57[illegible]

46:1733:17 ...		
widow Saukwell	pt. "Mount Hope"	150
Jacob Wooters	pt. "Smiths Clifts"	358
	~~pt. "Holow Hill"~~	~~62~~
Phill. Wooters	~~pt. "Smiths Clifts"~~	~~258~~
	pt. "Holme Hill"	50
Thomas Taylor	pt. "Turkey Neck"	275
	"Kings Creek Marsh"	50
	"Kingsberry Addition"	100
	pt. "Middle Spring"	25
	"Addition"	172
	"East Ottwell"	400
	"Warrilows Exchange"	326
46:1733:18 ...		
William Parrott	pt. "Marshey Addition"	100
	"Sallop"	167
John Harrington	pt. "Bugby" – for Sarah Phillips h/o Ann Phillips	150
	"Pasty Neck" – for Sarah Phillips h/o Ann Phillips	24
	"Hatton Garden" – for yourself	50
John Revell	"Strawberry Fields Addition"	50
	"Rathells Chance"	50
John Wooters	pt. "Smiths Clifts"	20
w/o Richard Hall	"Newnam"	50
	pt. "Cottingham"	50
46:1733:19 ...		
Samuel Broadway	"Dudley"	200
	"Ramah"	100
	"Sam's Fields"	102
	"Strawbridge"	100
Edward Clark	pt. "Parkers Farme"	350
	"Deleroy"	100
	"Parrotts Lott"	82
Jeremiah Jadwin	~~pt. "Hampton"~~	~~20~~
	~~pt. "Hampton" – from Robert Jadwin~~	~~250~~
	~~pt. "Parkers Range"~~	~~244~~
	pt. "Hampton" & pt. "Parkers Range"	44

Joshua Atkins	"Chance"	100
46:1733:20 ...		
MM Edward Fottrell & Benjamin Pemberton	"Partnership" – for h/o Robert Grundy	310
	"New Mill" – for h/o Robert Grundy	200
	"Graves" – for h/o Robert Grundy	100
	"Graves Resurvey" – for h/o Robert Grundy	280
	"Buckland" – for h/o Robert Grundy	250
	"Addition" – for h/o Robert Grundy	100
	pt. "Gurlington" – for h/o Robert Grundy	100
	"Murrey" – for h/o Robert Grundy	150
	"Rumley Marsh" – for h/o Robert Grundy	300
	"Grundys Inclosure" – for h/o Robert Grundy	171
	pt. "Sutton" – for h/o Robert Grundy	200
	pt. "Smiths Clifts" – for h/o Robert Grundy	232
	pt. "Eloms Addition" – for h/o Robert Grundy	14
	pt. "Lobbs Corner" – for h/o Robert Grundy	
	"Buckland Marsh" – for h/o Robert Grundy	50
	pt. "Marshland" – for h/o Robert Grundy	265
	"James Folly" – for h/o Robert Grundy	50
	"Greenland" – for h/o Robert Grundy	156
	"Turners Point" – for h/o Robert Grundy	200
	"Heworth" – for h/o Robert Grundy	205
	"Cumberland" – for h/o Robert Grundy	100
	pt. "Partnership" – for h/o Robert Grundy	1050
Jos. Holt	"Abbington" – for h/o Ja. Abbott, Jr.	100
	pt. "Buckrowe" – for h/o Ja. Abbott, Jr.	150
	pt. "Cattlins Plains" – for h/o Ja. Abbott, Jr.	10
	"Barren Ridge" a/s "Hull" – for h/o Ja. Abbott, Jr.	100
	"Mill Garden" – for h/o Ja. Abbott, Jr.	35
	"Hulls Addition" – for h/o Ja. Abbott, Jr.	100
	pt. "Broad Oak" – for h/o Ja. Abbott, Jr.	25
46:1733:21 ...		
John Alexander (cnp)	"Irish Freshes"	50
	"Alexanders Chance"	250
	pt. "Wales"	54
	"Yowell" – for Elizabeth Alexander	50

	"Lows Good Luck"	100
w/o John Abbott	"Bever Damms"	100
	pt. "Baildon"	167
~~James Anderson~~	~~pt. "Marshland"~~	~~70~~
h/o James Bampton – living with John Fisher	"These Keep Out"	72
	pt. "Sutton" – from (N) Taylor	100
Loftus Bowdle	"Mitchams Hall"	300
46:1733:22 ...		
William Anderson	"Prospect"	125
	"Knaps Lott"	150
William Anderson	pt. "White Phillips" – for h/o John Price	200
Hezekiah Mackey	"Holmby"	200
	pt. "Bullen"	60
	pt. "Broad Oak"	175
	pt. "Broad Oak" – from (N) Chaplin	200
John Barker	pt. "Lower Dover"	200
William Bush	pt. "Arcadia"	166
46:1733:23 ...		
Thomas Browne	"Parkers Point" – from (N) Long	75
Richard Hopkins	pt. "Nominy" – from (N) Forby	100
	pt. "Hopkins" – from (N) Hopkins	150
	pt. "White Phillips" – from (N) Dickenson	42
John Dickenson	pt. "Roadley"	150
Francis Chaplin	pt. "Roadley"	80
	"Broad Oak"	100
Ambros Ford	pt. "Partlett"	72
	pt. "Grissell & Ottwell" – from (N) Turbutt	28
46:1733:24 ...		
Samuell Dickenson (cnp)	"Cross Dower Marsh"	25
	"Cross Dower"	400
	pt. "Sutton"	50
	~~"Dickensons Lott"~~	~~216~~
	"Come Whitton"	200
	"Cross Dower Addition"	220
	"Dickensons Lott Addition"	95
	"Powells Island Resurveyed"	55

	pt. "Wales" – from (N) Alexander	46
	pt. "Compton" – from (N) Stevens	13
	pt. "Mount Hope" – from (N) Troth	200
	"Double Ridge" – from (N) Dean	100
	pt. "Mistake" – from (N) Armstrong	75
	"Good Luck" – from (N) Lowe	54
	pt. "Nominy" – from (N) Sharp	350
	pt. "Roadley" – from (N) Hadson	200
	"Hobsons Choice" – from (N) Price	100
	"Canterbury Mannor" – from (N) Troth	300
	"Canterbury Mannor" – from (N) Troth	50
	"Double Ridge" – from (N) Dean	60
	"Little Creek" – from (N) Sanders	150
	"Evan's Point" – from (N) Sanders	50
	pt. "Hir Dir Lloyd"	250
	pt. "Hir Dir Lloyd"	101
	"Mount Hope" – from (N) Troth	150
	"Banington" – from (N) Troth	50
	"Dickensons Lott"	113
	"Samuells Lott"	600
	pt. "White Phillips"	158
	"Eusam Point"	250
	pt. "Dover"	50
Nicholas Goldsborough	pt. "Hire Dire Lloyd"	400
46:1733:25 ...		
William Buckley	pt. "Lords Gift"	175
h/o Thomas Edmondson	"Neglect"	310
	"Edmondson's First Run"	400
	"Adjunction"	50
	"Upper Range"	100
	"James Reserve"	300
	pt. "Calfe Pasture" – from (N) Elston	150
Thomas Saukwell	pt. "Dover" – for h/o Robert Fortune	150
John Glover	pt. "Upper Dover"	344
William Harrison (cnp)	"Scarbrough"	1400
	pt. "Dover"	450

	"Roecliffť" – from (N) Trotter	170
	"Poplar Neck" – from (N) Bell	40
	"Poplar Levell" – from (N) Turner	160
	"Poplar Neck" – from (N) Bell	60
	"Gaskins Point" – from (N) Harrison	50
	pt. "Mount Misery"	12
	pt. "Mount Misery Addition"	50
	pt. "Dover"	75
	pt. "Prouse Point" & "Hap Hazard" – from (N) Harrison	<n/g>
	pt. "Dover" – from (N) Williams	114
46:1733:26 ...		
Walter Quinton	pt. "Goldsborough"	263
	pt. "Willingbrook" & pt. "Gurlington"	93
Fran. Harrison	pt. "Taylors Ridge"	100
	pt. "Hire Dire Lloyd"	75
	pt. "Taylors Ridge" – from (N) Watts	100
Robert Harding	pt. "Hire Dire Lloyd"	75
Richard Holmes	pt. "Sutton"	250
	"Sutton's Addition"	50
	"Buckrowe"	80
	pt. "Taylors Ridge"	100
Peter Webb	pt. "Roadley" – from (N) Berry	150
46:1733:27...		
h/o Robert Curtis	"Boone Hill"	250
Joseph James	pt. "Hickory Ridge"	75
	~~pt. "Hier Dier Lloyd"~~	~~200~~
Thomas Jenkinson	"Partricks Ridge"	1000
William Martin	"Swamptick"	100
William Martin	"Bullens Chance" – for William Moor	350
	"Conjunction" – for William Moor	25
John Altine	pt. "Hier Dier Lloyd" – for h/o Richard Moor	100
46:1733:28 ...		
Thomas Martin (cnp)	"Weeping Spring"	200
	"Armstrongs Delight"	50
	pt. "Hire Dire Lloyd"	200

	"Hard Measure Resurveyed"	94
	"Bullens Chance"	350
John Mullakin	"Partricks Plains"	300
	"Millican's Choice"	170
	"Casons Choice"	50
	"Partricks Choice"	200
Fran. Neale	~~pt. "Hiccory Ridge"~~	~~100~~
	"Cuba"	350
	pt. "Mounthope"	150
	"Adventure"	150
	"Fairefield"	200
	"Cuba Addition"	72
	"Hickory Ridge"	246
	pt. "Cuba" – from Perr. Neale	13
John Price	pt. "Hattfield" & "Hattfields Addition"	75
	~~"Edmondsons Freshes" – from (N) Edmondson~~	~~50~~
46:1733:29 ...		
Daniell Walker	pt. "Jamaico" – resurveyed	92
	"Enfield" – from (N) Collins	200
Morris Prisk	"Sydenburgh"	100
Henry Parrott	pt. "Canterberry Mannor"	520
Howell Powell	"Rigby Marsh"	300
	"Bever Neck" – from (N) Berry	259
	pt. "Advantage" – from (N) Alcock	42
	"Tryangle" – from (N) Dickenson	106
Daniell Powell	pt. "Boston Clifts"	550
William Rich	"Rich Park"	569
	"Nether Foston"	50
46:1733:30 ...		
John Pattison	pt. "Foston"	100
	pt. "Judiths Garden"	113
Richard Cooper	"Hamiltons Neck" in right of his wife (the) widow Skillington	250
Thomas Robins (cnp)	"Buckingham"	400
	"Robins Range"	300
	pt. "Jobs Content"	250

	"Jobs Content" – for Thomas Robins, Sr.	700
	"Chance"	100
	"Buckingham"	300
	pt. "Cooks Hope" – from (N) Edmondston	214
	"Hulls Neck" – from (N) Croneen	300
John Robinson	pt. "Goldsborough"	100
h/o George Royston (Patuxon)	"Begining"	300
46:1733:31 ...		
Kenelm Skillington	pt. "Turners Point"	200
Clement Sales	"Rich Range"	300
	"Delfe"	100
	~~"Edmondsons Green Cross"~~	~~400~~
	"Boon's Hope"	100
	"Woolsey Mannor"	1000
w/o William Turner	"Dawsons Fortune"	50
	pt. "Buckrowe"	50
	pt. "Cattlins Plains"	490
	"Stevens"	50
	"Compton"	300
	"Edmondsons Cove"	100
Nicholas Higgins	"Ware Point" – for h/o Cornelius Mullrain	50
Anthony Evans	pt. "Hire Dire Lloyd"	100
	pt. "Hire Dire Lloyd" – from (N) Edmondson	8
46:1733:32 ...		
William Thomas	pt. "Double Ridge"	130
	pt. "Double Ridge" – from (N) Lowe	80
	pt. "Double Ridge" – from (N) White	100
William Troth (cnp)	~~"Coles Bank"~~	~~300~~
	"Troths Fortune"	400
	"Acton"	300
	pt. "Jamaico"	50
	"Newington"	240
	~~"Mount Hope"~~	~~150~~
	"Actons Addition"	57
	"Troths Addition"	100
	"Hackney Marsh"	50

	"Troths Security"	109
	~~"Bonington" – from (N) Anderson~~	~~50~~
	"Bullen" & "Bullens Addition" – from (N) Taylor	350
Thomas Tate	"Tates Lott"	333
Thomas Alexander	"Poplar Hill"	50
46:1733:33 ...		
Tarrence Farrell	"Hawks Hill Addition"	100
John Sherwood	"Allambys Fields"	115
	"Petty France"	150
	pt. "Canterbury Manor"	130
	pt. "Westmoreland"	100
	~~pt. "Pitts Range"~~	~~200~~
	pt. "Killam"	229
William Jones	"Dicks Marsh"	200
John Cliftt	"Killingsworth" – for h/o (N) Burnyatt	50
	"Taylors Ridge" – from (N) Harrison for h/o (N) Burnyatt	100
	"Timber Neck Addition" – from (N) Swallow for h/o (N) Burnyatt	139
46:1733:34 ...		
John Whittington	pt. "Lower Dover"	200
	"Fishburn's Neglect"	130
	"Whittington's Addition"	35
	"Fishburn's Neglect" [!]	130
	"Boston Clifts" – from (N) Powell	130
w/o Richard Gorsuch	pt. "Hire Dire Lloyd"	200
Joseph Tonnard	pt. "Hire Dire Lloyd"	100
Richard White	pt. "Sutton Grange"	400
	pt. "Double Ridge"	220
	"Whites Gore"	40
John Wiggens	pt. "Parkers Point" – for h/o Phil. Jones	10
	pt. "Enlargement" – for h/o Phil. Jones	90
46:1733:35 ...		
William Cathrop	pt. "Mounthope"	100
	"Cathrop's Security"	205
	"Mounthope" – from (N) Wiles	67

Edmond Fish	"Fishes Range"	74
	~~"Stapleton"~~	~~77~~
	"Contention"	130
Silvester Abbott	"Hopson's Choice" – for h/o John Miller	50
	pt. "Sutton" – from (N) Miller for h/o John Miller	44
	"Partnership" – from (N) Brinsfield for h/o John Miller	36
William Shannahan	pt. "Timber Neck"	150
	"Browns Park" – George Shannahan from (N) Browne	119
Michaell Maginny	"Piney Point Advantage"	150
46:1733:36 ...		
w/o Dennis Connelly	"Kings Towne"	400
	"Timber Neck"	150
	~~"Hollands Addition"~~	~~50~~
John Fisher	pt. "Millers Hope"	101
	pt. "Fishers Chance"	125
William Carr	"Millers Purchase"	100
Henry Withgott	"Cornwell"	100
	"Josephs Lott"	100
~~Henry Frith~~	~~"Evans Point" – for h/o (N) Clement~~	~~250~~
46:1733:37 ...		
John Mullican	pt. "Taylors Ridge" – for h/o John Mitchell	100
w/o John Pope	"Goldstone"	50
William Curtis	"Springfield Grange"	64
	pt. "Dixon's Lott"	50
Peter Sanders	pt. "York" – for Christopher Battson	306
	"Bradford" – for Christopher Battson	50
Henry Bailey (cnp)	"Bettys Chance"	100
	"Marshey Point"	600
	"Bayleys Forrest"	135
	"Hogg Hole" – from (N) Seney	100
	"Hogg Hole" – from (N) Watts	50
	"Hogg Hole" – from (N) Morgan	200
46:1733:38 ...		

James Lord	"Wilderness" pt. "Hire Dire Lloyd"	100
	"Lords Chance"	100
	"Shoreditch" – from (N) Martin	100
	"Taylors Ridge" – from (N) Rich	100
Samuel Martingdale	pt. "Studds Point"	50
h/o John Allen	pt. "Collingham"	125
	~~"Parkers Freshes"~~	~~300~~
Robert Bryan	pt. "Hatfield" & "Hatfield Addition"	100
Philemon Armstrong	pt. "London Derry"	397
	"End of Controversey"	150
46:1733:39 ...		
Morris Giddens	"New Scottland" – for your son Benjamin	700
	"Hire Dire Lloyd" – from (N) Edmondson	10
Edward Combs	pt. "Hire Lloyd"	500
	~~"Long Point"~~	~~250~~
	"Goldstone"	50
	"Securety"	200
	pt. "Todcaster"	500
Mr. Nicholas Lowe	pt. "Hire Dire Lloyd"	105
	"Anderton"	600
	"Anderton's Addition"	100
	"Jacks Point"	100
	"Lowes Rumbles"	1440
	"Discovery"	530
	"Studds Point"	50
	"Good Luck"	26
	~~½ "Todcaster"~~	~~500~~
	pt. "Dover"	800
	"Devise" – from (N) Wintersell	440
	"Wintersell" – from (N) Wintersell	200
	pt. "Thornton" – from (N) Parrott	500
46:1733:40 ...		
Thomas Noble	pt. "Suttons Grange"	100
Henry Bullen	pt. "Bullen"	40
Thomas Taylor	"Timothys Lott"	300

~~Griffith Evans~~	~~"Moorefields"~~	~~100~~
	~~"Adventure"~~	~~100~~
Dennis Hopkins	pt. "London Derry"	103
	pt. "Hopkins Point"	100
	pt. "Coventry"	270
	pt. "White Phillips" – from Richard Hopkins	<n/g>
	"Hogsdon" – from Richard Hopkins	100
46:1733:41 ...		
Peter Sharpe	"Mount Pleasant"	500
	"Easons Neck"	100
	"Fancy"	50
	pt. "Conjunction"	25
	"Rattle Snake Point"	150
	pt. "Nominy"	402
	"Easons Lott"	50
	~~"Johns Neck"~~	~~400~~
	"Sharps Addition"	24
	"Chance"	40
	"Inclosure"	300
	pt. "Nominy" – from (N) Collins	100
William Hambertson	pt. "Sutton Grange"	50
h/o Foster Turbutt	"Ottwell"	500
	"Addition"	80
	~~"Fausley"~~	~~250~~
	pt. "Grissell"	122
	"Teagles Request"	125
	pt. "Partlett" – from (N) Ford	28
Thomas Stewart ~~Dr. John Carr~~	"Jordans Hill" – resurveyed	175
46:1733:42 ...		
Thomas Barnett	pt. "Bullen"	100
	pt. "Bullen" – from (N) Maccotter	50
	<n/g> – land adjoining to Pitts Mill	20
John Hendricks	pt. "Dover"	50
Stephen Rushoon	½ "Freshes"	100
	"Edmondson's Freshes Addition" – from Ja. Lord	100
h/o Benjamin Nobb	pt. "Lords Gift"	75

John Cox	"Spring Close"	50
46:1733:43 ...		
John King Miles	"Timber Neck"	120
	pt. "Betty Dowry"	150
	"Kings Plains"	158
	"Parsonage Addition"	100
	"Swineyard"	176
	pt. "Kings Forrest"	150
	pt. "Kings Neglect"	115
Mr. Robert Goldsborough	pt. "Ashby"	250
	pt. "Halls Neck"	100
	"Wyatts Fortune"	50
	pt. "Plains Dealing"	73
	"Peters Rest"	50
	"Chance"	50
	"Annual Peace" pt. "St. Michalls Fresh Runn"	50
	pt. "Four Square"	300
	pt. "Grundys Addition"	73
	pt. "Adventure"	100
	"Goldsborough Tryangle"	45
	"Woodland Neck"	100
	pt. "Cottingham" – from (N) Abrams	150
	"Newnam's Addition" – from (N) Crawly	50
	"Four Square" – from (N) Ungle	350
	"Benjamins Lott"	50
Richard Ratcliffe	"Jacobs & Johns Pasture" – from (N) Cockayne	170
46:1733:44 ...		
h/o Mr. Richard Carter (cnp)	"Craven"	300
	"Carter's Plains"	334½
	"Newnam's Thickett"	50
	"St. Michalls Fresh Runn"	350
	"Gore"	170
	"Good Chance"	50
	"Bodkin"	15[illegible]
	"Carters Range"	200
	"Carters Outworks"	19[illegible]

	"Carters Farme"	167½
	"Carter's Reserve"	200
	"Carters Sconce"	139
	pt. "Finneys Hermitage"	200
	"Carters Forrest"	420
	pt. "Carters Farme"	50
	"Carters Forrest"	326
	"Addition"	68
	"Carters Chance"	74
	pt. "Coston's Chance"	109
	"Carters Reserve"	164
	"Addition"	118
	"Addition"	21
	"Poplar Ridge"	400
Thomas Gulley	pt. "Ashby"	150
	~~"Babbs Hill"~~	~~100~~
46:1733:45 ...		
James Crawley	"Newnam's Addition"	50
Robert Morton	"Neglect"	100
	pt. "Ashby"	100
	"Hopewell"	50
Jos. Brascup	"Newnam's Range"	100
Peter Harwood	"Harwoods Hill"	100
	"Poplar Levell"	100
	"Millroad", "Millroad Addition", & "Millroad 2nd Addition"	150
	"Millroad Addition" – from (N) Smithson	80
	"Addition" – from (N) Blake	400
	"Lloyds Addition" – from (N) Blake	120
	pt. "Cottingham"	150
Thomas Eubancks	"Omalys Range"	200
	"Jacob & Johns Pasture"	120
Mark Williams	"Newnam's Folly"	50
46:1733:46 ...		
~~h/o John Wright~~	~~pt. "Mickle Mare"~~	~~100~~
Jos. Rogers	pt. "Cottingham"	200

Robert Golfe	"Millroad 2nd Addition"	200
Daniell Sherwood	~~"Potters"~~	~~50~~
	~~"Potters Delight"~~	~~50~~
	~~pt. "Cabbin Neck"~~	~~37½~~
	"Lurkey Hills"	100
	"Beggars Hall"	36
	"Anketell"	500
~~William Dixon (glover)~~	~~"Dixons Outlett"~~	~~200~~
	~~"Bennetts Hills"~~	~~50~~
	~~"Ending Controversey"~~	~~150~~
	~~pt. "Ashby"~~	~~60~~
46:1733:47 ...		
Edward Harding	"Coppins Coppice"	50
	pt. "Bite"	35
	"Parkers Addition"	50
	pt. "Hemsleys Arcadia" – from (N) Garey	376
	pt. "Tilghmans Fortune"	19
	pt. "Micklemore"	100
h/o Col. Thomas Smithson	"Holden"	225
	pt. "Holden's Addition"	50
	"Millroad", pt. "Millroad Addition", & pt. "Millroad 2nd Addition"	120
	"Holden's Range"	73
	pt. "Bite"	15
	pt. "Micklemore"	150
	"Gutterly More"	120
	"Gutterly More" [!]	120
Robert Hopkins	pt. "Cornelius Cool Spring" – for h/o (N) Russell	50
	"Cornelius Cove" – for h/o (N) Russell	50
	"Sharp's Fortune" – for h/o (N) Russell	100
	"Turkey Park" – for h/o (N) Russell	329
Thomas Bartlett	"Ratcliffe Manner"	920
46:1733:48 ...		
Edward Latham	pt. "Bettys Cove" – for h/o George Hurlock	30
James Hurlock	"Bettys Addition"	50
	"Addition"	50

Anthony Wise	"Gore"	45
	"Sheepshead Point Resurveyed"	246
	pt. "Dunsmoreheath" – from (N) Jadwin & (N) Edwards	200
	"Baintrees Addition" – from (N) Marlin	50
	"Frampton" – from (N) Robinson	122
John Tibballs	pt. "Sheepshead Point"	50
	"Tibballs Addition"	20
46:1733:49 ...		
Fran. Marlin	"Marlins Folly"	50
	"Marlins Chance"	50
	"Beantry"	500
	"Spring Close"	100
	pt. "Baintrees"	60
	"Batchelors Branch"	50
	pt. "Baintrees Addition"	10
James Dawson	"Frentry"	100
	"Frithland"	200
	"Long Point"	42
	"Cromwell" – from (N) Hawkins	300
John Lowe	"Piney Point" pt. "Graftons Mannor"	150
	pt. "Grafton Manner" – resurveyed	245
	"Piney Neck"	107
	pt. "Haddaways Lott"	27
	pt. "Haddaways Lott" – from (N) Haddaway	50
Stephen Isgate	pt. "Hopkins Point"	150
46:1733:50 ...		
John Valliant	"Maxwell Moore" — for h/o (N) Hopkins	250
	"Elams Addition" & "Lobbs Corner" – from (N) Grundy, etc.	85
	pt. "Yafford's Neck" – from (N) Aldarne	100
	pt. "Cumberland" – from (N) Colson & (N) Adams	50
	~~"Widows Lott" – from (N) Baynard~~	~~85~~
	<n/g> – from (N) Hudson	30
John Robson	"Jones Look Out"	50

William Hopkins	pt. "Hopkins Point"	100
	~~pt. "William & James"~~	~~35~~
	pt. "Marshy Point" – from Elizabeth Hopkins	100
James Hopkins	pt. "Hopkins Point"	100
	"Hopkins Point Addition"	25
	"Addition"	150
46:1733:51 ...		
Joseph Hopkins	pt. "Hopkins Point"	200
	"Hopkins Point Addition"	50
William Farrell	pt. "Stevens Range"	100
	"Port Rumney"	75
~~John Peck~~	~~pt. "Halls Neck"~~	~~60~~
Daniell Peck	pt. "Halls Neck"	184
Benjamin Peck	pt. "Halls Neck"	184
46:1733:52 ...		
h/o Mr. Robert Ungle	pt. "Plain Dealing"	100
	"Endeavour"	50
	"Grundys Lott"	46
	"Yorkshire"	250
	"Cabbin Neck"	80
	pt. "Arcadia"	150
	"Intention Resurveyed"	50
	"Stevens Range" – from (N) Chance	66
	"Stevens Range" – from (N) Sprye	120
	"Four Square" – from (N) Coursey	350
h/o Mr. Robert Ungle for lands of Richard Alderne	pt. "Yafford Neck"	300
	"Roystones Addition"	150
	"Clays Addition"	50
	"Aldern's Island"	41
Edward Baning	"Goose Neck"	50
Anne Fuller	"Intention"	50
	"Old Woman's Fancy"	50
46:1733:53 ...		
James Colson	"Clays Hope"	200
Peter Anderton (cnp)	pt. "Fox Hole"	100
	pt. "Fox Harbour"	50

	"Ealoms Addition" – from (N) Grundy & (N) Ungle	180
Arthur Rigby for h/o (N) Oram	pt. "Fox Hole"	200
	pt. "Fox Harbour"	50
	pt. "Adventure"	200
	"Fox Denn"	56
	"Anderby"	100
	"Crafford"	100
	"Rigbys Discovery"	105
	pt. "Adventure"	200
	"Rigbys Folly"	45
	"Anderbys Addition Resurveyed"	78
William Riggaway	"Westland"	140
Robert Kiddy for William Harris	½ "Ashford"	50
	"Long Neglect"	35
46:1733:54 ...		
Thomas Smith	"Lamberton"	150
	"Lambeth's Addition"	150
	"Goose Neck" pt. "Graftons Manner" – from (N) Lambden	<n/g>
John Bradshaw	"Cumberland"	200
Henry Wharton	"Hookland"	100
James Sandford	"Sandfords Hermitage"	250
	"Sandfords Folly"	45
Jasper Hall	"Prevention"	50
	"Wharton's Glade"	50
	"Couples Close"	100
46:1733:55 ...		
Robert Peirson	~~"Contention"~~	~~100~~
	"Bishopsick"	100
Edgar Webb	"Rockney Nook"	100
	"Rockney Nook Addition"	58
James Benson	"Maiden Point Addition"	100

Daniell Vinton	"Snellings Delight"	100
	"Edwards Hopwell"	100
Nathaniell Grace	"Rest Content"	100
	"Goodwin's Addition"	90
	pt. "Adventure"	115½
46:1733:56 ...		
William Skinner for (N) Fox	"Rays Point"	150
	"Enlargement"	50
w/o William Warrilow & John Cope	"Berrys Range"	130
	"Warrilow's Exchange"	326
Richard Hethrington	"Hethrington's Delight"	50
	pt. "Adventure"	115½
	pt. "Ashford"	50
	~~"Mount Misery"~~	~~12~~
	~~pt. "Mount Misery"~~	~~89~~
	pt. "Mount Misery"	9
George Taylor	"Chance"	100
	"Taylor & James Discovery"	100
	"Taylor & James Discovery" [!]	100
46:1733:57 ...		
Robert Harrison	"Haphazard"	120
	pt. "Crooked Intention"	50
James Auld	pt. "Elliots Folly"	50
	½ "Davenport"	100
	"Elliotts Addition"	200
Edward Elliott, Sr.	"Harleigh"	50
	"Beech"	50
	½ "Davenport"	10[illegible]
	"Elliotts Lott"	27[illegible]
	½ "Elliotts Folly"	5[illegible]
Edward Elliott, Jr.	"Macotter & Glover Addition"	10[illegible]
	"Point & Marsh"	5[illegible]
	"Macotter & Glover Resurveyed"	17[illegible]
Charles Bridges	"Boyden"	10[illegible]
	"New Building"	2[illegible]
46:1733:58 ...		

Richard Feddeman	pt. "Lancashire"	301
	"Addition"	50
	"Feddeman's Chance"	100
	~~"Withrington"~~	~~200~~
	pt. "Cabbin Neck"	13
	"Fortune"	121
	"Hazard"	200
Robert Fellow	pt. "Abrams Lott"	34
	pt. "Goffstone" – from (N) Goffe	100
George Cooley for Ra. Dawson, Sr.	pt. "Lostock"	600
John Camper	pt. "Lostock"	50
	"Lostocks Addition"	50
Peter Caulk	pt. "Lostock"	100
Alexander Larrimore	"Larrimores Neck"	100
	~~"Larrimores Lott"~~	~~50~~
	"Bamptshire"	50
	"Larrimores Addition"	50
	"Larrimores Prudence"	87
46:1733:59 ...		
David Fairbanck	"Wisbick"	60
	"Upholland"	50
	"Bellfast"	100
	"Camper's Neck"	100
	"Bradford"	62
	"Jones Hole"	36
	"Fairbanck's Chance"	195
	"Fairely"	100
John Hunt	"Content"	98
	"Divine St. Andrew"	200
	"Fools Parradice"	38
William Hambleton	"Willistone"	224
	"Martingham"	200
	"Hamiltons Addition"	100
	"Cambridge"	100
	"Hamilton's Neck"	300

Fran. Porter	~~"Lewis"~~	~~100~~
	½ "Hamersby"	200
	"Hazard"	70
46:1733:60 ...		
Fran. Sherwood	"Sherwoods Island"	20
	"Crooked Intention"	80
	"Middle Neck"	100
	½ "Hemersby"	200
	½ "Mount Misery"	50
	"Huckleberry Garden"	125
Edward & John Leeds	"Wades Point"	400
	pt. "Hatton"	410
	"Long Delay"	34
	"Leeds Landing"	65
	pt. "Sarahs Neck" – from (N) Bullock	3
Col. Mathew Til. Ward	"St. Michaells Point"	1000
	"Henriettas Purchase"	412
	"Court Road"	138
	pt. "Union Resurveyed"	611
	"Choptank Island Resurveyed"	1468
	"Three Necks Resurveyed"	165
46:1733:61 ...		
Robert Sands	"Sands Lott"	153
	"Chance"	50
	"Fishburn's Landing"	104
Thomas Lurty	"Barken Point"	100
	"Lancashire"	50
William Cooper for Rice Evans	pt. "Mile End"	75
John Kemp (cnp)	"Kemps Lott"	100
	"Mabell"	100
	"Bolton"	100
	"Bolton's Addition"	50
	"Mabells Addition"	50
	"Woolfe Harbour"	62
	½ "Kemps Lott Addition"	26

	pt. "Merchants Folly" – from (N) Haddaway	<n/g>
	"Hunt Keep Out"	28
George Collison	"Rehoboth"	50
	"Rehoboth's Point"	50
46:1733:62 ...		
William Landman	"Summerton"	200
	"Winterton"	50
	"William & Marys Addition"	152
	pt. "Grafton Manner" – from (N) Lowe	100
	pt. "Grafton Manner" – from (N) Lowe	275
George Haddaway	pt. "Mile End"	250
	~~pt. "Merchants Folly"~~	~~150~~
	"Kemps Lott" – from (N) Kemp	38
	~~pt. "Haddaways Lott"~~	~~123~~
Ralph Elstone	"Exchange"	100
	"Elstone"	50
	"Brooks Hall"	100
Nicholas Lurty	"Bridges"	100
	"Elston's Hazard"	52
	"Elston's Hazard" pt. "Grafton Mannor"	49
Enion Williams	"Enions Lott"	151
	"Fishburn's Lott"	302
	"Claybanck"	50
	pt. "Hatton"	90
	pt. "Enions Range"	170
	"Sybland"	200
	"Maxfield"	152
	pt. "Sybland Addition"	110
	pt. "Coallys"	100
46:1733:63 ...		
h/o Laurence Knowles	"Folly"	100
h/o Isaac Sasserson	"Abrahams Hermitage"	160
Capt. Thomas Sandiford (Liverpoole)	"Barn's Neck"	100
	"Barn's Neck Addition"	100
	pt. "Baggs Hole"	50
~~Mary Cooke~~	~~"Widow's Lott"~~	~~85~~

Charles Harbott	"Harbotts Choice"	100
	"Hobson's Choice" – from (N) Mullican	100
	pt. "Millers Hope" – from (N) Fisher	11
Matthew Griffin	"Griffins Adventure"	220
46:1733:64 ...		
Phill. Lloyd, Esq.	pt. "Carters Inheritance Resurveyed"	300
	"Outlett"	220
	pt. "Cedar Point"	48
	pt. "Moorsgate Addition"	69
	pt. "Woolmans Hermitage" & pt. "Woolmans Inheritance" – from several persons	316
	"Natts Point" – from (N) Smith	50
	"Knightlys Addition" – from (N) Garey	50
	~~pt. "Cottingham" – from (N) Clayland~~	~~140~~
	"Hemsleys Pasture" – from Madam Finley	655
James Powell	pt. "Powells Hazard"	70
Joseph Attwell	pt. "Bantry"	200
James Bishop	½ "Chance"	100
James Barber (KE)	pt. "Holden Addition"	50
46:1733:65 ...		
Samuel Crayker (ENG)	"Ramah"	300
William Dixon	"Cabbin Neck"	500
	"Dixon's Outlett"	200
	"Dixon's Lott"	200
John Dunn	"Winckles Ridge"	250
	"Burnistone"	170
Ralph & John Dawson	"Theife Keep Out"	50
	"Galloway"	150
	"Bryans Lott"	37½
	"Batchelor's Range Addition"	500
	"Harryton"	270
	"Cheetanck"	100
	"Haarbour Rouse"	110
	"Lizey Fortune"	16
	"Hattons Hope"	100
	"Shrigleys Fortune"	391

h/o William Edmondson	pt. "Hire Dire Lloyd"	112
	pt. "Hire Dire Lloyd"	170
46:1733:66 ...		
Magdalen Edmondson	~~"Eastwood"~~	~~300~~
	~~"Great Poplar Neck"~~	~~50~~
	"Barren Point"	200
	~~"Preghm"~~	~~100~~
	~~"Eastwood Point"~~	~~40~~
	~~"Jacks Cove"~~	~~50~~
	~~pt. "Cocks Hope"~~	~~58~~
	~~"Discovery"~~	~~250~~
	"North York" or "Norwich"	200
	~~pt. "Hewarth"~~	~~360~~
	"Edmondson Freshes Addition"	200
	"Edmondson's Fresh Runn"	400
	"Barren Point" [!]	200
h/o William Eldridge	"Eldridge Point"	100
James Tucker	pt. "Standforth" – from (N) Huett	100
William Gross	"Newnam's Fields"	50
	"Ashbys Addition"	200
William Gaskin	"Gaskins Pasture"	50
	"William & Margett"	100
46:1733:67 ...		
h/o Richard Howard	"Griffiths Addition"	50
h/o Thomas Hutcheson (Jersey)	"Beverly"	522
	"Beverlys Addition"	230
	"Hutchesons Discovery"	300
	"Hutchesons Point"	72
Daniell Croneen	pt. "Halls Neck"	60
John Bartlett	"Northumberland" – from (N) Hall	61
	pt. "Bensons Enlargement"	50
Mr. Samuel Jenings (London)	"Jenings Hope"	1000
Anthony Ivey	"Peaks Marsh"	300
46:1733:68 ...		
John Jadwin (cnp)	"Jadwins Choice"	300
	pt. "Chesnutt Bay"	400

	"Coventry"	250
h/o William Johnson (London)	~~"Desire"~~	~~200~~
	"Desire Addition"	60
	"Edmondson's Freshes"	100
h/o Robert Jones (PA)	pt. "Hall" & "Halls Addition"	140
William Kenting	"Bloomsberry"	200
John Keld	"Austin"	150
	"Alcocks Choice"	100
	"Hoggs Island"	140
Josias Lambert	"Lambert House"	50
46:1733:69 ...		
h/o Thomas Maning	"Tryangle"	55
	"Norwich"	200
Richard Dove	⅓ "Hattfield"	33¾
	⅓ "Hattfield Addition"	66¼
h/o William Moor	"Moore Land"	100
	"Chance Ridge"	150
George Merchant	pt. "Fair Play"	50
h/o Thomas Oliver	"Olive Branch"	100
Richard Poore	"Hooper Ensell"	200
	"Freeman's Rest"	50
Jos. Padley (ENG)	pt. "Chesnutt Bay"	600
Franc. Perkins	"Demeasn's Recovered"	136
46:1733:70 ...		
Capt. Richard Coward	"Plenhemmon" – from Mr. Coursey	600
	~~"Morgan's Point" – from Mr. Coursey~~	~~50~~
h/o Hannah Reynolds	"Reynold's Point"	300
h/o John Richardson	pt. "Willenbrough"	150
	"Jamaica's Addition"	50
Robert Register	pt. "Stevens Range"	14[illegible]
	"Durham"	7[illegible]
	"Parrotts Reserve" – from (N) Parrott	150
David & Sollomon Robinson (cnp)	"Davids Folly"	50
	pt. "Jamaica" – from <unr>	100
	pt. "Jamaica" – from (N) Dickenson	50
	pt. "Hall" – from (N) Atkins	70

	"Chance"	23
	"Robinsons Begining"	17
	"Long Point"	25
William Sweatnam	"Moore Fields Addition"	30
	"Brown's Lott"	200
	"Moorefields"	94
Christopher Stauper	"Stamper"	50
46:1733:71 ...		
James Steuart	"Fishing Bay"	200
Robert Welne	"Armstrongs Gift"	200
h/o Samuell Winstow	"Delight"	250
	"Plaine Dealing"	50
h/o John Whinfield	"Winfells Trouble"	200
~~Elisabeth Wise~~ Mathew Kirbye	"Swamp Hole"	100
Jos. Winslowe (NE)	"Duxbury"	680
h/o Thomas Vaughan	"Wakerford"	100
	"Anderbys Addition"	100
Daniell Crawley	pt. "Hire Dire Lloyd Resurveyed"	80
46:1733:72 ...		
Phill. Sherwood	"Sherwoods Neck"	268
John Meers	"Halls Neck" – from (N) Croneen	40
William Benstead	"Bensteads Adventure"	64
Benjamin Cook	"Benjamins Lott"	50
Charles Blake	"Sayers Forrest"	2250
	"Upper Range"	200
	"Adventure"	446
Samuell Turbutt	"Turbutts Fields Resurveyed"	168
	"Poplar Hill Resurveyed"	57
	pt. "White Phillips" & "Hogsdon" – from (N) Tucker	100
	"Marshland" – from (N) Berry	165
	pt. "Blessland" & "Bagg's Marsh" – from (N) Baggs	160
46:1733:73 ...		
Mark Noble	"Poor Hill"	37
	pt. "Sutton Grange"	100

Richard Wooters	"Richard & Marys Forrest"	80
Jonathan Miller	"Millers Chance"	85
George Robins	"First Hazard Resurveyed"	358
	"Partnership"	65
	pt. "Rich Range"	50
	pt. "Hatfield" & "Hatfields Addition"	25
Fran. Armstrong	"Surprise"	40
	"Cornelius's Neck"	50
	"Ireland"	500
	"Holland"	200
	pt. "Westmoreland"	200
	"Discovery"	80
Jacob Falconar	"Falconar's Hazard"	60
46:1733:74 ...		
James Myrick	"Hazards Addition"	9
	"Powells Hazard" – from (N) Powell	50
Hannah Oldham	"Addition"	32
William Dobson	"Dobsons Advantage"	35
	"Fork" – from (N) Sutton	250
	"Eagles Neck" – from (N) Parott	100
	"Worgans Reserve" – from (N) Clements	200
John Auld	"Newport Glasgowe"	258
William Aldern & Andrew Oren	"Hopewell"	200
Richard Borrough	"Schoolhouse Lott"	59
John Kersey	"Kerseys Good Luck"	37
46:1733:75 ...		
John Cooper	"Cooper's Lott"	52
William Grace	"Inlargement"	71
	"Halls Fortune"	50
~~John Gaskin~~	~~"Gurlington" – from (N) Greenwood~~	~~75~~
Jos. Clarke	"Clarks Folly"	101
	pt. "Johns Neck"	118
William Skinner, Jr.	pt. "Sarahs Garden"	13
	"Skinners Lott"	33

Phill. Banner	"Banners Hazard"	50
	"Falconars Square" – from Edward Carslake	100
Charles Lewis	"Chance"	79
John Newnam	~~"Benjamins Lott"~~	~~50~~
	"Newingham"	100
46:1733:76 ...		
h/o Thomas Miles	pt. "Mile End"	75
Richard Chance	"Cumberland" – from Col. Smithson	70
Mr. Ernault Hawkins	"Cudlington"	400
	"Cabbin Neck"	43
	"Cudlington's Addition"	50
	"Poplar Neck"	50
	"Sandy Bite"	50
	"Cudlingtons Encrease"	50
	"Good Luck" pt. "Grafton Manner" – from (N) Lowe	28
Daniell Phillips (CV)	pt. "Hire Dire Lloyd"	300
Thomas Booker	pt. "Tilghman's Fortune"	325
Robert Booker	pt. "Tilghmans Fortune"	75
h/o Phillip Massey	pt. "Tilghman's Fortune"	215
46:1733:77 ...		
John Battfield	pt. "Tilghman's Fortune"	88
	"Falconars Square" – from Edward Carslake	100
William Holmes	pt. "Tilghman's Fortune"	50
h/o James Courtney	"Hopewell"	100
Joseph Bunton for James Raglass	pt. "Dover"	225
Solomon Birkhead	"Little Bristoll"	1300
Jonathan Airey	pt. "Rockclift"	118
h/o Timothy Lindall	"Duxberry"	250
46:1733:78 ...		
Brett Delander	"Edmondsons Coven"	200
Robert Martin	"Rich Neck"	300
w/o Thomas Bennett	"Cove Hall"	100
	"Fort Adventure"	50
h/o John Barnes	"Barnes Chance"	100

h/o John Edmondson	"Enlargement"	100
	"Deep Point"	150
	"Norwich"	200
	"Desire" & pt. "Heworth"	603
	"Edmondsons Difficulty"	1253
George Gale (SO)	"Edmonds Range"	400
46:1733:79 ...		
Henry Mitchell	"Beach Blossom"	600
John Wright	"Middleton"	800
	"Poplar Neck"	100
Richard Talbot (AA)	"Rich Range Addition"	100
	"Parsons Ridge"	500
Thomas Hethod	"Plumb Point"	100
	"Timber Neck"	100
John Chaife	"Holehaven"	100
h/o Fran. Whittwell	"Addition"	300
46:1733:80 ...		
h/o John Drywood	"Drywoods Chance"	100
h/o (N) Sing	"Newnams Fortune"	100
~~Capt. Daniell Maud~~	~~"Holme Hill" – from (N) Alnutt~~	~~400~~
	~~"Rich Range" – from (N) Alnutt~~	~~250~~
	~~"Rich Range Addition" – from (N) Alnutt~~	~~100~~
h/o David Johnson	pt. "Waterton"	200
h/o William Brett	"Jamaicas Addition"	50
h/o Robert Harwood	pt. "Rich Farme Addition"	200
46:1733:81 ...		
John Jones (QA)	pt. "Roadway"	50
h/o Edward Roe	"Oxford Towne"	2
John & James Harrison	"Dover Marsh"	74
	"Dover Marsh"	150
	"Prouse Point" – from Robert Harrison	100
Rowland Henbridge	pt. "Buckby"	50
h/o John Stuart	"Abraham's Choice"	50
Andrew Abbington	"Warwick"	400
h/o John Rhodes	"Hogg Neck Addition"	50
46:1733:82 ...		

Thomas Foster	"Wells Outlett" – from (N) Sherwood	50
h/o William Glinn	"Bradford"	50
	"Tranquility" – from (N) Grundy	185
	~~"Timothy Lott" – from <unr>~~	~~85~~
	"Partnership" – from (N) Hamilton	34
	"Cross Haze" – from (N) Hamilton	50
	pt. "Cooks Hope" – from (N) Lowe	200
James Raglas for Samuell Farmer	"Rogue Keep Off"	50
	"Dividend" – from (N) Edmondson	50
Robert Clarke	pt. "Kemps Lott Addition"	26
h/o Patrick Macdaniell	"Patricks Delight"	65
h/o Thomas Cox	"Cox's Delight"	110
46:1733:83 ...		
William Harris	"Long Neglect"	35
	pt. "Ashford"	50
Robert Phillips (SM)	"Little Minories"	200
John Warner	"Poore Mann's Portion"	80
h/o George Sprouse	"Sprouses Fortune"	100
h/o Elizabeth Christian	"Widow's Chance"	50
h/o Jos. Mann	"Churley"	100
46:1733:84 ...		
Richard Bennett, Esq. (cnp)	"Morgan St. Michall"	300
	"Marron"	130
	"Claybourns Island"	700
	"Abbington"	200
	"Poplar Neck"	100
	pt. "Whettstone"	200
	"Planter's Increase"	100
	"Towne Road"	50
	"Henrietta Maria's Discovery"	216
	"Lobbs Creek Resurveyed"	679
	"Tobacco Pipe"	359
	"Turner's Ridge"	200
	~~"Morgans Choice"~~	~~300~~
	"Crouches Choice"	150
	½ "Abbington" – from (N) Banbury	200

	"Farmer" – from (N) Banbury	348
	"Sweatnams Hope" – from (N) Banbury	120
	"Daniells Addition"	30
	"Huntingtons Addition"	150
	"Timber Neck"	100
	~~"Clayburns Island"~~	~~700~~
	"Batchelors Delight"	100
	~~"Bodwell"~~	~~200~~
	~~"Indian Neck"~~	~~350~~
	~~"Winkleton"~~	~~185~~
	~~"Mitchells Lott"~~	~~200~~
	"Neglect"	100
	"Hern Island"	75
	~~"James Armour" – from (N) Carslake~~	~~180~~
	~~"Edmondsons Green" – from (N) Corse~~	~~400~~
	"Indian Neck Resurveyed"	913
	"Winkleton"	185
	"Mitchells Lott"	100
	~~"Whittington Neck"~~	~~475~~
	"Tryangle"	55
	"Advantage"	500
	"New Towne"	100
	"Freshes"	200
46:1733:85 ...		
h/o Seth Garrett	"Westford"	247
h/o Humphry Jennings	"Pitts Freshes"	200
h/o John Ingram	"Hunting Hill"	100
h/o Jonathan Syberry	"Towickam"	170
Charles Masters	"Vineyard"	250
John Clymer	"Ann's Chance"	50
h/o James Hall	"James Neck"	200
	"James Addition"	100
46:1733:86 ...		
h/o William Cross	"Branfield"	800
Henry Price & Johannes Dehoynoysa	"Copartnership"	37[illegible]

William Browne	"Dunn's Range" – from (N) Ringgold & (N) White	252
	"Tell Talles Loss" – from (N) Turner	125
	"Charloviles & Cork"	200
William Elbert	"Hemsley's Arcadia" – from (N) Thrift	150
	pt. "Normonton" – from (N) Hattfield	33
	pt. "Rebecca Garden" – from (N) Emerson	25
	"Loyd Costine"	659
	pt. "Rebecca's Garden" – from (N) Lloyd	<n/g>
Jane Blackwell now Sanders & John Pitts	pt. "Hamiltons Park" – from (N) Sheild	137
46:1733:87 ...		
James Barnwell	pt. "Badworth" – from (N) Shield	100
John Nailor	pt. "Brittamas" – from (N) Edwards	150
William Mitchell	"Turner's Hazard" & "Bullen's Addition" – from (N) Bullen	171
~~James Hollyday~~	~~"Falconar's Folly" – from (N) Falconar~~	~~100~~
Jane Curtis	"Dixons Lott" – from (N) Edmondson	100
Fardinando Callaghon	pt. "Brittania" – from (N) Storey & Elizabeth Williams	100
46:1733:88 ...		
Evan Price	a tract adjoining "St. Michalls Fresh Runn" – from John Start	100
William Salsberry	"Skinners Swineyard" – from (N) Skinner	200
	"Skeggs Spring" – from (N) Skinner	50
Mr. Phill. Lloyd, Jr.	"Brierlys Delight" – bought of John Carslake	150
	"Doughtys Lott" – bought of John Carslake	50
	"Doughtys Hope" – bought of John Carslake	50
Robert Stonestreete	"Dunn's Range Addition" – from Charles Walker	200
Woolman Gibson	"Leitts" – from Henry Jones	40
	"Edmondton" – from (N) Thorold	300
46:1733:89 ...		
Benjamin, John, & Andrew Kininmont	"Fools Parradice" – bought of John Kininmont	50
	pt. "Bartram" – bought of John Kininmont	150
	"Batchelor's Hope" – bought of John Kininmont	50
	"Hopewell" – bought of John Kininmont	80
	"Scotts Lott" – bought of John Kininmont	100
Jeffery Horney	pt. "Cottingham" – from (N) Abrams	50

Thomas Atkinson	pt. "Cottingham" – from (N) Abrams	37
Isaac Dixon	pt. "Cottingham" – from (N) Abrams	25
	"Cottingham" – from (N) Newton	<n/g>
	pt. "Carters Plains"	166¾
	pt. "Carters Farm"	83
	"Bennetts Hill"	50
	"Ending Controversey"	150
	pt. "Ashby"	66
	"Dixons Outlett"	150
Mary Horney & Catharine Willson	pt. "Dundee" – from Benjamin Kininmont	<n/g>
46:1733:90 ...		
Alexander Ray	pt. "Dundee" – from Benjamin Kininmont	30
John Loveday	"Midle Spring" – from (N) Trotter	150
Dennis Larey	"Beverdam Neck" – from (N) Montecue	70½
	"Austin" – from (N) Worley & (N) Smith	150
	"Parners Hazard" – from (N) Cook	142
Robert Lowther	"Beverdam Neck" – from (N) Skinner	70½
Roger Hunter	pt. "Dudleys Demeasne" – from (N) Thompson	85
	"Jacobs Begining" – from (N) Thompson	100
46:1733:91 ...		
John Berry	"Bever Neck" – from Thomas Berry	141
John Tomlinson	pt. "Roecliffe" – from (N) Needles	50
Edward Mann Sherwood	"Exchange" – from (N) Needles	200
	pt. "Highfield" – from (N) Russam	50
	"Pitts Range"	600
Caleb Clarke	pt. "Killam" – from (N) Bradbury	100
	pt. "Parker's Range" – from Robert Jadwin	256
	"Highfield" – from (N) Webb	100
	pt. "Hampton" pt. "Parkers Range"	200
	"Highfield Addition"	150
William Thompson	"Smiths Clifts" – from (N) Tippen	69
	"Hasco Green" – from (N) Tippen	50
46:1733:92 ...		
William Whittby	"Rich Range" – from (N) Purnell	150
Hannah Parrott	pt. "Middle Spring" – from Henry Parrott	150

William Marshall	"King Sale" – from (N) Lane	126
Jonathan Greenwood	"Parker's Farme" – from (N) Mansell	100
Thomas Pamphillion	"Ealoms Addition" & "Lobbs Corner" – from (N) Grundy & (N) Ungle	83
46:1733:93 ...		
Pierce Fleming	"Taylors Ridge" – from (N) Greenwood	100
Mary Ratcliffe	"Arcadia" – from (N) Fellows	34
	"Abrams Lott" – from (N) Fellows	66
James Ears	"Barmeston" – from (N) Cox	106
	"Cox Addition" – from (N) Cox	70
	"Cox Chance" – from (N) Cox	160
~~John~~ Thomas Bullen	"Newelyn" – from (N) Browne	140
	"Chance" – from (N) Fray	129
	"Lords Gift" – from (N) Browne	100
	"Lords Gift" – from (N) Floyd	60
Hezekiah Maccotter	"White Chappell" – from (N) Hues	100
	"Enlargement" & "Parkers Point" – from (N) Long	100
	pt. "White Phillips"	70
46:1733:94 ...		
James Dickenson	"Hatton" – from S. Dickenson	600
	"Crooked Lane" – from (N) Staplefort	116
	"Frankford St. Michael" – from Sam. Dickenson	616
	pt. "Hatton" – from (N) Thomas	112
James Chaplin	"Intention" – from (N) Dickenson	100
Hugh Spedden	"Hawks Hill Hope" – from (N) Ungle	100
	"Clifton" – from (N) Ungle	200
Isaac Kittson	"Upper Dover" – from (N) Glover	56
Daniell Maydier	pt. "Goldsborough" – from (N) Quinton	187
	"Fatterhurst" – from (N) Quinton	38
	"Jamaico"	150
	"Marshland"	70
	"Timothys Lott"	25
	"Hermitage" – from (N) Boyd	90
46:1733:95 ...		
George Brinsfield	<n/g>	<n/g>

~~John Collins~~	~~"Hire Dire Lloyd" – from (N) James~~	~~50~~
	~~"Hire Dire Lloyd" – from (N) Taylor~~	~~100~~
John & Hannah Neale	pt. "Hiccory Ridge" – from (N) Neale	50
John Oldham	"Comsberry" – from (N) Rich	100
	"Piney Runn" – from (N) Rich	100
	"Judiths Garden" – from (N) Pattison	80
	"Darlington" – from (N) Edmondson	225
Peirce Welch	"Stepney", "Cornelius Garden", "Salem", & "Quillen" – from (N) Young & (N) Craven	250
46:1733:96 ...		
Thomas Bozman	"Cardiff" – from (N) Alexander	100
	"Discovery"	200
	"Providence"	7
Edward Marsh	"Parkers Point" – from (N) Williams	50
John Berrye	pt. "Bever Neck"	150
	pt. "Broad Lane"	
~~Amy Elizabeth Libby~~	~~pt. "Mount Hope" – from (N) Cathrop~~	~~50~~
Elizabeth Barnwell	pt. "Mount Hope" – from (N) Cathrop	50
46:1733:97 ...		
James Taylor	pt. "Blissland" – from (N) Baggs	100
Aaron Parrott	pt. "Kingston" – from (N) Wilson	51
	pt. "Johns Neck"	26
Mary Bullen	pt. "Little Creek" & pt. "Evans Point" – from Wool. Gibson & his wife	<n/g>
John Herbert	"Mitchells Hermitage" – from Charles Herbert	100
Sarah & Jane Mullican	pt. "Roadley" – from Alice Mullican	150
Samuell Chamberlaine	pt. "Hire Dire Lloyd" – from (N) Lowe	70
	pt. "Hire Dire Lloyd" – from (N) Collins	150
	pt. "Hire Dire Lloyd" – from (N) Davies	200
	pt. "Halls Neck"	124
	"Barminston"	106
	"Cox Addition"	70
	"Cox Chance"	160
	"Contention"	100
46:1733:98 ...		

Fran. Cook	pt. "Nominy" – from (N) Lowe	250
	"Middle Neck" – from (N) Lowe	200
William Aires	pt. "Studs Point" – from (N) Cockeran	100
James Cockerin	pt. "Studs Point" – from (N) Odaly	100
Henry Connyers	"Maidstone" – from (N) Watts	250
	pt. "Warwick" – from (N) Squire	100
Jacob Palmer	pt. "Coventry" – from (N) Hopkins	30
	pt. "Mount Hope" – from (N) Edmondson	100
Thomas Richardson	"Addition" – from (N) Anderson	190
	"Adventure" – from (N) Willen	70
	"Mount Hope"	50
Richard Robinson	"Lords Gift" – from (N) Nobbs	100
46:1733:991 ...		
Samuell Cockayne	pt. "St. Michaells Fresh Runn" – from your mother	400
	pt. "St. Michaells Fresh Runn" – from your mother	401
Sarah Cockayne	"Carters Farme" – from your mother	500
William Cole	"Hilsdone" – from (N) Cockayne	200
	"Coston's Chance" – from (N) Cockayne	32
John Kemble	"Armstrongs Marsh" – from (N) Clayton	200
	pt. "Hazard" – from (N) Powell	70
David Davis	"Tilghman's Fortune" – from (N) Arnett	83
Charles Sinclare	pt. "Holsdons Range", "Mill Road", & "Mill Road Addition" – from (N) Smithson	120
John Williams	"Sharps Choice" – from (N) Wintersell	100
46:1733:100 ...		
Michaell Fletcher	"Darlington" – from (N) Green	280
	"Long Acre"	150
	"Sharps Choyce" – from (N) Wintersell & (N) Gray	200
John Wise	"Sheepshead Point" – from (N) Sanders	50
Rev. Mr. Henry Nicolls	"Micklemire" – from (N) Lindenham	230
	pt. "Maiden Point", "Maiden Point Addition", "Withers Range", & "Little Neck" – from (N) Benson	300
	"Galloway" – from (N) Carslake	150
	"Bryans Lott" – from (N) Carslake	12½
	"Batchelors Range" – from (N) Carslake	250
	pt. "Partnership"	500

John Porter	"Friths Neck" – from (N) Valiant	50
	"Wellens Good Luck" – from (N) Wellen	65
Thomas Greenwood	pt. "Adventure" – from (N) Rigby & (N) Sprignale	200
46:1733:101 ...		
Maur. Oram	pt. "Waistland" – from (N) Bartlett	40
	"Bartletts Tryangle" – from (N) Bartlett	
Thomas Lee	"Glades Addition" – from (N) Hall	71
Catharine Barrett	"Snellings Delight" – from (N) Vinton	50
Thomas Ball	"Long Point" – from (N) Ball	50
	"Long Neck"	180
	"Benjamin's Lott"	100
Robert Dawson	"Birchly" – from (N) Fellows	100
	"Theife Keep Out"	100
	pt. "Union" – from (N) Ward	170
Sarah Ratcliffe	"Goffstone" – from (N) Fellows	100
Lawrance Porter	"York" – from (N) Fairbancks	100
46:1733:102 ...		
John ~~Sandsbury~~ Poore	pt. "Union" – from (N) Stansbury	50
Michaell Cummings	"Lurty" – from (N) Lurty	50
	"Long Neglect" – from (N) Reynolds	100
	"Knave Keep Out"	180
John Kersey	"Webly" – from (N) Fishburne	300
	"Sarahs Neck" – from (N) Fishburne	50
Richard Dawson	"Jones Lott" – from (N) Lurty	50
Robert Roberts	"Ennions Range" – from (N) Williams	50
Thomas Ashcroft	~~"Wattson" – from (N) Reeder~~	~~150~~
	pt. "Stauper"	4
John Barber	pt. "Turner's" – from (N) Grundy	200
Henry Oldfeild	"Summerly" – from (N) Russam	300
46:1733:103 ...		
John Loockerman	"Kirkham" – from (N) Kenerly	350
Richard Townroe	pt. "Heworth" – from (N) Edmondson	22
	<n/g> – from (N) Edmondson	40
John Grozier	pt. "Edmondsons Freshes" & "Heworth" – from (N) Reston	110
Charles & Samuel Morgon	"Dudleys Clifts"	200

James Morgon	pt. "Morgon's Neglect" & "Morgon's Addition"	120
Edward Hopkins	pt. "William & James"	25
	pt. "Hopkins Addition"	25
Michaell Kirwick, Jr.	"Buck Range"	50
Richard Kirwick	"Venture"	37
46:1733:104 ...		
Samuell Dudley	pt. "Advantage" – from (N) Powell	19
Jonathan Taylor	"Piney Point" – from Thomas Taylor	150
	"Piney Point Advantage" – from (N) Alexander	125
William Wareing	pt. "Hampton" – from (N) Jadwin	200
Edmondson Stevens	pt. "Compton"	80
	"Edmondson's Lower Cove"	100
John Stevens	pt. "Compton"	20
	pt. "Edmondson's Lower Cove"	60
Joseph Harden	"Wilderness" – from (N) Welch	75
Rachell Turbutt	pt. "Bliss Land" & "Bagg's Marsh" – from (N) Baggs	300
	pt. "Bliss Land" & "Bagg's Marsh" – from (N) Baggs [!]	300
46:1733:105 ...		
William Shawe	"Halls Neck" – from (N) Abott	200
John Potts	"Near Carter's Bridge"	15
	pt. "St. Michall's Fresh Run" – from (N) Cockayne	15
Edward Eubancks	"Swifts Chance"	80
	"Jacob & John Pasture"	50
Nicholas Benson	~~"Bensons Enlargement"~~	~~370~~
	"Bogg Hole"	50
	~~"Fox Harbour"~~	~~50~~
	"Maiden Point"	150
	"Maiden Point Addition"	100
	"Withers Range"	224
	"Bensons Choice"	90
Phill. Skinner	pt. "Enlargement"	50
	"Skinners Point"	50
	"Skinners Addition"	25
46:1733:106 ...		

David Hughes	pt. "Davenport" & "Beech"	12
	pt. "Janes Progress"	35
Bartholomew Roberts	pt. "Janes Progress"	35
James Harvey	"Abrahams Lott"	100
Elizabeth Stanton	pt. "Bantry"	100
~~Bassell Nowell~~	~~pt. "Freshes"~~	~~100~~
John Vickers	pt. "Tell Tale Loss" – from (N) Browne	52
~~Thomas Stevens~~	~~pt. "Dover" – from (N) Sewell~~	~~75~~
46:1733:107 ...		
Batholomew Greenwood	pt. "Hampton" – from Bath. Jadwin	<n/g>
Matthias Docwra (QA)	"Storeys Park" – from (N) Storey	100
John Downes (QA)	pt. "Hemsleys Arcadia" – from (N) Garey	75
John Hill	"Greenhill" – from (N) Pratt	100
Sarah Seney	pt. "Sutton" & pt. "Hardship" – from Silvester Abbott	50
John Hodson	pt. "Roadly" – from (N) Dickenson	200
Thomas Wiles	pt. "Mount Hope" – from (N) Edmondson	50
	pt. "Chance" – from (N) Neale	62
46:1733:108 ...		
Elisabeth Kello	"Piney Point" – from Thomas Edmondson	250
Henry Henrix	pt. "Mount Hope" – from Thomas Edmondson	35
Thomas Curtis	pt. "Mount Hope" – from Thomas Edmondson	181
John Sprignall	<n/g> – tract of land bought of Phil. Morgon	100
Jacob Barnwell	pt. "Mount Hope" – from (N) Miles	27
Anthony Rumball	pt. "Lower Dover" – from (N) Powell	130
46:1733:109 ...		
John Sutton	pt. "Tilghmans Fortune"	81
Free School of Talbot County	pt. "Tilghmans Fortune"	100
John Laurance	pt. "Partnership"	180
Sarah Morgon wife of Capt. Edward Morgon	"Holme Hill" – from (N) Corney	62
	pt. "Smiths Clifts"	158
~~John Potts~~	~~pt. "St. Michaels Fresh Runn" – from (N) Cockayne~~	~~1[illegible]~~
46:1733:110 ...		
John Rousby, Esq.	"Morgons Hope"	30[illegible]
	"Morgons Choice"	30[illegible]

Fran. Connerly	"Hollands Addition"	41
John Kirbye	"Woolf Pitt Ridge"	50
William Stevens	"Williams Lott"	49
Nicholas Lurtey	"Cabbin Neck", "Potters Delight", & "Potters Lott Resurveyed"	150
Thomas Turner	"Turners Chance"	100
Daniell Royer	"Hermitage"	90
	pt. "Bartram"	30
	"Freshes" – from (N) Howell	200
Robert Fortune	pt. "Dover"	150
46:1733:111 ...		
William Elstone	"French Hazard"	41
Benjamin Pemberton	"Security"	406
Perry Benson	"Neglect"	96
	pt. "Bensons Enlargement"	170
~~John Price~~	~~pt. "Hattfield" & "Hatfield Addition"~~	~~775~~
James Williams	~~pt. "Dover"~~	~~50~~
	pt. "Dover" – from (N) Camper	86
David Kerby	pt. "Turners Ridge"	40
Tench Francis	"Addition"	50
	pt. "Bartram"	50
	"Addition" – from (N) Russam & (N) Thawley	250
	½ "Dixons Outlett"	50
	"Addition to Batchelors Branch" – from (N) Roberts & wife	33⅓
John Ray	pt. "Dundee"	133
	pt. "Addition to Batchelors Branch"	66⅔
46:1733:112 ...		
~~Thomas Roberts~~	~~pt. "Addition to Batchelors Branch"~~	~~33½~~
James Horney	"Batchelors Branch"	100
John Leverton	"Dudleys Choice"	100
John Higgins	"Borams Range"	177
Dennis Carey	pt. "Turky Neck"	100
	"Kingsburys Addition"	100
Thomas Purnell	pt. "Hampton"	80
John Baynard	"Hampton" & "Parkers Range"	130

John Camperson	"Hampton" & "Parkers Range"	<n/g>
46:1733:113 ...		
Bryan Seney	pt. "Sutton"	80
	pt. "Sutton" – from (N) Abbott	78
Daniel Carvan	pt. "Cuba"	100
Hugh Macdermod	pt. "Buckingham" & pt. "Jobs Content"	100
Robert Johnson	"Stapleton"	77
William Sharpe	"Moorefields"	100
	"Adventure"	100
Robert Rook	"Withrington"	200
	pt. "Lancashire"	70
Richard Borden	"Larramores Lott"	50
Sarah Corke	"Lewis"	100
Elisabeth Hadaway	pt. "Merchants Folly"	150
46:1733:114 ...		
Laughton Macdaniell	pt. "Fishburnes Lott"	100
William Thomas, Jr.	~~pt. "Hatton"~~	~~112~~
	pt. "Cottingham" – from (N) Chew	140
Charles Markland	"Morgon Point"	50
John Rocate	"Moorefields"	94
	"Moorefields Addition"	28
Mr. John Robins	"Holm Hill"	400
	pt. "Rich Range"	200
	"Rich Range Addition"	100
William Frampton	pt. "Rich Range"	50
Risdon Bozman	"Wattson" – from (N) Knowls	150
	"Partnership" – from (N) Knowls	
Robert Dodson	pt. "Bensons Enlargement"	120
46:1733:115 ...		
William Fooks	pt. "Hog Range" – from (N) Bennett	47
Robert Walker	<n/g> – on Kings Creek from (N) Berry	100
Robert Hunter	"Dudleys Demeasns" – from (N) Thompson	40
Charles Carroll, Esq.	<n/g> – from (N) Parran	1000
Edwin Godwin	"Parkers Freshes"	300
Andrew Price	½ "Todcaster"	500
Jerremiah Nicols	pt. "Partnership"	250

Nicholas Bartlett	pt. "Bartletts Inherritance"	100
46:1733:116 ...		
Thomas Keet	pt. "Brittania"	200
Anthony Richardson	"Hasely"	200
	"Widows Lott"	15
	½ "Partners Hazard" – from (N) Cook	<n/g>
	"Browns Lott" – from (N) Harper	100
Rachell Connelly	pt. "Hogg Hole"	142
Susannah Cockrin	pt. "Hogg Hole"	142
Edward Needles	pt. "Johns Neck"	4
Thomas Hutchinson	pt. "Johns Neck"	19
Henry Burgis	"Bobbs Hill"	100
46:1733:117 ...		
William Webb Haddaway	"Rich Neck"	150
	"Haddaways Lott"	70
Elizabeth Harrison	pt. "Bensons Enlargement"	190
James Spencer	pt. "Bensons Enlargement"	127
	"Fox Harbour"	50
Mary Parrott	pt. "Bensons Enlargement"	150
John Harrison, Sr.	"Prous Point" – from (N) Harrison	<n/g>
	pt. "Hap Hazard" – from (N) Harrison	<n/g>
William Mackey	<n/g> – from Phill. Casey & his wife, lying between two branches on Cornelius Neck	<n/g>
46:1733:118 ...		
Joseph Turner	pt. "Johns Hill" – from William Turner	90
Isaac Cox	pt. "Johns Hill" – for your wife from (N) Turner	90
John Neighbours	pt. "Edmondsons Freshes" – from John Price	50
Nicholas Goldsborough, Jr.	pt. "Halls Neck" – from (N) Peck	100
William Richardson	"Gurlington" – from (N) Gaskin	75
Thomas Frampton	"Framptons Begining"	96
Allemby Millington	"Nobles Meadows"	229
	"Betts Addition"	207
John Cannady	"Carradays Hazard"	29
John Ratcliffe	"Ratcliffs Highway"	113
46:1733:119 **<blank>**		
46:1733:120-2 **Recapitulation**		

54F:1 9 October 1734		**Acres**
George Robins	"Jennings <unr>"	718
John Ratcliffe	"Ratcliffs Choice"	109
Thomas Bozeman	"Tates Lott"	459
	"Timber Neck"	294
John Fairbank	"Good Happ"	23
John Morgon	"Morgons Addition"	137
Madam Henrietta Maria Lloyd	"Henrietta Maria Purchase"	412
William Michael	"Bullens Addition"	102
Michael Kerbye	"Buck Range Addition"	55
Philemon Skinner	"Skinners Discovery"	70
Richard Roberts	"Roberts Addition"	47
54F:2 ...		
Mary Cox	"Lewis"	290
Thomas Haddaway	"Haddaways Addition"	75
Daniell Bowyer	"Hermitage"	90
Solomon Horney	"Neglect"	126
Mary Wrightson	"Clays Neck"	102
John Cooper	"Coopers Lott"	52
John Stevens	"Edmonds Cove"	174
Robert Dawson	"Dawsons Composition"	282
William Harrison (Miles)	"Taylors Ridge"	100
Richard Bennett, Esq.	"Poplar Ridge"	249
John Mulican	"Mulicans Chance"	100
54F:3 ...		
James Kendrick	"Coventry"	250
Thomas Delahay	"Delahays Fortune"	100
54F:4 10 February 1735		
Robert Goldsborough	pt. "Four Square"	65[illegible]
John Bartlett (shipwright)	"Bartletts Inheritance"	14[illegible]
Edward Harding	"Hardings Endeavor"	20[illegible]
Capt. John Kemble	"Kemble Industry"	28[illegible]
Capt. James Dickenson	"Bennetts Freshes"	42[illegible]
Samuel Chamberlain	pt. "Four Square"	35[illegible]
Peirce Flemmin	"Flemmins Freshes"	21[illegible]
54F:5 10 February 1735		

Robert Goldsborough	pt. "Four Square"	650
John Bartlett	"Bartlett's Inheritance"	140
Isaac Marlin	"Marlin's Neglect"	57
Edward Harding	"Harding's Endeavour"	200
Capt. John Kemble	"Kemble's Industry"	283
Capt. James Dickenson	"Bennetts Freshes"	423
Samuel Chamberlain	pt. "Four Square"	350
Peirce Flemmin	"Flemmin's Freshes"	215
William Edmondson	"Edmondsons Pond"	9
Edmund Fish	"Fisher's Hazard"	18
Richard Bennett, Esq.	"Neglect"	107
~~Thomas Langley~~	~~"Langley"~~	~~200~~
54F:6 ...		
William Hemsly	"Hemsly upon Wye Addition"	146
Thomas Bullen	"Bullen's Discovery"	136
Edward Fottrell	"Fottrell's Discovery"	250
11 March 1736		
Anthony Richardson	"Addition"	229
Michael Fletcher	"Richmond"	41
Ann Goldsbrough wife of John Goldsbrough	"Peak's Marsh"	318
	"Marshy Peak"	132
Col. Ernault Hawkins	"Cabbin Neck", "Sandy Bite", & "Hall's Fortune"	238
54F:7 14 May 1738		
Samuel Broadway	"Broadway's Meadow"	100
John Hunt	"Fools Paradice"	38
Charles Banning	"Yorks Destruction"	50
Kenelm Skillington	"Skillington's Happ"	20
Michael Fletcher	"Dover Marsh"	348
Peter Caulk, Jr.	"Caulk's Addition"	236
Francis Harrison	"Minors Lott"	100
54F:<unnumbered> <blank>		
54F:8 ...		
William Edmondson	"Edmondsons Pond"	9
Edmond Fish	"Fishers Hazzard"	48
Richard Bennett, Esq.	"Neglect"	107

Thomas Langley	"Langley"	166
William Hemsly	"Hemsly Upon Wye"	146
Thomas Bullen	"Bullens Discovery"	136
Edward Fottrell	"Fottrells Discovery"	250
54F:9 11 March 1736		
Anthony Richardson	"Addition"	229
Michael Fletcher	"Richmond"	41
1738		
Robert Newcom	"Harbour Rouse"	130
William Harrison	"Dover"	395
Joseph Atkinson	"Atkinsons Chance"	43
William Barker	pt. "Lower Dover"	232
William Edwards	"Mistake"	51
Samuell Dickenson	"Little Creek"	200
Francis Neale	pt. "Hickory Ridge"	137
John Raynolds	"Raynolds Point"	148
James Dawson	"Bayleys Forrest"	113
54F:10 ...		
John Clift	"Clifts Addition"	100
11 March 1736		
Ann Goldsbrough wife of John Goldsbrough	"Peaks Marsh"	318
	"Marshy Peak"	132
Col. Ern. Hawkins	"Cabbin Neck", "Sandy Bite", & "Halls Fortune"	238
14 May 1738		
Samuel Broadway	"Broadways Meadows"	100
John Hunt	"Fools Parradice"	38
Charles Banning	"Yorks Destruction"	50
Michael Fletcher	"Dover Marsh"	348
Peter Caulk, Jr.	"Caulks Addition"	236
Francis Harrison	"Minors Lott"	100
Kenelm Skillington	"Skillingtons Hap"	20
54F:11 ...		
David Kirby	"Kirby's Interest"	38
Thomas Turner	"Stoppard Moore"	100
Robert Rolls	"Dorothy's Enlargement"	45

Rizdon Bozeman	"Neglect"	34
Michael Fletcher	"Richmond's Addition"	282
George Robins	"Buckingham"	903
54F:12 14 March 1740/1		
Mr. Ridso. Boseman	"Warsons Addition"	73
Robert Newcom	"Partnership Distruction"	208
John Harrisson	"Harrissons Security"	167
Inclosed to Mr. Boseman & received per Mr. Jeremiah Nicholls on 17 April 1741.		
Ralph Dawson	"Jones's Lott Addition"	50
54F:13 29 January 1741/2		
William Harper	"Bite the Biter"	35
John Carslake	"Carslake's Discovery"	109
Robert Hall	"Hall's Range"	353
David Jones	"Jones's Interest"	40
Thomas Purnell	"Fragment"	20
Daniel Lambden	"Bridges"	176
Robert Rolls	"Rolls Range"	237
Thomas Sherwood	"Daniel & Mary"	375
John Studham	"Studham's Chance"	18
Inclosed to Mr. Thomas Boseman & forwarded to Mr. Thomas Muire per Mr. Jeremiah Nichols on 3 February 1741/2.		
54F:14 25 February 1742/3		
Peter Denny	"Denny's Content"	85
Richard Feddeman	"Feddeman's Discovery"	408
Thomas Perkins	"Perkins Discovery"	193½
Isaac Cox	"Joce's Hazard"	103
Robert Harwood	"Harwood's Neglect"	38
James Ratcliff	"Maple Branch"	40
John Kenneday	"Kennedy's Addition"	23
Thomas Bozman	"Tate's Lott"	449
Matthew Tilghman Ward	"But Neck"	577
Sent by Mr. Robert Hall & forwarded to Mr. Bozman on 11 March 1742/3.		
54F:15 30 January 1743/4		
John Carslake	"Carslake's Content"	60
William Ayres	"Ayres Venture"	96
John Arrington	"Pasty Nuke"	24

John Stevens	"John's Lott"	60
David Davis	"Bite the Biter"	33
Arthur Rigby	"Rigby's Choice"	101½
Inclosed to Mr. Thomas Bozman & sent by Mr. Jeremiah Nicols on 3 March 1743/4.		
54F:16 7 February 1744/5		
John Potts	"Potts's Discovery"	60
Edmond Blades	"Matthew Circumvented"	334
Thomas Bozman	"Browns Park"	119
Richard Gresson	"Gresson's Discovery"	106½
Edward Neale	pt. "Nanticoke Mannor"	171
Richard Bennett, Esq.	"Tobacco Pipe" & "Hackers Oldfield"	745
Frances Camperson	"Frances's Delight"	48
Samuel Hopkins	"Ealom"	90
Inclosed to Mr. Thomas Bozman & sent to Mr. Edward Lloyd on 5 March 1744/5.		
54F:17 23 February 1744/5		
Richard Chance	"Chance"	167
5 March 1745/6		
Ralph Dawson	"Rest Content"	45
John Powell	"Boston Clift"	520
William Vickers	"Piccadilly"	150½
John Fairbank	"Goodhap"	23
12 February 1746/7		
Anthony Lecompt	"Anthony's Inlargement"	108½
Edward Oldham	"Oldham's Discovery"	115½
James Edge	"Scrapps"	60
54F:18 ...		
William Martin	"Martin's Purchase"	5
John Silvester	"Horse Point"	21
Col. Edward Lloyd	"Lloyd's Addition to Brorely"	380
	"Bennetts Kind Caution"	322¾
Richard Bennett, Esq.	"Elizabeth's Venture"	192½
Edward Clark	"Pigg Point"	40
Robert Stonestreet	"Tillberry"	376
Mr. Robert Goldsborough	"Conjunction"	279
Samuel Mullikin	"Mullikin's Delight"	63¾
Joseph Turner	"Turner's Discovery"	122¾

John Sherwood	"Allemby's Fields"	124¾
Richard Kirby	"Kirby's Outlett"	47
54F:19 27 February 1747/8		
Michael Kirby	"Bows's Range"	235
George Beswick	"Christopher's Lott"	286¼
John Chambers	"Chambers's Adventure"	132¾
6 February 1748/9		
Col. Edward Lloyd	"Lloyd's Lott"	141
Robert Hall	"Hall's Addition"	12
Thomas Bozman	"Bozman's Addition"	393¾
David Kirby	"David Kirby"	98
Andrew & Richard Skinner	"Tanner's Choice"	769
54F:20 ...		
William Adams	"Adam's Right"	n/g
William Wilson	"Wilsons Lott"	190
John Barwick	"Barwick's Discovery"	123
Enclosed to Mr. Thomas Bozman & sent by Rev. Mr. Archbull on 15 February 1748		
12 February 1749		
John Barwick	"Discovery Addition"	10
George & Philemon Noble	"Nobles Addition" surveyed for Robert Noble on 25 March 1731	350
John Register	"Kingsberry Addition"	159¼
Rizdon Bozman	"Moor & Casell" surveyed for Thomas Bullen on 20 October 1747	84
54F:21 ...		
William Gale	"Fishers Discovery"	5
John Glover	pt. "Upper Dover"	114¾
William Troth	"Bonnington"	38
13 February 1750		
John Dickinson	"Dickinsons Field"	18¾
William Thomas	"Fortune"	93¾
Thomas Loveday	"Knave Stand Off"	68
Jacob Gore	"Dunsmore Heath" surveyed for John Wooters on 4 June 1682	200
54F:22 ...		
John Fairbank	"Tobacco Pipe"	9¾

Francis Register	"Francis's Plains"	64½
William Taylor	"Turkey Neck Addition"	35
54F:23 18 February 1752		
John Dixon	"Dixon's Discovery"	20¼
Sarah Beswick	"Sarah's Addition"	50
Henry Richardson	"Point Look Out"	8½
Thomas Ashcroft	"Devenport"	114¾
Anthony Gregory	"New Begun"	91¼
John Auld, Jr.	"Auld's Security"	47
Col. Edward Lloyd	"Bennett Lloyd"	384½
Henry Martin	"Crooked Ramble"	75
Edward Knott	"Pooley's Discovery"	75
Thomas Stevens	"Compton"	108
Robert Lowther	"Forrest & Dike"	116
54F:24 ...		
James Benson	"Fishing Bay" surveyed for Perry Benson on 29 February 1747	126¾
Jacob Gore	"Frampton" surveyed for Robert Frampton on 24 February 1685	122
William Wintersell	"Wintersell" surveyed for William Winters on 20 October 1684	200
Simon Keld	"Kelds Inheritance"	271
Sent to Mr. John Bozman on 19 August 1752.		
54F:25 22 February 1753		
Thomas Dudley	"Broad Lane Addition"	41[illegible]
Peter Harwood	"Addition"	284[illegible]
John Lookerman, Jr.	"Skeemers Neglect"	44
Samuel Chamberlaine	"Rockey Nook Addition"	39[illegible]
Nathaniel Conner	"Brufferton"	74
Abram Falkener	"Neighbours Keep Out"	46
Arthur Rigby	"Lamberton"	109[illegible]
Robert Harwood	"Harwoods Hill"	62[illegible]
Thomas Powell	"Powell's Meadows"	34[illegible]
Edmond Ferrill	"Portumney"	179[illegible]
Edward Clark	"Parkers Farm Addition"	4[illegible]
Inclosed to Mr. John Bozman & forwarded by Mr. James Earle on 26 February 1753.		

54F:26 28 February 1754		
Robert Newcomb	"Robart & Margarett"	441½
Daniel Powell	pt. "Troth's Fortune"	246½
7 April 1755		
John Cox	"Cox's Venture"	38
James Benny	"Level Luck"	60
Thomas Powell	"Powell's Misfortune"	42½
Edward Elliott	"Elliotts Purchase"	361
Samuel Chamberlaine	"Grundy's Lott"	55
Thomas Frampton	"Framptons Chance"	34¾
Enclosed to Mr. Henry Hollyday on 10 April 1754.		
54F:28 16 March 1756		
Mr. James Tilghman	"Fausley Meadow"	50½
Impey Dawson	"Cromwell"	470¾
Samuel Chamberlaine, Esq.	"Rome"	138½
James Broadaway	"Dudley" surveyed for Richard Dudley on 12 February 1679.	200
James Kemp	"Kemps Discovery"	9½
Col. Thomas Chamberlaine	2 lots in town of Oxford surveyed for Samuel Chamberlaine, Esq. On 3 June 1735	1½
18 March 1757		
Daniel Sherwood, Jr.	"Allembys Fields Addition"	7¾
Henry Burgess	"Neighbours Stand Off"	18¼
Jonathan Neale	"Neales Advantage"	403
54F:28[!] 28 February 1758		
Cornelius Daley	"Cornelius's Coole Spring Addition"	11¾
Dr. Henry Murray	"Gatterly Moor"	206½
Rigbey Foster	"Fosters Chance"	27¼
John Goldsborough	"Orems Delight"	56¾
17 February 1759		
Robert Harwood	"Harwoods Addition"	4

46:1738:1	**Island Hundred**	**Acres**
William Clayton	pt. "Waterton"	290
	"Wishbeck"	100
	"Poplar Hill"	200
	pt. "Normonton"	167
	pt. "Bettys Dowry" – from (N) King	2
	pt. "Kings Neglect" – from (N) King	107
	"Addition" – from (N) King	200
Rachell Finney	"Finney Range"	225
	pt. "Waterton"	170
Philip Emmerson	½ "Widdows Chance"	320
	"Harwood Lyon"	600
	pt. "Wellston"	100
	"Hambletons Park"	263
	"Keilding & Buckingham"	393
	"Addition"	63
John Millar	½ "Newmans Lott" – for h/o C. Stevens	100
	½ "Planters Delight" – for h/o C. Stevens	100
	pt. "Nobles Chance" – for h/o C. Stevens	100
	"Stevens Addition" – for h/o C. Stevens	75
	pt. "Nobles" – for h/o C. Stevens	<n/g>
John Swett	pt. "Planters Delight" – for h/o Robert Noble	100
	"Nobles Addition" – for h/o Robert Noble	150
	pt. "Nobles Ridge" – for h/o Robert Noble	75
46:1738:2	**Island Hundred ...**	
Daniel Baker	pt. "Bettys Chance"	100
	pt. "Stevens Plains"	50
Oliver Millington	pt. "Betts Chance"	100
	"Epsom"	100
Mary Morgan	pt. "Morgans Neglect", pt. "Ramsey Forrest", & pt. "Morgans Addition" – for h/o John Morgan	106
Mr. John Davis (cnp)	"Hope Chance"	50
	"Knave Keep Out"	50
	"Personage"	100
	"Batchelors Point"	100
	pt. "Ashby"	147

	pt. "Bettys Cover"	20
	"Addition"	350
Mrs. Hannah Davis	½ "Widdows Chance"	320
	"Peventure"	50
	"Whartons Glade"	50
	"Couple Close"	100
	"Addition"	32
Christopher Santee	"Chance"	100
	"Knave Sand of"	50
46:1738:3 Island Hundred ...		
George Prouse	pt. "Cumberland" & pt. "Chances Help" – from (N) Chance	157
Dennis Larey	pt. "Parkers Hazard"	142
	"Beverdam Neck" – from (N) Mounteque	70½
John Sprignal	<n/g> – tract bought of Capt. Edward Morgan	100
	pt. "Chesnut Bay"	
Thomas Turner (miller)	"Turners Chance"	100
Thomas Purnell	pt. "Hampton"	8
	pt. "Rich Range"	150
William Kirbey	"Kirbey Adventure" – from his father	49
46:1738:4 Island Hundred ...		
Thomas Bruff	"Daniels Addition"	70
	"Walkers Tooth"	147
	"Daniels Rest"	50
	"Partnership"	106
	"Walkers Corner"	18
	"Millington"	50
James Hollyday, Esq.	"New Design Bettys Branch"	325
	"Stock Range"	400
	"Granny"	100
	<n/g> – another tract of land of (N) Woolman	150
	"Faulkners Folly"	100
George Grason	"Tannars Hope"	50
	"Skinners Outlett"	50
	"Infancy" – for Robert Grason	65

Mr. Robert Lloyd	"Rickburn"	200
	"Elliotts Discovery"	100
	"Adjunction"	50
	"Scotland"	50
	"Loyds Discovery"	96
	"Hope" – from (N) Collins	100
	pt. "Turners Point" – from (N) Turner	200
	pt. "Partnership"	1200
	"Widdow Chance"	50
	"Tallifawn"	100
	"Rumbley Marsh"	300
	"Murry"	150
	"Partnership"	310
	"New Mill"	200
	"Addition"	100
	"Buckland Marsh"	50
	"Buckland"	250
	pt. "Gurlington"	100
	"Grundeys Inclosure"	176
	pt. "Marshland"	265
	"Graves"	100
Lewis Jones	"Triangle"	100
46:1738:5	**Island Hundred ...**	
Richard Skinner	"Skinners Choice"	340
	"Skinners Borders"	100
	"Skinners Vineyard"	75
	"Skinners Addition"	150
	"Skinners Security"	103
Mr. Jacob Gibson	"Rebaccas Gardon"	150
	"Champenham & Benden"	550
	"Champenhams Addition"	50
Robert Hall	"Parkers Thickett"	100
	"Leinrick"	70
Perry Benson	pt. "Huntinton"	76
	"Neglect"	96
	pt. "Partnership"	308

46:1738:6	**Island Hundred ...**	
George Gary	"Dirty Wedden"	100
	"Fortunes Addition"	52
	"Dirty Weddens Addition"	100
	"Brafferton"	100
	"Fortune"	150
	"Little Britinia"	150
	"Todd Upon Dowen" – from (N) Thorld	80
William Elbert	pt. "Rebbecca Garden" – from (N) Emmerson	25
	"Lloyds Costine"	659
	pt. "Rebbeccas Garden" – from Mr. Loyd	25
	pt. "Gratham" – from Richard Marlin to Mrs. Frances Elbert	106
James Sanders & John Pitts	pt. "Hambletons Park" – from (N) Sheild	137
	"Damses Outlet"	50
Fardinando Callaghan	pt. "Britinia" – from (N) Story & Elizabeth Williams	100
Woolman Gibson	"Leigh" – from Henry Jones	40
	"Edmondton" – from (N) Thorld	300
	pt. "Bendon" – from (N) Thorld	17
	pt. "Bryans Lott"	12½
46:1738:7	**Island Hundred ...**	
Robert Stonested	"Dunns Range Addition" – from Charles Walker	200
John & Andrew Kinonmont	"Fools Parridice"	50
	pt. "Bartram"	150
	"Batchelors Hope"	50
	"Hopewell"	80
	"Scotts Lott"	100
William Cole	"Hilsdon" – from (N) Cockayn	200
	"Costins Chance" – from (N) Cockayn	32
	pt. "Britinia"	230
John Vickers	pt. "Tell Tales Loss" – from (N) Brown	52
	"Vickers Lott"	52
James Horney	"Batchelors Branch"	100
	"Batchelors Branch Addition"	100
46:1738:8	**Island Hundred ...**	

Thomas Keeld	pt. "Britinia" & pt. "Stevens's Range"	200
Mr. Edward Lloyd	"Meersgate"	300
	"Thrimbey Grange"	500
	"Natts Point"	50
	"Lynton"	600
	"Grange"	150
	"Salters Marsh"	100
	"Long Neglect"	133
	"Meersgate Addition"	267
	pt. "Crouches Choice"	50
	"Inlett"	88
	"Roadway"	50
	"Addition"	100
	"Scotts Close" – from (N) Start	200
	pt. "Woolmans Hermitage"	55
	pt. "Woolmans Enheritance"	104"
	"Breileys Deligt"	150
	"Doughtys Lott"	50
	"Doughtys Hope"	50
	"Ceedar Point"	48
	"Meersgate Addition"	69
	"Knightleys"	100
	"Soldiers Delight"	100
Samuell Kininmont	⅓ "Dundee"	133
Aron Higg	"Pattingham"	100
46:1738:9 **Island Hundred ...**		
Sollomon Warner	"Pools Discovery"	168
William Warner	pt. "Nobles Chance"	100
Lambert Sheild & James Sanders	pt. "Bedworth"	100
	"Rich Farm Addition"	200
John Kininmont	"Kininmonts Delight"	244
Margery Smallcorn	"Faulkeners Level"	150
Richard Gibson	pt. "Gallaway"	54
	pt. "Bryans Lott"	12½
46:1738:10 **Island Hundred ...**		
Benjamin Stuart	pt. "Fishing Bay"	200

John Ray	pt. "Dundee"	133
Francis Pickrin, Jr.	"Sarahs Lott"	50
Alice Hewey	pt. "Carters Inheritance" – for h/o Robert Hewey	100
George Beswicks	pt. "Christophers Loot"	100
	pt. "Stevens Plains"	50
Richard Besswicks	pt. "Christophers Lott"	100
	pt. "Stevens's Plaines"	50
46:1738:11 Island Hundred ...		
Robert Beswicks	pt. "Harrises Lott"	111
William Hemsley	"Hemsley upon Wye"	1160
	"Hemsley upon Wye Addition" composed of: • "Virgins Inn" • "Virgin Inn Addition"	146
Thomas Hopkins	pt. "William & James"	33
	pt. "Maxwell Moor"	100
46:1738:12 Island Hundred ...		
Mrs. Hen. Mar. Chew	"Timber Neck"	120
	"Betty Dowry"	150
	pt. "Kings Plains"	158
	pt. "Kings Forrest"	150
	pt. "Carters Inheritance"	300
	"Outlett"	220
	pt. "Woolmans Hermitage"	109
	pt. "Woolmans Inheritance"	206
	"Knightleys Addition"	50
	pt. "Kings Neglect"	<n/g>
	"Parsonage Addition"	<n/g>
46:1738:13 Island Hundred ...		
Richard Bennett, Esq. (cnp)	"Morgan St. Michalls"	300
	"Marron"	130
	"Claybourns Island"	100
	"Abbington"	400
	"Poplar Neck"	100
	pt. "Wellston"	150
	"Town Road"	50
	"Henritts Marr. Discovery"	216

	"Lobbs Crook on Resurvey"	679
	"Tobbacca Pipe"	359
	pt. "Crouches Choice"	100
	"Farme"	348
	"Sweetnams Hope"	120
	"Batchelors Delight"	100
	"Hern Island"	75
	"Bodwells Indian Neck Resurveyed"	913
	"Winkleton"	185
	"Mitchells Lott"	200
	"Triangles"	55
	"Advantage"	500
	"New Town"	100
	"Planters Increase", "Turner's Ridge", & others – resurveyed	504
	"Poplar Ridge" – on escheat	249
	"Free Neglect" – on resurvey	107
	"Kimbles Industry"	283
	"Stevens's Lott"	19
46:1738:14	**Island Hundred ...**	
Harris Clayland	"Skipton"	300
	pt. "Ramsey Forrest"	43
	pt. "Finnleys Hermitage"	200
Samuell Wright	"Harrises Range"	400
Will Russell	pt. "Huntington" – by your fathers will	76
Thomas Russell	pt. "Huntington" & pt. "Huntingon Grange" – by your fathers will	200
William Edwards	pt. "Addition" & pt. "Fishing Bay" – by will of Michaell Russell to your wife	90
	"Mistake"	51
Mary Sherwood	pt. "Huntington" & pt. "Addition" – by your fathers will	90
46:1738:15	**Island Hundred ...**	
Mr. William Dawson (cnp)	"Batchelors Range"	250
	"Batchelors Range Addition"	500
	"Hatton Hope"	100
	pt. "Shrigleys Fortune"	170

	pt. "Gallaway"	100
	pt. "Huntington" & pt. "Addition"	90
William Hadder	pt. "Ramsey Forrest"	107
Vincent Jones	pt. "Nobles Chance"	100
Robert Noble, Jr.	pt. "Newmans Lott"	100
46:1738:16 **Island Hundred ...**		
John Bolton (QA)	"Inclosure"	150
Joseph Kininmont	⅓ "Dundee"	133
46:1738:17 **Island Hundred ...**		
Adam & Richard Eubanks	pt. "Omeleys Range"	150
	"Jacob & Johns Pasture"	120
John Tibbles	pt. "Sheepshead Point"	50
	"Tibbls Addition"	20
Thomas Robson	"Jones Look Out"	50
	pt. "Partnership" – from (N) Benson & (N) Valiant	125
James Hopkins	pt. "Hopkins Point"	100
	"Hopkins Point Addition"	25
	"Addition"	150
John Barwick	"Newmans Folly" – from (N) Williams	50
46:1738:18 **Island Hundred ...**		
Henry Wharton	"Hookland"	100
Ralph Person	pt. "Bishoprick"	50
Nathaniell Grace	"Rest Content"	100
	"Goodwins Addition"	90
	pt. "Adventure"	113½
Richard Herrington	"Hetheringtons Delight"	50
	½ "Adventure"	113½
George Taylor	"Chance"	100
	"Taylor & James Discovery"	100
John Fellows	pt. "Abrahams Lott", pt. "Goffton", & pt. "Mill Road 2nd Addition"	65
	pt. "Abrahams Lott" – from John Jones, Jr.	58
Mary Attwell	pt. "Bantry"	200
46:1738:19 **Island Hundred ...**		
John Bartlett (cnp)	pt. "Bensons Enlargment"	50
	"Rockney Nook"	100

	"Rockey Nook Addition"	58
	pt. "Bartletts Inheritance"	30
Matthew Kirby	"Swamp Hole"	100
Jacob Faulkenor	"Faulkenors Hazard"	60
James Myrick	"Hazard Addition"	9
	"Powells Hazard" – from (N) Powell	50
Philip Banning	"Bannings Hazard"	50
	"Faulkenors Square" – from Edward Carslake	100
Ralph Holmes	pt. "Tilghmans Fortune"	50
46:1738:20 Island Hundred ...		
Jeffery Horney	pt. "Cottingham" – from (N) Abrahams	50
Isaac Dixon	pt. "Cottingham" – from (N) Abrahams	25
	pt. "Cottingham" – from (N) Newton	50
	pt. "Carters Plains"	206
	"Bennetts Hill"	50
	"Ending Controversie"	150
	pt. "Ashby"	60
	pt. "Dixons Outlett"	156
Mr. Samuell Cockayne	pt. "St. Michalls Fresh Run" – from your mother	401
Thomas Perkins	pt. "Carters Farm" – from your wives mother	500
46:1738:21 Island Hundred ...		
John Williams	"Sharps Choice" – from (N) Wintesell	100
	pt. "London Derry" – from (N) Armstrong	1½
John Loockerman	"Kirkham" – from (N) Kemnery	350
	pt. "Shregleys Fortune"	100
	"Harrington"	270
Morris Oram	pt. "Waitland & Bartletts Tryangle" – from (N) Bartlett	40
	pt. "Foxhole"	145
	pt. "Fox Harbour"	50
	"Fox Denn"	56
	"Waterford" – from (N) Vaughn & (N) Robins on 9 November 1734	100
John Potts	"Near Carters Bridge"	15
	pt. "St. Michalls Fresh Run"	60

Elizabeth Eubanks	"Swifts Chance" – for h/o Edward Eubanks	80
	"Jacob & Johns Pasture" – for h/o Edward Eubanks	50
46:1738:22 Island Hundred ...		
Fran. Stanton	pt. "Bantry"	100
Henry Henrix	pt. "Mount Hope" – from Thomas Edmondson	35
John Sutton	pt. "Tilghmans Fortune"	81
Free School of Talbot County	pt. "Tilghmans Fortune"	100
Mr. Tench Francis	"Addition"	50
	pt. "Bartram"	50
	pt. "Addition" – from (N) Russam	100
	pt. "Dixons Lott" or "Outlett"	250
	"Addition Batchelors Branch" – from (N) Roberts & ux	33½
	"Fausley"	250
	"Edmondson Range" – from (N) Gale	400
	"Parkers Park" – from (N) Richardson	500
William Thomas, Jr.	pt. "Cottingham" – from (N) Chew	140
	pt. "Cottingham" – for your wife	125
	"Morefeild" – from (N) Turner	280
46:1738:23 Island Hundred ...		
Henry Burges	"Bobbs Hill"	100
	"Hopewell"	50
James Ratcliff	"Ratcliff High Way"	113
	pt. "Jacob & John Pasture" – from your father	85
	pt. "Addition" – from (N) Cockayne	52
	pt. "Jacob & Johns Pasture" – from John Ratcliff on 18 March 1737	85
John Neighbours	pt. "Edmondsons Freshes" – from John Price	50
Mr. Nicholas Goldsborough, Jr.	pt. "Halls Neck" – from (N) Peck	100
Joseph Hix	pt. "Ashford"	50
John Booker	pt. "Tilghmans Fortune"	75
46:1738:24 Island Hundred ...		
John James, Jr.	"Arcadia"	34
	pt. "Abrahams Lott"	8
	pt. "Abrahams Lott" – from (N) Fellows	58
George Palmer	pt. "Mount Hope"	100

Edward Pirkins	"Newmans Range"	100
Francis Pickering	pt. "Ashby" – from (N) Melton to your wife per will	100
Thomas Spry	pt. "Maxwell Moor"	150
William Bennett	"Easons Addition" & "Lobbs Corner"	83
	pt. "Cumberland"	50
	"Cove Hall"	100
	"Forth Adventure"	50
46:1738:25	**Island Hundred ...**	
Richard Eaton	pt. "Fox Hole"	100
	pt. "Fox Harbour"	50
	"Eatons Addition" – from (N) Grundey & (N) Ungle	180
John Wise	"Gore"	45
	"Sheeps Head Point Resurveyed"	246
	"Baintrees" – from (N) Marlin	50
Benjamin Hopkins	pt. "Hopkins Point"	66¾
Peter Denney	pt. "Hopkins Point"	66¾
James Millis	pt. "Adventure" – for h/o Peter Russam	100
Richard Aldern	pt. "Yaffords Neck"	300
	"Roystons Addition"	150
	"Clays Addition"	50
	"Alderns Island"	41
	pt. "Cumberland"	150
46:1738:26	**Island Hundred ...**	
William Harrison (Irish Creek)	½ "Ashford"	50
	"Longe Neglect"	35
Edmund Ferrell	pt. "Stevens Range"	100
	pt. "Tamney"	75
	pt. "Coventry" – from (N) Hopkins on 6 June 1734	60
John Ratcliff	"Goffston" – from (N) Fellow to your wife	100
Robert Hopkins	pt. "Turkey Point"	159
46:1738:27	**Island Hundred ...**	
Mrs. Elizabeth Davis	pt. "Tilghmans Fortune"	83
	"Sandfords Hermitage"	250
	"Sandfords Folly"	45

James Harvey	"Abrams Lott"	100
Edward Hardin	pt. "Bite"	25
	pt. "Tilghmans Fortune"	19
	"Mukley Mire"	100
	pt. "Hier Dier Loyd"	10
	pt. "Coventry" – from (N) Hopkins	40
	"Hardins Endevour"	200
Thomas Winchester	"Marlins Folly"	50
	"Marlins Chance"	50
	"Bantry"	500
	pt. "Baintrees"	60
	"Marlins Neglect"	57
	"Spring Close"	100
	pt. "Baintrees Addition"	10
46:1738:28 **Island Hundred ...**		
John Valiant	pt. "Gafford Neck" – from (N) Aldern	50
	½ "Partnership"	308
Mrs. Frances Ungel	"Old Womans Folly"	50
William Banning	"Goos Neck"	50
William Skinner	"Clays Hope" – for h/o James Colson	200
46:1738:29 **Island Hundred ...**		
Arthur Rigbey	"Rigbeys Folly"	45
	"Anderbey Addition Resurveyed"	78
	"Anderbeys"	100
	"Crafford"	100
	"Rigbeys Discovery"	105
	pt. "Fox Hole"	65
	"Lemberton"	150
William Riggaway	"Westland"	100
Edward Elliott	"Maccotter & Glover Resurveyed"	355
	"Chance"	223
	"Point & Marsh"	50
	pt. "Londony" – from (N) Armstrong	2
Nathaniel Grace, Jr.	"Inlargement"	71
46:1738:30 **Island Hundred ...**		

Thomas Atkinson	pt. "Cottingham" – from (N) Abrahams	37
	pt. "Cottingham" – from Ja. Atkins	100
	"Newman" – from Ja. Atkins	50
Richard Hopkins	pt. "Nominie" – from (N) Fairby	100
	pt. "Hopkins Point"	150
	pt. "White Philips" – from (N) Dickinson	12
Thomas, John, & James Bartlett	pt. "Ratcliff Mannor"	770
Andrew Oram	pt. "Anderton"	200
46:1738:31 Island Hundred ...		
James Clayland	"Storys Lott" – from William Clayland on 13 April 1734	56
Edward Harding, Jr.	"Ratcliff Choice" – from John Ratcliff on 26 February – 2nd May 1735	109
46:1738:32 Island Hundred ...		
John Eubanks	pt. "Omeleys Rang" – from Thomas Eubanks per will	52
George Dullin	pt. "Partnership" – from George Robins	65
Mr. John Goldsborough	"Peaks Marsh" – on resurvey 25 March 1715; patented 9 August 1738	318
	"Mashey Peak" – surveyed 18 June 1719; patented 9 August 1736	132
John Brascerop	pt. "Coventry" – from (N) Palmer	30
John Booker	a tract of land adjoining to "St. Michalls Fresh Run" for h/o Evan Price	100
Mr. Thomas Corkayne	pt. "Carters Plaines"	94

46:1738:33	**Tuckahoe Hundred ...**	
William Turner	pt. "Turners Ridge" or "Range"	10
	"Moorefields Addition"	65
	"Mays Dowrey" – from (N) Rogers	200
	pt. "Johns Hall"	90
William Stacey	pt. "Turkey Neck"	100
	pt. "Turkey Neck" – from (N) Taylor	25
James Willson	"Kingsberry"	70
Rebbecca Durden	"Johns Neck"	700
Rogger Bradbery	⅓ "Pitts Range"	200
46:1738:34	**Tuckahoe Hundred ...**	
Richard Hall	pt. "Smiths Clifts"	372
John Ratherell	"Strawberrys Field Addition"	50
	"Ratherells Chance"	50
46:1738:35	**Tuckahoe Hundred ...**	
Samuell Broadaway	"Dudley"	200
	"Ramah"	100
	"James Fields"	102
	"Strawbridge"	100
	"Broadaway Meddows" – 1 May 1732	100
Edward Clarke	pt. "Parkers Farm"	350
	"Parrotts Lott"	82
Joshua Clarke	"Clarks Folly"	101
	pt. "Johns Neck"	118
	pt. "Middle Spring" – for h/o William Parratt	150
Jonathan Ayree	pt. "Roeclift"	118
	"Davids Ridge"	125
John Nailer	pt. "Britania"	150
	pt. "Duns Range"	100
	"Moorefields Addition" – from (N) Swett	30
William Michall	"Turners Hazard" & "Bullens Addition" – from (N) Bullen	171
	pt. "Morgans Addition", pt. "Morgans Neglect", & pt. "Ransey Forrest"	101
46:1738:36	**Tuckahoe Hundred ...**	
Sarah Loveday	"Middle Spring" – from (N) Trotter	150

Robert Lowther	"Bever Dam Neck" – from (N) Skinner	70½
John Tomlison	pt. "Roeclift" – from (N) Needles	50
Caleb Clark	pt. "Parkers Range" – from (N) Jadwin	56
	"Highfields" – from (N) Webb	100
	pt. "Hamton" & pt. "Parkers Range"	200
	pt. "Parkers Range" – another part from (N) Jadwin	2
	"High Fields Addition"	150
46:1738:37 **Tuckahoe Hundred ...**		
Aron Parrott	pt. "Kingstown" – from (N) Willson	51
	pt. "Johns Neck"	264
Henry Oldfield	"Summerly" – from (N) Russam	250
Charles & Samuell Morgan	"Dudles Clifts"	200
Michele Kirbey	"Buck Range"	50
	"Buck Range Addition"	55
	pt. "Dunns Range" – for your son	100
	"Bowses Range"	227
James Morgan	pt. "Morgans Neglect" & "Morgans Addition"	120
Richard Kirwick	"Venture"	37
	½ "Dudleys Demeasens"	50
46:1738:38 **Tuckahoe Hundred ...**		
Samuell Dudley	pt. "Advantage" – from (N) Powell	18
	pt. "Roeclifts" – for h/o (N) Needles	100
	"Bever Neck" – from Thomas Dudley per will	100
	pt. "Smiths Clifts" – for h/o Richard Tompson	94
	pt. "Hucker Green" for h/o Richard Tompson	50
William Warren	pt. "Hampton" – from (N) Jadwin	200
Sarah Morgan wife of Capt. Edward Morgan	"Holm Hill" – from (N) Corney	62
	pt. "Smiths Chance"	258
Isaac Dopson	"Wolf Pitt Ridge" – for h/o John Kerby	50
	"Strawberry Fields" – for h/o John Kerby	100
	pt. "Turners Discovery" – for h/o John Kerby	30
John Leverton	"Dudleys Choice"	100
46:1738:39 **Tuckahoe Hundred ...**		
David Kerbey	pt. "Turners Range"	40
	"Limbrick"	60
Frances Camperson	pt. "Hampton" & pt. "Parkers Range"	100

Mr. John Robins	"Holm Hill"	400
	pt. "Rich Range"	200
	pt. "Rich Range Addition"	100
William Frampton	pt. "Rich Range"	50
John Walker	<n/g> on Kings Creek from (N) Berry	100
Robert Hunter	"Jacobs Beginning"	100
46:1738:40 Tuckahoe Hundred ...		
Thomas Hutchenson	pt. "Johns Neck"	19
	pt. "Bugbey" – from (N) Bradbery	200
Thomas Frampton	"Framptons Begg"	96
	"Collins Pasture"	50
Allunby Millington	"Nobles Meddows on Resurvey"	229
	"Betts Addition"	207
John Cannaday	"Cannadays Hazard"	29
Joseph Turner	pt. "Johns Hill"	90
Isaac Cox	pt. "Johns Hill"	90
Henry Buckingham	pt. "Middle Spring"	100
46:1738:41 Tuckahoe Hundred ...		
William Scott	"Salop Resurveyed"	167
Jonathan Tylor	pt. "Kingstown" – from (N) Southenlby to your father on 18 June 1684	100
William Tharp	pt. "Austen" – from (N) Loney	50
	pt. "Austen" – from (N) Keild	50
John Burges	"Bever Neck"	141
	"Bever Neck" & pt. "Broad Laine"	150
James Kendrett	"Coventry"	250
46:1738:42 Tuckahoe Hundred ...		
Thomas Vickers	pt. "Charlevale"	50
	"Morefields" – from (N) Swett	94
William Vickers	pt. "Dunns Rang" – for your daughter Sarah	50
	"Pickadella" a/s "Padingtown" – from (N) Hemsley	200
Mary Brown	"Teltales Loss"	125
	pt. "Charlevale" & "Cork"	150
Jane Turner	"Hascoegreen" – from (N) Parys	160
	"Sought Out" – from (N) Laswell	100

Mr. Edward Needles	⅓ "Pitts Range"	200
	⅓ "Kellem"	369
	pt. "Kellem" – from (N) Sherwood	140
	pt. "Johns Neck"	4
	½ "Exchange"	100
	pt. "Roeclift" – from h/o (N) Groazier	50
46:1738:43	**Tuckahoe Hundred ...**	
James Willson, Jr.	pt. "Middle Spring"	50
	pt. "White Oak Swamp"	100
Thomas Turner (carpenter)	"Turners Discovery" – per will of Edward Turner	65
	"Parrotts Reserve"	50
	pt. "Johns Hill"	90
James Berry	"White Marsh" – per will of (N) Pitt	760
Thomas Dudley	pt. "Broadlain"	1103
William Dudley	"Dudles Demensens"	115
	pt. "Bugbey" – from (N) Bradberry	50
	pt. "Collyn" – from (N) Ball	200
John Compton	pt. "Middle Spring"	100
46:1738:44	**<does not exist>.**	
46:1738:45	**Tuckahoe Hundred ...**	
John Hetherinton	pt. "Bugbey"	150
Frances Williams	"Sybland"	200
	"Maxfield"	152
	"Sybland Addition"	110
	pt. "Collin"	100
Thomas Keet	pt. "Austin"	100
	"Alcock Choice"	100
Francis Regerster	"Parrotts Reserve" – from (N) Parrott	150
John Ervan	"Dobsons Advantage"	35
	"Fork" – from (N) Sutton	250
	"Eagles Neck" – from (N) Parrott	100
	"Worgans Reserve" – from (N) Clemons	200
46:1738:46	**Tuckahoe Hundred ...**	
Joseph Durdin (cnp)	"Kings Creek Marsh" – from James Taylor	50
	pt. "Blessland" – from James Taylor	100
	"Kingsberry Addition" – from James Taylor	130

	pt. "Turkey Neck" – from (N) Cary	100
William Robbins	pt. "Smiths Clifts" – from (N) Wooters	201
	pt. "Holm Hill" – from (N) Wooters	34
Mr. Grundey Pemberton	pt. "Smiths Clifts"	232
	"Elms Addition" & "Lobs Corner"	14
	pt. "Cumberland"	30
	pt. "Heworth"	205
46:1738:47 Tuckahoe Hundred ...		
Andrew Bandey	pt. "Kingstown"	100
Henry Clift	"Dudleys Inclosure" – for h/o James Dudley	104
	pt. "Dudleys Addition" – for h/o James Dudley	37
Sarah Greenwood w/o Barth. Greenwood	pt. "Parkers Farme"	100
John Regester	"Kings Berry Addition"	100
Anthony Booth	pt. "Blomsberry"	100
46:1738:48-9 <do not exist>		
46:1738:50 Tuckahoe Hundred ...		
Charles Gannon	pt. "Blomsberry" – from James Kenting	44
Thomas Mathews	pt. "Blomsberry" – from Solomon Kenting	44
Daniel Ward	pt. "Bloomsberry" – for wife from (N) Oldfield & wife	50

46:1738:51	**Thirdhaven Hundred ...**	
Duges Chace	"Abbington" – for h/o Samuel Abbott, Sr.	100
	pt. "Buckroe" – for h/o Samuel Abbott, Sr.	150
	pt. "Catlins Plaines" – for h/o Samuel Abbott, Sr.	10
	"Walnut Garden" – for h/o Samuel Abbott, Sr.	50
	"Halls Addition" – for h/o Samuel Abbott, Sr.	100
William Martin	"Mitchams Hall" – for h/o Loftus Dowdle	300
William Bush	pt. "Arcadia"	166
Thomas Foard	pt. "Parlett"	72
	pt. "Gressell" & pt. "Otwell" – from (N) Turbut	28
Mr. Nicholas Goldsborough	pt. "Heer Dier Loyd"	400
	"Ottwell"	500
	"Addition"	80
	pt. "Gressell"	122
	pt. "Parlett" – from (N) Ford	28
46:1738:52	**Thirdhaven Hundred ...**	
Henry Parrott	pt. "Canterbury Mannor"	500
Kenelm Skillenton	pt. "Turners Point"	200
James Ferrell	"Hawks Hill" – for h/o Terrance Terrell	100
Edmund Fish	"Fishes Range"	74
	"Contention"	130
James Hickey	pt. "Poiney Point Advantage" – for h/o Michaell Magenny	150
William Skinner, Jr.	"Sarahs Garden"	13
	"Skinner Lott"	33
	pt. "Bensons Enlargement" – from (N) Parrott on 6 November 1735	150
46:1738:53	**Thirdhaven Hundred ...**	
Ferrell Gallerher	pt. "Tilghmans Fortune" – for h/o John Botfield	88
Solomon Robinson	"Rich Neck"	300
	"Shore Ditch"	25
William Mershall	"Kings Sale" – from (N) Lain	126
Thomas Pamphillion	"Eatons Addition" & "Lobbs Corner" – from (N) Ungel	83
Pearce Flemon	"Flemons Freshes Resurveyed"	215
46:1738:54	**Thirdhaven Hundred ...**	

Mr. Samuell Chamberlain	pt. "Hier Dier Loyd" – from (N) Lowe	70
	pt. "Hier Dier Loyd" – from (N) Collins	150
	pt. "Hier Dier Loyd" – from (N) James	200
	pt. "Halls Neck"	124
	pt. "Barmston", pt. "Coxes Addition", & pt. "Coxes Chance"	224
	"Contention"	100
	"Goldston"	50
	"Rome"	100
	pt. "Hier Dier Loyd"	300
	½ "Bishopreck" – from (N) Pearson	50
	pt. "Four Square on Resurvey"	350
	pt. "Halls Neck" – from Daniell Peck on 22 July 1734	462
	~~"<unr> Neck"~~	~~<unr>~~
	pt. "Bishoprick"	50
	pt. "Plain Dealing"	100
	"Endeavour"	50
	"Grundys Lott"	46
	"Cabbin Neck"	50
	"Stevens's Range"	180
	"Yorkshire"	280
	"Intention Resurveyed"	50
Michell Fletcher	"Darlington" – from (N) Green	229
	"Long Acre"	150
	"Sharps Choice" – from (N) Wintersell	200
	"Richmond"	40
John Frith	pt. "London Derry"	1½
46:1738:55	**Thirdhaven Hundred ...**	
William & Solomon Sharp	"Morefields"	100
	"Adventure"	100
	"Easons Neck"	100
	"Fancey"	50
	"Conjunction"	25
	"Rattle Snake Point"	150
	"Mount Pleasure"	500

	pt. "Nomince"	402
	"Eason Lott"	50
	"Sharps Addition"	24
	"Chance"	40
	"Inclosure"	300
	pt. "Nominie" – from (N) Collins	100
	"Dicks Marsh"	200
Charles Markland	pt. "Plemhommon" or "Morgan Point"	50
James Millar	pt. "Canterberry Mannor"	130
Thomas Browning	pt. "Hier Dier Loyd" – surveyed for Daniell Crowley	80
	pt. "Hier Dier Loyd" – from (N) Dawsey	75
Robert Lowrey	pt. "Lostock"	184½
46:1738:56	**Thirdhaven Hundred ...**	
Vincent Lowe	pt. "Hier Dier Loyd"	105
Philip Jenkins	pt. "Edmondsons Freshes"	300
	pt. "Dudley Clifts"	16
	pt. "Chesnut Bay"	300
Gaberel Sailes	"Rich Range"	300
	"Dolph"	100
James Barnes	"Boons Hope" – for h/o Clement Sailes	100
Joshua Grason	"Stapleton"	77
	"Fish Hazard"	18
46:1738:57	**Thirdhaven Hundred ...**	
Francis Parrott	"Lords Chance"	100
Joseph Parrott	pt. "Abrahams Lott", pt. "Mileroad 2nd Addition", & pt. "Gosston" – from (N) Fellows	230
Richard Giles	"Swamptick"	100
	pt. "Shore Ditch"	75
William Harrison (Miles Creek)	pt. "Taylor Ridge"	100
Nicholas Glenn	pt. "Cooks Hope"	200
Adam Brown	pt. "Hier Dier Loyd"	100
	pt. "Parkers Point" & pt. "Enlargement"	75
46:1738:58	**Thirdhaven Hundred ...**	
Joseph Eason	pt. "Hier Dier Loyd" – for h/o Frances Harrison	75
	pt. "Taylor Ridge" – for h/o Frances Harrison	100

Philip Martin	"Bullens Chance"	350
	pt. "Conjuntion"	25
Thomas Martin	pt. "Hier Dier Loyd"	200
	"Hard Measure Resurveyed"	94
	"Ottwell" – from (N) Parrott on 21 May 1735	100
	"Tawney Close" – from (N) Parrott on 21 May 1735	50
James Walker	"Enfield"	200
Thomas Skillinton	"Hambletons Neck"	300
Ralph Elston	"Edmondsons Freshes" & pt. "Heworth" – for h/o William Elston	110
	"French Hazard" – for h/o William Elston	41
46:1738:59	**Thirdhaven Hundred ...**	
John Lurty	"Bridges"	100
	pt. "Elstons Hazard" & pt. "Grafton Mannor"	49
	"Cabbin Neck", "Potters Delight", & "Potters Lott on Resurvey"	150
Mr. Edward Oldham	"Comsberry" – from (N) Rich	100
	"Piney Run" a/s "Judiths Garden" – from (N) Rich	100
	pt. "Judiths Garden" – from (N) Pattison	80
	"Rich Range" – from (N) Rich	569
	pt. "Neither Forrest" – from (N) Rich	50
Mr. Thomas Bozman	"Cardiff" – from (N) Alexander	100
	"Discovery"	231
	"Providence"	7
	pt. "Timber Neck"	150
	"Browns Park"	119
	"Teates Lott on Resurvey"	459
	"Timber Neck on Resurvey"	294
	"Poiney Point" – for h/o Jonathan Taylor	150
	"Poiney Point Advantage" – from (N) Alexander	125
	"Ottwell"	400
	"Bullen" & "Bullen Addition"	350
	"Timothys Lot"	300
William Buckley	pt. "Lords Gift"	175
John Robinson	pt. "Goldsborough"	100
46:1738:60	**Thirdhaven Hundred ...**	

John Coward	"Bemhomon" – from (N) Rousbey	600
John Pattison	pt. "Judiths Garden"	63
	pt. "Anderton"	100
Mr. John Sherwood	"Allumbey Fields"	115
	pt. "Westmor Land"	100
John Clift	pt. "Taylors Ridge" – from (N) Harrison	100
	"Timber Neck Addition" – from (N) Swallow	139
Elizabeth Baley	pt. "Marshy Point"	300
William Combs	pt. "Hier Dier Loyd"	500
46:1738:61	**Thirdhaven Hundred ...**	
Capt. Nicholas Lowe	pt. "Anderton"	500
	"Anderton Addition"	100
	"Jacks Point"	100
	"Lowes Rambles"	1126
	"Discovery"	530
	"Wintersell" – from (N) Winters	145
	pt. "Nominie" – from (N) Cook	250
	"Middle Neck" – from (N) Cook	200
Dennis Hopkins	pt. "Londonderry"	103
	pt. "Hopkins Point"	90
Jeffery Cox	"Spring Close"	50
46:1738:62	**Thirdhaven Hundred ...**	
William Edmondson	pt. "Hier Dier Loyd"	112
	pt. "Hier Dier Loyd" – from (N) Eason	17[illegible]
	pt. "Hier Dier Loyd" – from (N) Evans	20[illegible]
	pt. "Hier Dier Loyd" – on escheat	[illegible]
David Robinson	pt. "Hall" – from (N) Atkins	7[illegible]
	"Davids Folly"	5[illegible]
	"Chance"	2[illegible]
	"Robinsons Beginning"	1[illegible]
	"Long Point"	25[illegible]
Mr. George Robins (cnp)	"First Hazard Resurveyed"	35[illegible]
	pt. "Hatfield" & "Hatfield Addition" – from (N) Price	2
	"Jobs Content"	100
	pt. "Buckingham"	40

	"Robins's Range"	300
	pt. "Cooks Hope"	214
	pt. "Halls Neck"	300
	pt. "Hatfield" & "Hatfields Addition" – from (N) Dood	100
	"Dun More Heat" – from (N) Wise	200
	"Frampton" – from (N) Wise	122
	pt. "Jemaicoe" – from (N) Walker	92
	pt. "Marshy Point" – from (N) Bailey	300
	pt. "Tilghmans Fortune" – from (N) Stanton	325
	pt. "Turkey Neck" – from (N) Hopkins	170
	"Jennings's Hope" – on escheat	718
Fra. Armstrong	"Surprize"	40
	"Discovery"	80
	"Huntington Grange"	100
	"Curnelious Cool Spring"	100
	pt. "Londonderry"	382
46:1738:63	**Thirdhaven Hundred ...**	
Mr. John Edmondson	"Desire" & pt. "Heworth on Resurvey"	603
	"Edmondsons Difficulty"	1253
	"Desire Addition"	60
	"Inlargment"	100
	"Jacks Cove"	50
	pt. "Tilghmans Fortune"	524
Edwardman Sherwood	"Exchange" – from (N) Needles	100
	pt. "Highs Fields" – from (N) Russam	50
	⅓ "Pitts Range"	200
	pt. "Kellem"	229
Abednegoe Botfield	pt. "Faulkenors Square"	100
	"Betty Cove Addition" – for h/o (N) Hurlock	50
	"Addition"	52
	pt. "Bettys Cove"	30
John Love	pt. "Hatton"	63
46:1738:64	**Thirdhaven Hundred ...**	
Thomas Bowdle	pt. "Hier Dier Loyd"	200

John Jones (tanner)	pt. "Chance Helpe" & pt. "Cumberland" – from Richard Chance on 26 May 1736	80
James Webster	pt. "Barmston", pt. "Cox Addition", & pt. "Coxes Chance" – from Francis Scale on 25 April 1737	112
46:1738:65 **<does not exist>**		
46:1738:66 **Thirdhaven Hundred ...**		
Henry Bailey	"Betty Chance"	100
Thomas Skinner	pt. "Marshy Point"	100

46:1738:67	**Bullenbrook Hundred ...**	
William Anderson	"Prospect"	125
	"Knaps Lott"	150
John Dickinson	pt. "Roadley"	150
	pt. "Scarborough"	200
Daniell Powell	pt. "Bostons Clifts"	550
John Carr	"Millars Purchas"	100
	pt. "Lowes Rambles"	114
46:1738:68	**Bullenbrook Hundred ...**	
Thomas Stuart	"Jurdans Hill Resurveyed"	175
	½ "Upper Range"	50
John Nicols (DO)	"Poor Hill"	37
	pt. "Sutton Grange"	100
	pt. "Sutton Grange" – from Thomas Noble	100
John Millar	"Millars Chance"	85
	"Hobsons Choice"	150
Solomon Birkhead	"Little Bristol"	1300
James Barnwell	pt. "Bedworth" – from (N) Shield	100
	pt. "Mount Hope" – as heir to Elizabeth Cathrop	50
	pt. "Mount Hope" – from (N) Miles	27
46:1738:69	**Bullenbrook Hundred ...**	
Thomas Bullen	"Newellyn" – from (N) Brown	140
	"Chance" – from (N) Fray	129
	"Lords Gift" – from (N) Brown	100
	"Bullens Discovery on Resurvey"	136½
James Dickinson	"Hatten" – from (N) Dickinson	322
	"Crookedlain" – from (N) Stapleforde	116
	"Frankford St. Michaels" – from Samuell Dickinson	616
	pt. "Hatton" – from (N) Thomas	112
	pt. "Baildon" – from (N) Byard	30
	"Bennetts Freshes" – from (N) Byard	423
Mr. Daniell Maynadier (cnp)	pt. "Goldsborough" – from (N) Quinton	187
	"Tatterhouse" – from (N) Quinton	38
	"Jamacoe"	150
	pt. "Marshland"	70

	"Timmothys Lott"	25
	"Hermitage" – from (N) Boyerd	90
	"Partnership"	34
	"Cross Haize"	50
	pt. "Fatrills Discovery"	76
Edmond Marsh	"Parkers Point" & pt. "Enlargment" – from (N) Williams	75
46:1738:70 **Bullenbrook Hundred ...**		
William Aires	pt. "Studs Point" – from (N) Cockrin	100
	"Intention" – from (N) Dickinson	100
	pt. "Roadley"	80
Mrs. Rachell Turbutt	pt. "Bessland" & pt. "Baggs Marsh" – from (N) Baggs	300
	"Turbuts Fields Resurveyed"	168
	"Poplar Hill Resurveyed"	57
	pt. "Hogsdon"	100
	"Marshland"	165
	pt. "Blessland" & pt. "Baggs Marsh" – from (N) Baggs	160
Robert Wiles	pt. "Mount Hop" – from (N) Edmondson	53
	pt. "Haws Hill Addition" – from (N) Edmondson	50
46:1738:71 **Bullenbrook Hundred ...**		
Bryan Seney	pt. "Sutton", pt. "Suttons Addition", & pt. "Partnership" – from (N) Abbott	219
	pt. "Sutton" & pt. "Suttons Addition" – from Selvesture Abbott on 6 August 1735	54
William Fooks	pt. "Hogg Range" – from (N) Barnett	47
	pt. "Turkey Neck" – from (N) Taylor on 25 February 1735	16
Jeremiah Nicols	pt. "Partnership"	250
Mr. Anthony Richardson	"Haseley"	200
	"Widdows Lott"	85
	"Partners Hazard" – from (N) Cook	142
	"Browns Lott" – from (N) Hopper	200
	pt. "Mount Hope"	50
	<n/g> – land belonging to "Pitts Mill" formerly of Thomas Barnett	20
	pt. "Worgans Reserve"	300

William Connerly	pt. "Hogg Hole" – for the wife of Richard Connery	142
Mill. Mackey	"Holmbey"	200
	pt. "Bullen"	60
	pt. "Broad Oak" – from (N) Chaplin	175
46:1738:72	**Bullenbrook Hundred ...**	
William Richardson	"Gurlington" – from (N) Gasken	75
Christopher Birkhead	pt. "Scarbrough" – from (N) Harrison to your wife	100
William Barker	pt. "Lords Gift" – for h/o Richard Robinson	100
46:1738:73	**Bullenbrook Hundred ...**	
John & James Barnett	pt. "Bullen"	100
	pt. "Bullen" – from (N) Maccotter	50
Robert Cutcart for h/o Thomas Kirk	"Cornelous Garden" – for h/o (N) Malrain	50
Park Webb	pt. "Hicory Ridge" – from (N) Neal for h/o Jonathan Neal	50
John Hixon	pt. "York"	153
Dennis Morris	pt. "York"	102
46:1738:74	**Bullenbrook Hundred ...**	
William White	pt. "Sutton Grange"	280
	"Killingswort"	50
	pt. "Willingbrook" & pt. "Gurlington Resurveyed"	93
	pt. "Goldsborough"	113
James White	pt. "Double Ridge"	120
	"Whites Gore"	40
	pt. "Sutton Grange"	120
William Taylor	"Middle Spring"	50
	pt. "Turkey Neck"	259
Thomas Metcalf	"Chance"	100
Richard Cooper	"Woolsey Mannor" – for h/o George Sailes	1000
Sarah Webb	pt. "Roadley" – to your husband from (N) Harrison	150
46:1738:75	**Bullenbrook Hundred ...**	
James Corkrin	pt. "Hogg Hole"	142
John Shaw	pt. "Halls Neck" – from (N) Abbott	200
Joseph Bunton	pt. "Dover"	112½
John Holt	pt. "Broadoak" – from (N) Chaplain	25
Elizabeth Anderson	pt. "Studs Point" – for h/o Samuell Martendale	150

Henry Harris	pt. "Millars Hope" – for h/o Simond Fisher	121
Edward Brenney	pt. "Parkers Point" & pt. "Inlargment"	75
46:1738:76	**Bullenbrook Hundred ...**	
Mathew Jenkins	pt. "Patricks Ridge"	560
Thomas Barnett	pt. "Patricks Ridge"	100
Mary Welch or John Angely	pt. "Salem, Stepney, & Quillen"	45
Thomas Mackingham	pt. "Salem, Stepney, & Quillen"	45
James Chaplain	pt. "Broadoak"	300
46:1738:77	**Bullenbrook Hundred ...**	
Thomas Stevens	pt. "Cattlins Laines" tbc Elizabeth Stevens for h/o William Stevens	250
	"Williams Lott" – for h/o William Stevens	49
	pt. "Compton" – for h/o William Stevens	80
John Alexander	"Fish Freshes"	50
	"Alexanders Chance"	250
	pt. "Wades"	54
	"Lowes Goodluck"	100
George Brinsfield	pt. "Thief Keep Out"	36
	pt. "Sutton"	56
46:1738:78	**Bullenbrook Hundred ...**	
Samuell Dickinson (cnp)	"Cross Dover"	400
	"Samuells Lott"	600
	"Dickinsons Lott Addition Resurveyed"	113
	"Powells Island"	55
	pt. "Wades" – from (N) Alexander	46
	"Lowes Good Luck" – from (N) Lowe	55
	pt. "Compton" – from (N) Stevens	13
	pt. "Mount Hope"	350
	pt. "Double Ridge"	50
	pt. "Nomince" – from (N) Sharp	350
	pt. "Reedley" – from (N) Hudson	200
	"Hobsons Choice"	100
	pt. "Conveniency Mannor" – from (N) Troath	350
	"Little Creek" – from (N) Sanders	150
	"Evans Point" – from (N) Sanders	300
	pt. "Hier Dier Lloyd"	101

	"Dickinsons Lott"	216
	pt. "White Philips"	150
	pt. "Dover"	50
	pt. "Salem & Quillen"	45
	"Fishers Chance Resurveyed" – from (N) Fisher	125
	pt. "Millars Hope" & pt. "Herberts Choice" – from James Herbert on 7 May 1734	100
	pt. "Little Creek"	100
John Glover	pt. "Mount Hope"	75
	½ "Upper Range"	50
Richard & Mary Holmes	pt. "Sutton"	250
	"Suttons Addition"	50
	"Buckrowe"	80
Robert Welch	"Sydingbrough"	100
	"Plausley"	100
46:1738:79	**Bullenbrook Hundred ...**	
William Harrison (Dover)	pt. "Dover"	450
	"Roeclift" – from (N) Trotter	170
	"Poplar Level" – from (N) Turner	116
	pt. "Poplar Level" – from (N) Stevens	75
	pt. "Poplar Level" – from (N) Williams	114
	pt. "Poplar Level" – from (N) Edmondson	112
John Price	pt. "Hatfield" & pt. "Addition"	25
Frances Neale	pt. "Hicory Ridge"	296
	pt. "Hicory Ridge" – in His Lordships Mannor	137
Howell Powell	"Rigbeys Marsh"	300
	"Bever Neck" – from (N) Berry	259
	pt. "Advantage" – from (N) Alcock	42
46:1738:80	**Bullenbrook Hundred ...**	
William Thomas, Sr.	"Double Ridge"	150
	pt. "Double Ridge" – from (N) Lowe	80
Lemon John Cathrop	"Calthrops Security"	205
	pt. "Mount Hope" – from (N) Wilis	67
Morris Giddons	"New Scotland"	700
46:1738:81	**Bullenbrook Hundred ...**	

Hezekiah Macetter	"White Chaple"	100
	pt. "White Philips"	70
John Stevens	pt. "Compton"	20
	"Edmondsons Cove"	174
	"Dawsons Fortune"	50
	pt. "Buckrow"	50
	pt. "Catlins Plaines"	240
	"Acton" – for h/o Mary Troatter	300
	pt. "Strawberry"	163
	½ "Dudley Choice"	100
John Higgen	"Boarams Range"	177
Thomas Dellahay	pt. "Taylors Ridge"	100
	pt. "Halls Neck" – for h/o (N) Meer	40
Samuell Abbott	"Beverdam"	100
	"Hutchinsons Addition"	150
46:1738:82	**Bullenbrook Hundred ...**	
Edward Neal	pt. "Mount Hope"	50
Walter Jenkins	pt. "Patricks Ridge"	240
William Adrey	pt. "Mount Hope" – for h/o Joseph Banon	50
	pt. "Lowes Rambles" – for h/o Joseph Banon from (N) Lowe on 5 November 1737	200
Thomas Elsbey	pt. "Parkers Point" & pt. "Enlargment"	175
William Mullican	pt. "Taylors Ridge"	100
Samuell Mullican	pt. "Patricks Plaines" & pt. "Easons Choice"	175
Sarah Mullican	pt. "Roadley"	150
46:1738:83	**Bullenbrook Hundred ...**	
Mary Mullican	pt. "Mullicans Choice"	70
Hugh Linch	pt. "Mullicans Choice"	100
Patrick Mullican	pt. "Patricks Plaines" & pt. "Inlargment"	175
	pt. "Taylors Ridge" – for your wife Mary Lord	100
David Johnes	"Wilderness" – from (N) Hardin	75
Edward Hargiton	pt. "Patrick Ridge"	100
46:1738:84	**Bullenbrook Hundred ...**	
Joseph Withgot	"Cromwell"	100
	"Josephs Lot"	100

William Adams	pt. "Hatfield" & pt. "Hatfields Addition" – from John Price & Richard Dove on 20 November 1734	50
Turance Connerry	"Hollands Addition"	41
	"Kingston"	400
William Carey	pt. "Partnership" – from (N) Abbott	18
	pt. "Sutton" & "Suttons Addition" – from (N) Abbott	115
John Dannilin who married coheir of James Trayman	pt. "Studs Point"	50
Hezekiah Maccotter, Jr. who married coheir of James Trayman	pt. "Studs Point"	50
<unr>	<unr>	<unr>
46:1738:85-6 **<blank>**		

46:1738:87	**Bay Hundred ...**	
John Camper	pt. "Lostock"	50
John Hunt	"Content"	98
	"Fools Parridice"	38
	"Devine St. Andrew"	200
Peter Caulk	pt. "Lostock"	100
	"Caulks Addition" – resurvey of pt. "Lostock" on 22 July 1736	256
Thomas Lurty	"Parkin Point"	100
	"Lankesheir"	50
George Collison	"Rehoboth"	50
	"Rehoboths Point"	50
George Haddaway	pt. "Lostock"	172
	"Fishburns Landing" – from (N) Sanders	104
46:1738:88	**Bay Hundred ...**	
John Auld	"New Port Glasgow"	258
Thomas Adcock	"Coopers Lott"	52
John Porter	"Friths Neck" – from (N) Valliant	50
Catherine Barrett	pt. "Snelling Delight" – from (N) Vinton	50
	pt. "Snelling Delight"	100
Robert Dawson	"Dawsons Composition on Resurvey"	283
Laurance Porter	"York" – from (N) Fairbank	100
46:1738:89	**Bay Hundred ...**	
John Poor	"Union" – from (N) Sandberry	50
Solomon Horney	"Neglect"	126
Richard Dawson	"Jones Lott" – from (N) Lurty	50
Edward Hopkins	"William & James"	25
	pt. "Hopkins Addition"	25
	pt. "Deventport", "Beach", "Elliotts Lott", & "Stopper" – from (N) Ashcraft & wife on 30 July 1735	100
46:1738:90	**Bay Hundred ...**	
Nicholas Benson	"Bogg Hole"	50
	"Bensons Choice"	90
	pt. "Bensons Enlargment"	43
Philip Skinner (cnp)	pt. "Enlargment"	50
	"Skinners Point"	50

	"Skinners Addition"	23
	"Skinners Discovery"	70
David Hughs	"Dain Port & Beach"	12
	pt. "James's Progress"	35
Bartholomew Roberts	pt. "James's Progress"	35
	"Enions Range" – to your father from (N) Williams	50
	"Robert Addition"	47
John Fairbank	pt. "York"	51
	"Bellfast"	100
	"Camper Neck"	100
	"Beadford"	62
	"Jones Hole"	36
	"Fairbanks Choice"	195
	"Fairley"	100
	"Goos Neck"	23
46:1738:91 **Bay Hundred ...**		
Robert Roole	"Witherington"	200
	pt. "Lancasheir"	70
	pt. "Cabbin Neck"	13
Mr. Rizon Bozman	"Wattson & Partnership" – from (N) Knowles	150
	"Hemmersbey on Resurvey"	273
	"Sherwood Neck"	268
	"Folly"	100
Robert Dodson	pt. "Bensons Enlargment"	120
Nicholas Bartlett	pt. "Bartletts Inheritance"	110
46:1738:92 **Bay Hundred ...**		
William Webb Haddaway	"Rich Neck" pt. "Grafton Mannor"	150
	"Haddaway Lott" pt. "Grafton Mannor"	73
	"Karsey Good Luck" – for h/o John Kersey	37
	"Welley" – for h/o John Kersey	300
	"Sarahs Neck" – for h/o John Kersey	50
	"Marchants Folly"	150
	"Miles End"	250
John Harrison (cnp)	"Prouce Point" & pt. "Haphazard" – from (N) Harrison	100
	pt. "Lostock"	172

	"Miles End" – for h/o William Cooper	75
Daniell Lambdon	pt. "Sand Lott"	50
	"Winterton"	50
John Herrington	"Hatton Garden"	50
Thomas Richardson	"Adventure"	70
46:1738:93	**Bay Hundred ...**	
Joseph Dawson	pt. "Lostock"	150
Joseph Hopkins	pt. "Hopkins Point"	66¾
	"Bay Point"	150
	"Enlargment"	50
William Lambdon	pt. "William & Marys Addition"	52
	"Summerton"	200
Thomas Smith (schoolmaster)	pt. "Goos Neck" & pt. "Grafton Mannor" – from (N) Lambdon	100
John Lambdon	pt. "Grafton Mannor"	100
Thomas Cummings	"Knave Keep Out"	180
	"Lurty" – from (N) Lurty	50
John Porter, Jr.	"Wellings Good Luck"	65
46:1738:94	**Bay Hundred ...**	
John Ball	"Long Point"	50
	"Long Neck"	180
	"Benjamin Lott"	100
William Harrison (bay side)	"Poplar Neck"	10
	"Mount Miserys Addition"	12
	pt. "Mount Miserys"	2
	pt. "Prouse Point" & pt. "Haphazard"	5
	pt. "Bensons Enlargment"	19
Edward Auld	pt. "Elliotts Folly"	5
Henry Swording	pt. "Kemps Lott Addition"	2
Sarah Colk	"Lewis on Resurvey"	29
46:1738:95	**Bay Hundred ...**	
Thomas Haddaway	"Haddaways Addition"	7
John Wills	"Bantly Bay"	5
Mr. Daniell Sherwood	"Lurkeys Hills"	10
	"Beggars Hall"	3
	"Anketell"	49

John Lowe	pt. "Grafton Mannor Resurveyed"	245
	"Piney Neck"	107
	"Haddaways Lott"	50
	pt. "Fishbourns Landing"	100
	pt. "Ratcliff Mannor"	150
James Dawson	"Crammell"	300
	"Cudlington"	400
	"Cudlingtons Addition"	50
	"Cudlingtons Increase"	50
	"Poplar Neck"	50
	"Baleys Forrest"	113
46:1738:96 **Bay Hundred ...**		
Robert Harrison	"Happ Hazard"	50
	"Crooked Intention"	50
Charles Bridges	"Blogden"	100
Richard Feddaman	pt. "Lancasheir"	30
	"Feddemans Choice"	100
	"Discovery"	56
Robert Larrimore h/o Alexander Larramore	"Larramores Neck"	100
	"Bampsheir"	50
	"Larramores Prudence"	87
William Hambleton	"Wettstone"	224
	"Mortenham"	200
	"Hambletons Addition"	100
	"Cambridge"	100
	pt. "Adventure" – from (N) Grace	113½
46:1738:97 **Bay Hundred ...**		
Francis Porter	pt. "Hamersbey"	100
Francis Sherwood	"Sherwood Island"	20
	"Middle Neck"	100
	½ "Mount Misery"	50
	"Huckelberry Garden"	125
John Leeds (cnp)	"Wades Point"	400
	pt. "Hatton"	410
	"Long Delay"	34
	pt. "Scarbrough"	200

	pt. "Hatton"	90
Col. Matthew Tilghman Ward	"Rich Neck on St. Michalls Point"	1000
	"Henrittas Marias Purchase Resurveyed"	412
	"Court Road"	138
	pt. "Union Resurveyed"	611
	"Choptank Island Resurveyed"	1468
	"Three Necks Resurveyed"	165
	"Wellens Outlett"	50
46:1738:98 **Bay Hundred ...**		
Robert Sands	pt. "Sands Lott"	103
	"Chance"	25
John Kemp	"Bolton"	100
	"Boltons Addition"	50
	"Wolfe Harbour"	62
	"Hunt Keep Out"	28
Rev. Henry Nicols	"Micklemore"	230
	pt. "Maiden Point", "Maiden Point Addition", "Wethers's Range", & "Little Neck" – from (N) Benson	300
	pt. "Gallaway"	96
	pt. "Partnership"	500
	"Holdon"	225
	pt. "Bite"	15
	"Forked Neck" – for the Vestry	50
	pt. "Hopkins Point" – from Dennis Hopkins	86
	pt. "Bryans Lott"	12½
James Spencer, Jr.	pt. "Bensons Enlargment"	137
	"Fox Harbour"	50
46:1738:99 **Bay Hundred ...**		
John Spedding	pt. "Hawks Hill Hope" & pt. "Clofton"	150
Edward Spedding	pt. "Hawks Hill Hope" & pt. "Clofton"	150
Daniell Vinton	"Edwards Hopewell"	100
46:1738:100 **Bay Hundred ...**		
Edmond Fish, Jr.	"Garterly Moor" – from your father	120
John Ackels (cnp)	"Mable" – for h/o William Kemp	100
	"Mables Addition" – for h/o William Kemp	50

	"Kemps Lott" – for h/o William Kemp	100
	"Kemps Lott Addition" – for h/o William Kemp	26
John Hopkins	pt. "Beach, Elliotts Lott, Elliotts Folly, & Harley" – from (N) Ashcraft on 29 July 1735	100
Thomas Ashcraft, Jr.	pt. "Deventport, Beach, & Elliotts Lott" – from (N) Ashcraft on 29 July 1735	380
Thomas Sudham	"Fairplay" – from (N) Bartlett & (N) Spencer	25
	pt. "Mainsale" – from Charles Spencer	49
46:1738:101 **Bay Hundred ...**		
Henry Richardson	"Pasly Neck"	24
James Spencer	"Foresaile"	12
John Reynolds	pt. "Renolds Point"	148
Susanah Slaughter	pt. "Middle Spring" – per will of your husband William Parrott on 8 May 1720	50
Mr. Arnold Hawkins	"Good Luck" & pt. "Grafton Mannor"	28
	"Cabbin Neck, Sandey Bite, & Halls Fortune"	238
46:1738:102 **Bay Hundred ...**		
Joseph Elliott	pt. "Coventry"	120
Kenelnm Skillington	"Skillingston Help"	20
Joseph Atkinson	"Atkinsons Choice"	43
Robert Newcomb	"Harbour Rome" – on escheat	130
Charles Baning	"Yorks Destruction"	50

47:1739:1 ...		**Acres**
John Salter	"Salters Marsh" tbc Mr. Edward Lloyd	200
William Grange	"Grange" tbc Mr. Edward Lloyd	150
Henry Morgan	"Morgan Saint Michaell" tbc Richard Bennett, Esq.	300
Zachary Wade	"Wades Point" tbc Mr. John Leeds	400
William Hatton	"Hatton" tbc Mr. John Leeds	500
47:1739:2 ...		
Dennes Scott	"Scotts Close" tbc Mr. Edward Lloyd	200
Edward Lloyd	"Linton" tbc Mr. Edward Lloyd	600
Henry Morgan	"Marron" tbc Richard Bennett, Esq.	130
Henry Morgan	"Harryton" tbc John Loockerman	270
Anthony Griffin	"Harbour Rouse" – escheated by Robert Newcomb by the same of 130 a. (f. 141)	60
47:1739:3 ...		
Nicholas Pickard	"Pickburn" tbc Mr. Robert Lloyd	200
Henry Taylor	"Talyfarn" tbc Mr. Robert Lloyd	100
Thomas Bennett	"Bendon" – escheated by Jacob Gibson by the same name (f. 117)	100
William Champ	"Champenham" – this with "Bendon" abovesaid was resurveyed for Jacob Gibson under the name of "Champenham" (f. 117)	200
William Champ	"Williston" – William Hambleton purchased this from Robert Martin in July 1665; resurvey & quantity as in f. 108	224
William Lewis	"Lewis" – resurveyed for Peter Caulk & patented to Sarah Caulk (f. 134)	100
47:1739:4 ...		
Martin Kirk & John Hill	"Kirkham" tbc John Lockerman	350
William Hamilton	"Martingham" tbc William Hambleton	200
Edmond Webb	"Webley" tbc William Webb Haddaway for h/o John Kersey as guardian	300
Thomas Miles	"Mile End" tbc: • John Harrison for h/o John Cooper being guardian – 75 a. • William Webb Haddaway – 250 a. • disclaimed by George Haddaway on 12 May 1736 – 250 a.	400
Greston Cromwell	"Cromwell" tbc James Dawson	300
Cuthbert Phelps	"Cudlington" tbc James Dawson	400

47:1739:5 ...		
Richard Bruges	"Bruges" tbc John Lurkey	100
Edward Lloyd, Esq.	"Hir Dier Lloyd" tbc: • Vincent Lowe – 105 a. • William Combes – 500 a. • Samuel Chamberlaine – 720 a. • Jep. Eason for h/o Fran. Harrison – 75 a. • Thomas Martin – 200 a. • William Edmondson (DO) – 382 a. • Loftus Bowdle – 200 a. • Nicholas Goldsborough – 400 a. • Solomon Volintine for h/o Samuel Martin – 100 a. • Adam Brown – 100 a. • Thomas Browning – 75 a. • Edward Harding – 10 a. • pt. escheated by Daniell Crowley – 80 a. • pt. resurveyed by William Dickinson – 101 a. • pt. escheated by name of "Wilderness" & granted to William Edmondson by the "Edmondsons Ponds" – 9½ a.	3050
Edward Lloyd, Esq.	"Cross Dower" – tbc Samuell Dickinson	400
Thomas Read	"Readley" tbc: • Thomas Ayres for h/o Fra. Chaplin – 80 a. • John Dickinson – 150 a. • Sarah Webb – 150 a. • Sarah & Jane Mullican – 150 a. • Samuell Dickinson – 200 a. • wanting supposed the bounds will not include the amount of the original survey – 70 a.	800
47:1739:6 ...		
Henry Bullen	"Bullen" tbc: • John & James Barnett – 150 a. • Phil. Kersey – 60 a. • Mr. Thomas Bozman for h/o Jonathan Taylor – 350 a. • h/o (N) Bullen alleges it will not be found in the survey – 240 a.	800
Henry Morgan	"Winhimmon" tbc John Coward	600
John Anderton	"Anderton" tbc: • Mr. Nicholas Lowe – 500 a. • John Pattison – 100 a.	600

Anthony Griffin	"Grissell" tbc: • Thomas Foard – 28 a. • Mr. Nicholas Goldsborough – 122 a.	150
William Parratt	"Nartlett" tbc: • Mr. Nicholas Goldsboroug – 28 a. • Thomas Foard – 72 a.	100
47:1739:7 ...		
William Taylor	"Otwell" tbc Mr. Nicholas Goldsborough	500
Thomas Taylor	"East Oatwell" tbc Thomas Bozman for h/o Jonathan Taylor	400
William Turner	"Turners Point" tbc: • Robert Grundy – escheated 200 a. • Kenelm Skillington – 200 a.	400
Samuell Graves	"Graves" tbc Mr. Robert Loyd	100
Andrew Skinner	"Anderby" tbc Arthur Rigbey	100
47:1739:8 ...		
Thomas Seymour	"Summerton" tbc William Lambdon	200
Peter Anderton	"Lostock" tbc: • George Haddaway – 172 a. • John Harrison – 172 a. • Robert Lowrey – 184 a. • John Camper – 50 a. • Peter Caulk – 236 a. resurveyed as "Calks Addition" (f. 141) • Joseph Dawson – 150 a.	828
William Hamilton	"Hamiltons Neck" tbc Thomas Millington	300
James Adams	"Marshy Point" tbc: • Elizabeth Bailey – 400 a. • George Robins – 300 a.	700
Richard Tilghman	"Canterbury" tbc: • Henry Parrott – 320 a. • James Miller – 130 a. • Samuell Dickinson – 350 a.	1000
47:1739:9 ...		
Samuel Tilghman (cnp)	"Tilghmans Fortune" tbc: • George Robins – 325 a. • John Booker – 75 a. • Elizabeth Davis – 83 a. • Ralph Holmes – 50 a. • Ferrell Gallahar in right of his wife – 88 a. • Free School – 100 a. • Edward Hardin – 19 a.	1000

	• John Sutton – 81 a. • Philip Massey (the last possessor is dead & no person that claims under his title) – 215 a. • John Edmondson – 524 a.	
Capt. Robert Morris	"Ratcliffe Mannor" tbc: • Thomas, John, & James Bartlett – 770 a. • John Lowe – 150 a.	800
Phillip Calvert, Esq.	"Woolsey or Chancellors Point" tbc Richard Cooper guardian to h/o George Sailes	1000
Thomas Todd	"Todd upon Dirvan" tbc: • George Garey – 80 a. • Jacob Gibson (alleges this land in included in elder surveys & will disclaim) – 320 a.	400
Richard Williss	"Thrmby Grange" tbc Mr. Edward Lloyd	500
47:1739:10 ...		
Robert Hopkins & Thomas Hopkins	"Hopkins Point" tbc: • James Hopkins – 100 a. • John Leonard for h/o Stephen Esgate who refuses to pay – 150 a. • Richard Hopkins – 150 a. • Mr. Henry Nichols – 86 a. • Dennis Hopkins – 90 a. • Joseph Hopkins – 66¾ a. • Peter Denny – 66¾ a. • Benjamin Hopkins – 66¾ a. • <wanting> – 23½ a.	800
Andrew Skinner	"Spring Close" – tbc Isaac Marlin to Thomas Winchester	100
Edmund Webb	"Edmundton" tbc Woolman Gibson	300
Richard Jennings	"Jennings Hope" – escheated by George Robins for 718 a. (f. 132)	1000
Job Nutt	"Jobs Content" tbc Mr. George Robins	1000
William Hemsley	"Mersgate" tbc Mr. Edward Loyd	300
47:1739:11 ...		
William Lewis	"Sarrahs Neck" tbc William Webb Haddaway guardian to h/o John Kersey	50
Seth Foster	"Choptank Island Part" – resurveyed for Col. Math. Ward for 1468 a (f. 125)	300
Alexander Macotter & Daniell Glover	"Macotters Glover" – resurveyed for Edward Elliott for 355 a. (f. 123)	100

Richard Lurkey	"Lurkey" tbc John Wrightson	250
Henry Morgan	"Morgans Hope" – bounds of this land being very doubtful, John Rousby, Esq. who has right to the land will not pay rent	300
Thomas Manning	"Hopewell" – taker up not known nor any person that does claim under his title	100
Thomas Manning	"Exchange" tbc: • Edward Man Sherwood – 100 a. • Edward Needles – 100 a.	200
47:1739:12 ...		
Melacholan Clee	"Shoreditch" tbc: • Solomon Robinson for h/o Samuel Martin – 25 a. • Richard Giles in right of his wife of William Martin – 75 a.	100
William Evan	"Evans Point" tbc Samuell Dickinson	300
Francis Armstrong	"Armstrongs Delight" – resurveyed for Thomas Martin with "Weeping Spring" & called "Hard Measure" 94 a. (f. 120)	50
Henry Cattline	"Cattline Plains" tbc: • Thomas Stevens for h/o William Stevens – 250 a. • John Stevens – 240 a. • Dugles Chace for h/o Samuell Abbott – 10 a.	500
Henry Skinner	"Sutton" tbc: • Richard Holmes for self & Thomas Metcalfe in right of his wife – 250 a. • Samuel Dickinson – 50 a. resurveyed with other lands & called "Samuells Lott"	300
Attwell Badwell	"Attwell" tbc Thomas Martin	100
John Eason	"Rattlesnake Point" tbc William Sharp	150
47:1739:13 ...		
Andrew Skinner	"Rich Range" tbc Gaberil Sailes	300
Robert Bullen	"Bullens Choice" tbc Philip Martin	350
John Eason	"Moorfields" tbc William Sharp	1200
Andrew Skinner	"Foston" – John Pattison alleges land is included in elder survey & will disclaim	100
Andrew Skinner	"Piney Point" tbc Thomas Bozman for h/o Jonathan Taylor	150
Andrew Skinner	"Tannershope" tbc George Gresham	50

Bartholomew Glosier & Andrew Skinner	"Dicks Marsh" tbc William Sharp	200
47:1739:14 ...		
William & John Shaw	"Cottingham" tbc: • William Thomas, Jr. – 265 a. • Jeffery Horney – 50 a. • Thomas Atkinson – 137 a. • Isaac Dixon – 75 a. • Robert Goldsborough – 150 a. • Peter Harwood – 150 a. • supposed to lost in the water – 73 a.	900
Andrew Skinner	"Nether Foster" tbc: • Edward Oldham – 50 a. • alleged to lie in elder survey called "Hier Dier Loyd" – 150 a.	200
Henry Parker	"Parkers Point" tbc: • Thomas Elsbey – 30 a. • Edward Brenney – 30 a. • Adam Brown – 30 a. • Edward Marsh – 30 a.	120
Roger Gross	"Ashby" tbc: • Robert Goldsborough – 250 a. • Francis Pickrin – 100 a. • Thomas Gulley – 150 a. • Isaac Dixon – 60 a. • John Davis – 147 a. • supposed to be lost by the water – 93 a.	800
Roger Gross	"Fausley" tbc Tench Francis	250
James Forbus	"Wales" tbc: • Samuell Dickinson – 46 a. • John Alexander – 54 a.	100
47:1739:15 ...		
Henry Alexander	"New Scotland" tbc Morris Giddons	700
Henry Clay	"Clays Hope" tbc William Skinner for h/o James Colson	200
William Hamilton	"Cambridge" tbc William Hambleton	100
George Peake	"Peaks Marsh" – escheated for Foster Turbot & patented to Ann Goldsborough 318 a. (f. 139)	300
John Kinnemont	"Dundee" tbc: • John Ray – 133⅓ a. • Samuell Kininmont – 133⅓ a. • John Wilson (Dundee) – 133⅓ a.	400

Henry Woolchurch	"Midle Spring" tbc: • John Loveday – 150 a. • John Compton/William Wilson – 100 a. • Josua Clarkson for h/o William Parrott – 150 a. • James Willson, Jr. – 50 a. • Henry Buckingham – 100 a. • William Taylor – 50 a. • Susanah Slater – 50 a.	600
47:1739:16 ...		
William Jones	"Batchellors Point" tbc John Davis	100
Daniell Jennefer	"Dover" tbc: • William Harrison – 751½ a. • Thomas Bunton – 112½ a. • Samuell Dickinson – 50 a. • Thomas Hinson Wright for creditors James Davis (QA) – 40 a.	800
William Eldridge	"Eldridge Point" – taker up not known nor any person that does claim	100
Francis Armstrong	"Weeping Spring" – with "Armstrongs Deligh" was resurveyed for Thomas Martin & called "Hard Measure" 94 a. (f. 120)	200
Thomas Biss	"Little Bristoll" tbc Solomon Burket	1300
Francis Armstrong	"Cornelius Neck" – let fall	50
47:1739:17 ...		
Andrew Skinner	"Rock Cliffe" tbc: • Jonathan Airey – 118 a. • William Harrison – 170 a. • John Tomlinson – 50 a. • Elizabeth Grousher – 50 a. • Samuell Dudley for h/o William Needles – 100 a.	320
Timothey Lindall	"Duxbury" – taker up not known nor any person that does claim	250
Timothy Lindall	"Salem" tbc: • Samuel Dickinson – 16½ a. • Mary Welch – 16½ a. • Susanna Welch – 16½ a.	50
Sarah Marsh	"Marsh Land" tbc: • Mr. Robert Loyd – 265 a. • Rachell Turbott for h/o Samuell Turbott – 165 a. • Mr. Daniell Maynadier – 70 a.	500

Hopkins Davis	"Buckrow" tbc: • John Stevens – 50 a. • Dugles Chase for h/o Richard Holmes – 150 a.	200
47:1739:18 ...		
Francis Armstrong	"Holland" – Fra. Armstrong (heir) alleges this land included in elder survey & will disclaim	200
Francis Armstrong	"Westmoreland" tbc: • Maj. John Sherwood – 100 a. disclaimed on 9 May 1739 • Rogger Bradberry – 100 a. disclaimed on 24 December 1736 • no person will own – 200 a.	400
Francis Armstrong	"Edmunds Cove" – resurveyed for John Stevens for 174 a. (f. 134)	200
John Smith & William Robinson, etc.	"Nominey" tbc: • Richard Hopkins – 100 a. • William Sharp – 502 a. • Samuell Dickinson – 350 a. • Nicholas Lowe – 250 a.	1100
Thomas Manning	"Triangle" – taker up not known nor any person that does claim	55
John Alley & Nicholas Berkeley	"Rich Neck" tbc Solomon Robinson for h/o Samuell Martin	300
47:1739:19 ...		
Andrew Skinner	"Compton" tbc: • Thomas Stevens for h/o William Stevens – 80 a. • John Stevens – 20 a. • Samuell Dickinson – 13 a.	100
John Edmondson	"Edmundsons Lower Cove" – James Elvert to whom this land was patented not known nor any person that does claim	100
Thomas Studds	"Studds Point" tbc: • William Ayres – 100 a. • Elizabeth Anderson for h/o (N) Martindall – 50 a. • John Dalinell – 50 a.	200
John Edmundson	"Edmundsons Cove" – James Elvert to whom this land was patented not known nor any person that does claim.	100
Ralph Elston	"Elston" – no person will own this land; supposed to lie in elder surveys	50

Ralph Elston	"Long Point" tbc John Ball	50
Joseph Winslow	"Plain Dealing" tbc: • Samuell Chamberlain – 100 a. • Mr. Robert Goldsborough – 100 a.	200
47:1739:20 ...		
John Ingram	"Hogsdon" tbc: • Rachell Turbutt for h/o Samuel Turbutt – 70 a.	100
Patrick Mullikin	"Patricks Choice" tbc: • John Mullikin s/o Patrick Mullikin let this land fall & took it up again by name of "Mullicans Choice" for 170 a. (f. 82)	200
Thomas Miles	"Millington" tbc: • Richard Bruff to whom land belongs says he will disclaim; lines running into Miles River.	50
John Kennement	"Bennett Hill" tbc Isaac Dixon	50
John Kennement	"Fentry" tbc Grundey Pemberton (QA)	100
Henry Mitchell	"Mitchams Hall" tbc Ann Bowdle for h/o Loftus Bowdle	300
John Nevill & Margery Hathcott	"Irish Freshes" tbc John Alexander	50
47:1739:21 ...		
Ralph Willson	"Beaver Neck" tbc: • Howell Powell – 259 a. • Samuell Dudley – 100 a. • John Burges – 241 a.	600
James Rigby	"Rigbys Marsh" tbc Howell Powell	300
Thomas Vaughan & Richard Gurling	"Buckland" tbc Mr. Robert Loyd	250
Thomas Phillips & Richard Whitte	"Whitte Phillips" tbc: • Hezekiah Maccotter – 70 a. • Samuel Dickinson – 150 a. • Richard Hopkins – 42 a. • wanting – 38 a.	300
James Hall	"Cove Hall" tbc William Bennett	10
John Hollingsworth	"Clay Banks" tbc John Williams h/o Enion Williams (CE)	5
Thomas Maning & John Ingram	"Norwick" – taker up of this land not known nor any person that does claim	20
47:1739:22 ...		

John Edmundson	"Edmundsons Fresh Run" – h/o Thomas Edmundson knows nothing of this land	400
Andrew Skinner	"Tanners Choice" tbc Richard Skinner	340
Andrew Skinner	"St. Michaels Fresh Run" tbc: • Robert Goldsborough – 50 a. • John Potts – 60 a. • Samuell Cockayn – 401 a. • h/o Richard Carter (ENG) – 639 a.	1150
John Boon	"Boons Hope" tbc James Barnes for h/o Clement Sailes	100
Andrew Skinner	"Yaffords Neck" tbc: • Richard Alden – 300 a. • John Valliant – 100 a.	400
Andrew Skinner	"Hopewell" – h/o Andrew Skinner allege this land is included in "Hopkins Point" an elder survey & therefore refuse to pay	100
Andrew Skinner	"Sheppards Point" – resurveyed for Anthony Wise for 246 a.	100
47:1739:23 ...		
Nathaniel Cleeve	"Nathaniell Point" tbc Mr. Edward Loyd	50
Andrew Skinner	"Piney Point Advantage" tbc: • Thomas Bozman for h/o Jonathan Taylor – 100 a. • James Hickey for h/o Arthur Megenny – 150 a.	250
Elizabeth Brewer	"Widdows Choice" tbc: • Philimon Emerson – 320 a. • Hannah Davis for h/o Tamerlan Davis – 320 a.	640
William Crouch	"Crouchs Choice" tbc: • Richard Bennett, Esq. – 100 a. • Edward Loyd – 50 a.	150
Thomas Manning	"Hogg Hole" tbc: • William Connerly in right of his wife – 142 a. • James Cockrin in right of his wife – 142 a.	200
Mathias Worgan	"Worgans Reserve" tbc: • John Evin for h/o William Dobson – 200 a. • Anthony Richardson – 300 a.	500
Thomas Camplire	"Campliers Neck" tbc John Fairbank	100
47:1739:24 ...		

John Powick	"Patricks Ridge" a/s "Powicks Ridge" tbc: • Mathew Jenkins – 560 a. • Thomas Barnett – 100 a. • Walter Jenkins – 240 a. • Edward Hargiton – 100 a.	1000
Samuell Winslow	"Intention" – resurvey by Mr. Robert Ungle for 66 a. (f. 114)	50
Samuell Winslow	"Prevention" tbc Hannah Davis	50
Andrew Skinner	"Long Point" tbc David Robinson	250
Samuell Winslow	"Cabbin Neck" tbc Samuell Chamberlain	50
Richard Woolman	"Addition" tbc Mrs. H. M. Chew	200
Joseph Winslow	"Boston Clift" tbc: • Susannah Powell for h/o Daniell Powell – 550 a. • Thomas Whittington – 130 a.	680
John Shaw	"Huntington Grange" tbc Francis Armstrong in right of his wife	100
47:1739:25 ...		
John Knight	"Knightly" tbc Mr. Edward Lloyd	100
William Smith	"Soldiers Delight" tbc Mr. Edward Loyd	100
William Jones	"Batchellors Hope" tbc John & Andrew Kininmont	50
Josias Lambert	"Lambert House" – taker up of this land not known nor any person that does claim	50
Henry Parker	"Enlargement" tbc: • Thomas Elsbey – 15 a. • Edward Brenney – 45 a. • Adam Brown – 45 a. • Edm. Marsh – 45 a.	180
Andrew Skinner	"Double Ridge" tbc: • William Thomas – 230 a. • Samuell Dickinson – 50 a. • James White – 120 a.	400
Andrew Skinner	"Forked Neck" tbc Mr. Henry Nicols for Vestry of St. Michells Parish	50
47:1739:26 ...		
Andrew Skinner	"Timber Neck" tbc Mrs. Hen. Mar. Chew	120
William Jones	"Bartram" tbc: • John & Andrew Kinimon – 150 a. • Mr. Tench Francis – 50 a.	200
William Moore	"Chance Ridge" – taker up of this land not known nor any person that does claim	150

John Hollingsworth	"Beech" tbc Thomas Ashcraft	50
Henry Hooper	"Hoopers Ensitt" tbc John Hawkins, Jr. who married heir living in QA	200
Henry Wharton	"Hookland" tbc Henry Wharton	100
Josias Lambert	"Lamberton" tbc Arthur Rigbey	150
Robert Curtis	"Bonehill" tbc h/o Robert Curtis living in VA	250
47:1739:27 ...		
Thomas Hammond	"Hampton" tbc: • William Warren – 200 a. • Thomas Purnell – 8 a. • Caleb Clark – 100 a. • John Baynard – 50 a. • John Camperson – 50 a. • wanting supposed in elder survey – 62 a.	550
Thomas Vaughan	"Blessland" tbc: • Joseph Durder – 100 a. • Rachell Turbott for h/o Samuell Turbott – 100 a. • Rachell Turbott – 300 a.	500
Robert Knapp	"Knaps Lott" tbc William Anderson	150
Henry Frith	"Frithland" – escheated & resurveyed for Edward Fotril as "Fotrills Discovery" 250 a. (f. 138)	200
Thomas Oliver	"Olives Branch" – taker up not known nor any person that does claim	100
Thomas Heathcote	"Midle Neck" tbc Fra. Sherwood	100
John Barns	"Barns Neck" – with other land escheated & resurveyed for Edward Elliott as "Chance" 233 a. (f. 132)	100
47:1739:28 ...		
Alexander Larramore	"Larramores Neck" tbc Robert Larramore	100
George Prows	"Prows's Point" tbc: • William Harrison – 40 a. • Robert Harrison – 50 a. • lost by elder survey – 10 a.	100
Ralph Dawson	"Mabell" tbc John Ackles for h/o William Comb	100
Hannah Reynolds	"Reynolds Point" – escheated for John Reynold 148 a. (f. 142)	300
Francis Bettus	"Holden" tbc Mr. Henry Nichols for Vestry of St. Michells Parish	225
Francis Bettus (cnp)	"Boggs Hole: tbc: • Nicholas Benson – 50 a.	100

	• escheated by Edward Elliott & called "Chance" 223 a. (f. 132)	
James Scott	"New Mill" tbc Mr. Robert Lloyd	200
James Magregor	"Choetank" – William Dawson (heir) says the bounds of this land can not be found, but will make further inquery	100
John Barns	"Barns Chance" – taker up no known nor any person that does claim	100
47:1739:29 ...		
Henry Hawkins	"Hope" tbc Mr. Robert Lloyd	100
John Edmundson	"Devidend" – resurveyed for Fran. Connerly as "Hollands Addition" 41 a. (f. 126)	50
John Jadwin	"Jadwins Choice" – taker up not known nor any person that does claim	300
John Edmundson	"Enlargment" tbc John Edmondson	100
Francis Armstrong	"Deep Point" – let fall	150
John Edmundson	"Adjunction" – h/o Thomas Edmondson say they know nothing of this land	50
John Edmundson	"Upper Range" tbc: • John Glover – 50 a. • Thomas Stuart – 50 a.	100
John Edmundson	"Edmund Range" tbc Mr. Tench Francis	400
John Kinnament	"Fools Parradice" tbc John & Andrew Kininmont	50
47:1739:30 ...		
Thomas Emerson	"Long Point" – no person claims this land; presume it is included in elder surveys	50
William Hamilton	"Lancashire" tbc: • Robert Role – 70 a. • Richard Fiddeman – 30 a.	100
Francis Armstrong	"Bettys Cove" tbc: • John Davis – 20 a. • w/o James Hurlock – 30 a.	50
John Pitt	"Pitts Chance" tbc Ann Darbey (ENG)	400
William Jones & Peter Sides	"Lobbs Crook" – resurveyed for Richard Bennett, Esq. for 679 a. (f. 126)	550
Roger Gross	"Abbington" tbc Richard Bennett, Esq.	400
William Smith	"Poplar Neck" tbc Richard Bennett, Esq.	100
William Snaggs	"Battchellors Delight" tbc Richard Bennett, Esq.	100
47:1739:31 ...		

Stephen Whettstone	"Whettstone" tbc: • Richard Bennett, Esq. – 150 a. • Phil. Emerson – 150 a.	300
Peter Sharp	"Chesnutt Bay" tbc: • Philip Jenkins – 300 a. • John Sprignal – 100 a. • Joseph Padley (ENG) – 600 a.	1000
John Newman	"Newmans Lott" tbc: • John Millar for h/o Charles Stevens – 100 a. • Robert Noble – 100 a.	200
Robert Noble	"Nobles Chance" tbc: • William Warner who married the heirs [!] – 100 a. • Vincent Jones – 100 a. • John Millar for h/o Charles Stevens – 100 a.	300
Francis Bettar	"Rocky Nook Addition" tbc John Bartlett for h/o Edger Webb	50
William Taylor	"Taylors Ridge" tbc: • Joseph Eason for h/o Fra. Harrison – 100 a. • John Clift – pt. resurveyed as "Clifts Addition" 100 a. (f. 143) • Mary Lord – 100 a. • William Harrison – pt. resurveyed for 100 a. (f. 135) • John Mullican – pt. resurveyed as "Mullicans Choice" for 100 a. (f. 135) • Thomas Delahay – pt. resurveyed as "Dellehays Fortune" for 100 a. (f. 135) • Peirce Fleming – pt. resurveyed as "Flemmings Freshes" for 215 a. (f. 137)	700
47:1739:32 ...		
Peter Pitt	"St. Johns Neck" tbc Rebecca Durden for h/o Stephen Durden	700
Robert Curtis	"Adventure" tbc William Sharp	100
Henry Parker	"Rocky Nook" tbc John Bartlett for h/o Edger Webb	100
John Edmundson	"Wastland" tbc William Ridgway	100
John Edmundson	"Norwich" – John Edmundson (son of John Edmundson) refused to pay; says included in "North York"	200
Thomas Hopkins	"Addition" tbc James Hopkins; disclaimed	150

William Islinsworth	"Turkey Neck" tbc: • Dennes Carey – 100 a. • William Taylor – 259 a. • William Fooks – 16 a. • William Stacey – 125 a	500
Henry Parker	"Poplar Ridge" – resurveyed for Richard Bennett, Esq. for 249 a. (f. 135)	400
Richard Acton	"Acton" tbc John Stevens for h/o Henry Froath	300
47:1739:33 ...		
Francis Armstrong	"Londonderry" tbc: • Francis Armstrong – 382 a. • Dennes Hopkins – 103 a. • Richard Feddeman – 3 a. • Edward Elliott – 2 a. • John Frith – 1½ a. • John Williams – 1½ a.	500
Robert Wallne	"Armstrongs Gift" – taker up not known nor any person that does claim	200
Henry Parker	"Bite" tbc Edward Hardin as pt. resurveyed as "Hardins Endeavour" for 200 a. (f. 137)	50
Henry Mitchell	"Peach Blossom" tbc h/o Henry Mitchell (CV)	600
Henry Mitchell	"Gouldstone" tbc Mr. Samuell Chamberlaine	50
William Dell	"Delph" tbc Gabelil Sailes	100
John Wright	"Skipton" tbc Rogger Clayland	300
47:1739:34 ...		
John Wright	"Middleton" – taker up not known nor any person that does claim	80[illegible]
John Wright	"Poplar Neck" – taker up not known nor any person that does claim	10[illegible]
John Homewood	"Holm Hill" tbc: • John Robins – 400 a. • William Robins – 34 a. • Sarah Morgan – 62 a.	50[illegible]
Charles Holdsworth	"Maiden Point" tbc Mr. Henry Nichols	15[illegible]
John Eason	"Easons Neck" tbc William Sharp	10[illegible]
Daniell Walker	"Chance" tbc Nathaniell St. Tee	10[illegible]
Thomas Hethod	"Mount Misery" tbc: • William Harrison (bayside) – 25 a. • Fra. Sherwood – 50 a. • lost by elder survey – 25 a.	10[illegible]

Ralph Elston	"Thief Keep Out" – resurveyed for Robert Dawson as "Dawsons Composition" for 202 a. (f. 134)	100
47:1739:35 ...		
Ralph Elston	"Long Neck" tbc: • John Ball – 180 a. • wanting presumed to be lost in elder surveys – 20 a.	200
Thomas Hethod	"Plumb Point" – taker up not known nor any person that does claim	100
Thomas Hethod	"Timber Neck" – taker up not known nor any person that does claim	100
William Jones	"Planters Delight" tbc: • John Millar for h/o Charles Stevens – 100 a. • John Swett for h/o Robert Noble – 100 a.	200
Abraham Bishop	"Champenhams Addition" tbc Jacob Gibson	50
Francis Armstrong	"Cornelius's Cool Spring" tbc Francis Armstrong in right of his wife	100
Thomas Vaughan	"Merchants Folly" tbc William Webb Haddaway	150
Thomas Vaughan	"Rich Neck" tbc William Webb Haddaway	150
47:1739:36 ...		
John Burk	"Barken Point" tbc Thomas Lurey	100
Robert Humphreys	"Harly" – taker up not known nor any person that does claim	50
John Edmundson	"Hatt Field" tbc: • George Robins – 75 a. • William Adams – 12½ a. • John Price – 12½	100
Henry Wharton	"Whartons Glade" tbc Hannah Davis	50
John Edmundson	"Mount Hope" tbc: • Samuell Dickinson – 350 a. • James Barnwell – 75 a. • Robert Wiles – 53 a. • Henry Henrix – 35¼ a. • George Palmer – 100 a. • Lemon John Cathrop – 67 a. • Anthony Richardson – 50 a. • Edward Neal – 50 a. • William Adrey for h/o Joseph Barron – 50 a. • h/o Robert Finley (ENG) – 200 a.	700
John Chafe	"Hole Haven" – let fall	100

Samuell Winslow	"Delight" – taker up not known nor any person that does claim	250
Samuell Winslow	"Witherington" tbc Robert Roles	200
47:1739:37 ...		
William Shears	"Rich Neck" – taker up not known nor any person that does claim	50
John Edmundson	"Little Creek" tbc Samuell Dickinson	150
William Smith	"Smiths Clifts" tbc: • Samuell Dudley for h/o Richard Thompson – 94 a. • Sarah Morgan wife of Capt. Edward Morgan – 258 a. • Richard Hall – 390 a. • William Robins – 221 a. • Grundy Pemberton – 232 a. • Thomas Thompson – 94 a. • William Dudley who will disclaim – 138 a. • John Wooters (QA) – 20 a. • Jacob Wooters (QA) – 95 a. • lost – 458 a.	2000
Patrick Millican	"Patricks Plains" tbc: • Samuell Mullican – 150 a. • Patrick Mullican – 150 a.	300
Thomas Phillips & Richard White	"Fox Hole" tbc: • Morris Oram – 145 a. • Arthur Rigbey – 65 a. • Richard Eaton – 100 a.	300
William Moore	"William & James" – resurveyed for Thomas Hopkins for 58 a. (f. 127)	50
John Edmundson	"Addition" – Fran. Whitewell the last possessor not known nor any person that does claim	300
47:1739:38 ...		
Daniell Jennifer	"Advantage" tbc: • Richard Bennett, Esq. – 500 a. • Howell Powell – 42 a. • Samuell Dudley – 18 a.	500
Howell Powell	"Powells Island" – resurveyed for William Dickenson for 655 a. (f. 120)	50
James Scott	"Scotts Lott" tbc John & Andrew Kininmont	100
Daniell Jennifer (cnp)	"Rich Range" tbc: • William Whiteley (QA) – 100 a. • John Robins – 200 a.	500

	• William Frampton – 50 a. • Thomas Purnell – 150 a.	
Phill. Loyd & Henry Parker	"Addition" tbc Peter Harwood	400
Nicholas Berkley	"Netty France" – disclaimed by James Millar on 18 November 1737	150
47:1739:39 ...		
John Edmundson	"Discovery" – with other lands included in resurvey by John Edmundson called "Edmondsons Difficulty" (f. 130)	250
William Moore	"Moorland" – taker up not known nor any person that does claim	100
William Smith	"Brain Tree" tbc Thomas Winchester for h/o Isaac Martin	500
John Edmundson	"Caerdiffe" tbc Mr. Thomas Bozman	100
John Drywood	"Drywoods Chance" – taker up not known nor any person that does claim	100
William Dawson	"Dawsons Fortune" tbc John Stevens	50
John Richardson	"Jamaico" tbc: • Mr. Daniel Maynadier – 150 a. • lost & presumed in elder surveys – 3 a. • Daniell Walker – pt. escheated & resurveyed for 92 a. (f. 119)	250
47:1739:40 ...		
John Edmundson	"North York" – John Edmundson the heir of the taker up of the land alleges he will disclaim	200
John Edmundson	"Edmundsons Freshes" tbc: • John Webb for h/o William Elston – 110 a. • Philip Jenkins – 300 a. • John Neighbours – 50 a.	250
Edward Hull	"Hulls Neck" tbc: • Mr. George Robins – 300 a. • John Shaw – 200 a. • Thomas Dellehay for h/o John Mears – 40 a.	400
Richard Howard	"Griffiths Addition" – taker up not known nor any person that does claim	50
Edward Roe	"Andertons Addition" tbc Mr. Nicholas Lowe	100
Edward Low	"Rumley Marsh" tbc Mr. Robert Lloyd	300
Henry Hawkins	"Addition" tbc Mr. Edward Lloyd	100
Attwell Badwell	"Tawny Close" tbc Thomas Martin	50

47:1739:41 ...		
John Niell	"Niells Range" tbc: • Mr. Edward Man Sherwood – 200 a. • Edward Needles – 200 a. • Rogger Bradberry – 200 a.; disclaimed	600
Edward Roe	"Chance" tbc Thomas Metcalf in right of his wife	100
Francis Armstrong	"Armstrongs Marsh" – resurveyed for Capt. John Kemble as "Kembles Industry" for 283 a. (f. 137)	200
John Edmundson	"Addition" tbc Mr. Tench Francis	100
John Edmundson	"Bantry" tbc: • Mary Attwell for h/o Joseph Attwell – 200 a. • Fra. Stanton in right of his wife – 100 a.	300
Francis Armstrong	"Mistake" – included in a resurvey for Samuell Dickinson called "Samuels Lott" (f. 130)	75
Richard Gurling	"Addition" tbc Mr. Robert Lloyd	100
Robert Bullen	"Conjunction" tbc: • Phil. Martin – 25 a. • William Sharp – 25 a.	50
47:1739:42 ...		
William Hamilton	"Hamiltons Park" tbc: • Philip Emerson – 263 a. • James Sanders & John Pitts – 137 a.	400
Alexander Ray	"Enlargement" tbc: • Philemon Skinner – 50 a. • Joseph Hopkins – 50 a.	100
Arthur Emory	"Chance" tbc George Taylor	100
Henry Parker	"Enfield" tbc James Walker	200
Henry Alexander	"Kingston" tbc Peirce Fleming for h/o Dennes Connerly	400
Thomas Mears	"Midle Neck" tbc Mr. Nicholas Lowe	200
Peter Sharp	"Ending of Controversy" tbc Isaac Dixon	150
Robert Landman	"Rehoboth" – resurveyed for George Collison as "Rehoboth's Point" for 50 a. (f. 130)	50
John Anderton	"Birchley" – with other lands resurveyed for Robert Dawson & called "Dawsons Composition" (f. 134)	100
47:1739:43 ...		
Alexander Larrimore	"Larrimores Lott" tbc h/o Richard Burden (Long Island)	50
Thomas Hethod	"Poplar Neck" tbc William Harrison (bay side)	100

Henry Frith	"Friths Neck" tbc John Porter	50
Henry Frith	"Addition" tbc Richard Fiddeman	50
William Gaskin	"William & Margaret" – taker up not known nor any person that does claim	100
George Prouse	"Prouses Fortune" – disclaimed by George Sprouse on 3 December 1736	100
Thomas Camplire	"Fairly" tbc John Fairbank	100
Ralph Dawson	"Up Holland" tbc Bridget Shehawn (DO) sold to Richard Manfield	50
William Rich	"Comsberry" tbc Mr. Edward Oldham	100
47:1739:44 ...		
Nicholas Holmes	"Holmby" tbc William Mackey	200
John Kininement	"Addition" tbc Mr. Tench Francis	50
William Dickenson	"Cross Dover Marsh" – included in a resurvey by Samuell Dickinson called "Samuells Lott" (f. 130)	25
Peter Sides	"Wisbick" tbc William Clayland	100
Henry Hawkins	"Poplar Hill" tbc William Clayton	200
Richard Carter	"Carters Inheritance" – resurveyed for Phil. Lloyd, Esq. for 400 a. (f. 116)	300
Hopkins Davies	"Fox Harbour" tbc: • Richard Eaton – 50 a. • Morris Oram – 50 a.	100
Thomas Vaughan	"Ashford" tbc: • William Harris (Irish Creek) – 50 a. • Joseph Hix – 50 a.	100
Thomas Vaughan	"Waterford" tbc Morris Oram	100
47:1739:45 ...		
Thomas Vaughan	"Crawford" tbc Arthur Rigbey	100
Christopher Staper	"Stauper" tbc: • Thomas Ashcraft – 4 a. • taker up not known nor any person that does claim – 46 a.	50
John Reynolds	"Fox Harbour" tbc James Spencer, Jr. in right of his wife	50
William Godwin	"Rest Content" tbc Nathaniell Grace	100
John Ingram	"Cornwell" tbc Joseph Withgott	100
Richard Carter	"Chance" tbc Mr. Robert Goldsborough	50
William Taylor	"Addition" tbc Mr. Nicholas Goldsborough	80
John Elliott	"Elliotts Discovery" tbc Mr. Robert Loyd	100

John Edmundson	"Johns Neck" tbc: • Joshua Clark – 113 a. • Aron Parrott – 264 a. • Edward Needles – 4 a. • Thomas Hutchenson – 19 a.	400
47:1739:46 ...		
John Newman	"Newmans Folly" – taker up not known nor any person that does claim	100
James Scott	"Adjunction" tbc Mr. Robert Lloyd	50
James Scott & James Pascall	"Partnership" tbc Mr. Robert Lloyd	310
James Shanklady	"James's Reserve" – John Edmundson to whom this land was assigned said he knew nothing of it; after his decease, his son likewise refused to pay the rent for the same reason; supposed to be included in elder surveys	300
Francis Armstrong	"Uper Range" tbc Mr. John Blake (QA)	200
Francis Armstrong	"Adventure" – included in "Hicory Ridge"	150
Thomas Cole	"Coles Bank" tbc William Clayton (QA) who pays the rent there	300
47:1739:47 ...		
William Shirt	"Watterton" tbc: • William Clayton – 290 a. • Rachell Fenney for h/o William Fenney – 170 a. • h/o David Jonson not known nor any person that does claim – 200 a.	660
Phillip Stevenson	"Harwood Lyon" – Phill. Emerson	600
Nathaniell Ashcomb	"Compton" tbc h/o Nathaniel Ashcomb (Clifts, CV)	300
John Winfield	"Winfields Trouble" – taker up not known nor any person that does claim	200
Jonathan Hopkins	"Hopton" – included in survey for Mr. William Hemsley of "Hemsley upon Wye" for 1160 a. (f. 130)	32
George Aldridge	"Indian Neck" – included in survey for Richard Bennett, Esq. of "Badwells Indian Neck" for 913 a. (f. 130)	35
Francis Armstrong	"Cornelius's Cove" tbc h/o Michaell Russell who allege cannot find the bounds but will make further inquiry	5
Edmund Winckle	"Fortune" tbc George Garey	15
47:1739:48 ...		

Timothey Freeman	"Freemans Rest" – presume belongs to John Hawkins who married h/o Richard Poor (QA)	50
William Eason	"Easons Choice" tbc: • Samuell Mullican – 25 a. • Patrick Mullican – 25 a.	50
John Eason	"Fancy" tbc William Sharp	50
Thomas Goddard	"Forth Venture" tbc William Bennett	50
James Hall	"Halls Neck" – resurveyed for Robert Hall & patented to Benjamin Peck for 476 a. (f. 138)	400
John Edmundson	"Todcaster" – lies in QA & possessor lives there	1000
William Gaskin	"Gaskin's Point" – resurveyed for Col. Math. Ward as "Three Necks" for 165 a. (f. 126)	100
Ralph Elston	"Rays Point" tbc Joseph Hopkins	150
John Richardson	"Jamaicos Addition" – taker up not known nor any person that does claim	50
47:1739:49 ...		
John Richardson	"Cuba" – lies in His Lordships Mannor in TA	150
Samuell Hall	"Halls Fortune" – escheated & resurveyed for Arnold Hawkins with other lands as "Cabbin Neck, Sandy Bite, & Halls Fortune" for 238 a. (f. 138)	50
Phillip Calvert, Esq.	"Whitte Marshes" tbc: • James Berry – 760 a. • lost being included in elder surveys – 240 a.	1000
Phill. Calvert, Esq.	"Four Square" tbc: • pt. resurveyed for Robert Goldsborough for 650 a. (f. 136) • pt. resurveyed for Samuell Chamberlain for 350 a. (f. 137)	1000
John Edmundson	"Uper Dover" – lies in His Lordships Mannor	400
John Edmundson	"Lower Dover" – lies in His Lordships Mannor	400
John Edmundson	"Freshes" – John Edmundson the heir of Thomas Edmundson will disclaim	300
Thomas Phillips	"Highfield" tbc: • Edward Man Sherwood – 50 a. • Caleb Clark – 100 a.	150
47:1739:50 ...		
Richard Royston	"Roystons Addition" tbc Richard Aldren	150
John Richardson (cnp)	"Willenbrough" tbc: • h/o John Richardson (PA) – 150 a. • pt. resurveyed for Walter Qunton – 50 a.	200

	(f. 122)	
William Finney	"Finneys Range" tbc Rachell Fenney for h/o William Finney	225
Richard Carter	"Carters Farm" tbc Thomas Perkin in right of his wife	500
Edward Winckles	"Winckleton" tbc Richard Bennett, Esq.	185
Richard Woolman	"Grunny" tbc Mr. James Hollyday	100
Thomas Phillips	"Highfield Addition" tbc Caleb Clark	150
George Watts	"Maidston" tbc h/o Henry Conner (DO)	250
Richard Carter	"Carters Preserve" tbc h/o Richard Carter (ENG)	200
Henry Parker	"Parkers Range" tbc: • Caleb Clark – 256 a. • John Baynard (QA) – 130 a. • John Camperson – 100 a.	500
47:1739:51 ...		
Henry Parker	"Parkers Park" tbc Mr. Tench Francis	500
Richard Carter	"Carters Farm" tbc: • Isaac Dixon – 83 a. • h/o Richard Carter (ENG) – 167 a.	250
Bryan Omaly	"Thief Keep Out" – William Dawson who is the heir can't find the bounds, but will make further inquiry	50
Andrew Skinner	"Rich Farm Addition" a/s "Rich Range Addition" tbc John Robins	100
John Davis	"Hope Chance" tbc John Davis	50
William Sharp	"Mount Pleasure" tbc William Sharp	500
John Morgan	"Cabbin Neck" – taker up of this land not known nor any person that does claim	500
James Rigby	"Cabbin Neck" – resurveyed for Col. Ernault Hawkins with other land called "Cabbin Neck, Sandy Bite, & Halls Fortune" for 258 a. (f. 138)	43
47:1739:52 ...		
John Parson	"Parsons Ridge" tbc Mr. John Talbott (AA)	500
Robert Harwood	"Rich Farm" tbc: • h/o Robert Finly (ENG) – 200 a. • Robert Walker from James Berry – 100 a. • supposed to be included in elder surveys – 150 a.	450
George Cowley	"Sutton" tbc: • Bryan Sieney – 200 a. • William Carey – 100 a.	300

Attwell Bowdwell	"Green Hill" tbc John Hill (QA)	100
John Richardson	"Hattfield Addition" tbc: • Robert Bryan, but no heirs appear nor any person that does claim – 100 a. • George Robins – 100 a.	200
John Richardson	"Jamaicos Addition" – supposed to belong to h/o John Richardson (PA)	50
William Stevens	"Spring Close" tbc Jeffery Cox	50
Richard Skeggs	"Skeggs Spring" tbc Col. Arnold Hawkins & Mr. Tench Francis (QA)	50
Francis Brook	"Nottingham" tbc Aron Higgs	100
Robert Harwood	"Harwood Hill" tbc Peter Harwood	100
47:1739:53 ...		
Samuell Abbott	"Abbington" tbc Dugles Chace in right of h/o (N) Abbott	100
Robert Harwood	"Rich Farm Addition" tbc: • William Shield & James Sanders – 200 a. • lost in elder surveys – 200 a.	400
William Finney	"Finneys Hermitage" tbc: • h/o Richard Carter (ENG) – 200 a. • Roger Clayland – 200 a.	400
Edward Roe	"Galston" – William Combs the heir will disclaim	50
Edward Winckles	"Winckles Ridge" – John Dun the possessor found it was taken by elder survey & disclaimed it	250
Henry Parker	"Kingston" tbc: • Aron Parrott – 51½ a. • Andrew Bandey in right of his wife – 100 a. • Aron Parrott – 100 a., will disclaim • John Compton (NE) – 49 a.	300
Henry Parker	"Mill Road" tbc: • Peter Harwood – 100 a. • h/o Col. Smithson (ENG) – 50 a. • Charles Skinner – 50 a.	200
Ralph Elston	"Brook Hall" – Ralph Elston will disclaim, as taken by elder survey	100
47:1739:54 ...		
Samuell Hatton	"Hatton" tbc: • James Dickinson – 434 a. • George West for h/o John Love – 63 a. • h/o John Preston (Carolina) – 103 a.	600

George Dawley	"Normanton" tbc: • William Clayton – 767 a. • included in survey of William Elberst called "Loyds Costine" for 659 a. (f. 128) – 33 a.	800
Thomas Taylor	"Kingsberry" tbc: • Joseph Durden – 130 a. • James Willson – 70 a.	200
Rebecca Woolman	"Rebecca Garden" tbc: • Jacob Gibson – 150 a. • William Elbert – 50 a.	150
Simeon Stevenson	"Nobles Ridge" tbc John Swett for h/o Robert Noble	150
Thomas Larey	"Franckforde St. Michell" tbc James Dickinson	616
Nicholas Holmes	"Suttons Addition" tbc Thomas Metcalfe & Richard Holmes	50
Andrew Skinner	"Roadway" – resurveyed for Col. Edward Lloyd for 50 a. (f. 117)	50
47:1739:55 ...		
Richard Gurlington	"Gurlington" tbc: • pt. resurveyed for Walter Quinton as pt. "Willenbrough" & pt. "Gurlington" – 25 a. • pt. resurveyed for Capt. William Greenwood – 75 a. (f. 124)	200
Andrew Skinner	"Skinners Out Lett" tbc George Gresham	50
Bryan Omaly	"Galloway" tbc: • Mr. Henry Nichols – 96 a. • William Dawson – 100 a. • Richard Gibson – 52 a. • John Wrightson – 52 a.	300
Edward Roe	"Oxford Towne" – bounds of this land lost; heir will disclaim	2
John Edmundson	"Swamp Hole" tbc Mathew Kirbey	100
William Berry	"Berrys Range" – taker up not known nor any person that does claim	130
Richard Gurling	"Morrey" tbc Mr. Robert Loyd	150
John Douty	"Doutys Lott" tbc Mr. Edward Lloyd	50
John Douty	"Doutys Hope" tbc Mr. Edward Lloyd	50
47:1739:56 ...		
Daniell Walker	"Daniels Rest" tbc Thomas Bruff – 50 a.	100

Henry Parker	"Holden Addition" tbc: • James Barber who purchased land from Henry Parker – 50 a., let fall • h/o Thomas Smithson (ENG) – 50 a.	100
Henry Parker	"Parkers Addition" – included in resurvey of Edward Harding called "Hardens Endeavour" (f. 137)	50
John Newman	"Newmans Field" tbc Capt. John Carpenter (Annapolis)	50
Timothy Goodridge	"Timothys Lott" tbc Thomas Bozman for h/o Jonathan Taylor	300
Nathaniell Theagle	"Theagles Reg." – Nicholas Goldsborough who married heiress of this land says it is included in elder surveys & will disclaim	125
William Froth	"Froths Fortune" – lies in the Mannor	400
Thomas Vaughan	"Contention" tbc Mr. Samuell Chamberlain	100
47:1739:57 ...		
George Hurlock	"Bettys Addition" tbc w/o James Hurlock for h/o James Hurlock	50
Thomas Martin	"Swamptick" tbc Richard Giles in right of his wife	100
Francis Brooke	"Town Road" tbc Richard Bennett, Esq.	50
Humphry Daventport	"Maiden Point" tbc Mr. Henry Nichols	100
Richard Carter	"Carters Plains" tbc: • Isaac Dixon" – 206 a. • h/o Richard Carter (ENG) – 294 a.	500
John Eason	"Easons Lott" tbc William Sharp	50
William Froth	"Froths Addition" – lies in His Lordships Mannor in TA	100
Henry Parker	"Fishing Bay" tbc Benjamin Stuart	200
Humphry Daventport	"Daventport" tbc Thomas Askinafter	200
47:1739:58 ...		
Thomas Taylor	"Kingsbys Addition" tbc John Register	100
Richard Carter	"Carters Range" tbc h/o Richard Carter (ENG)	200
John Stanley	"Chance" – several heirs of John Stanley say that this land is included in elder survey & disclaim	100
Bryan Omely	"Bryans Lott" tbc: • Mr. Henry Nichols – 12½ a. • Woolman Gibson – 12½ a. • John Wrightson – 12½ a. • Richard Gibson – 12½ a.	50

John Squires	"Killinsworth" tbc William White	50
William Sharp	"Sharps Fortune" – heirs of Michell Russell to whom this land belongs say they cannot find the bounds, but will make further inquiry	100
William Sharp	"Sharps Chance" tbc: • John Williams – 100 a. • Michell Fletcher – 200 a.	300
Phill. Loyd	"Loyds Addition" tbc Peter Harwood	120
47:1739:59 ...		
Phill. Loyd	"Bettys Branch" tbc Mr. James Hollyday	325
Thomas Lurkey	"Lancashire" tbc Thomas Lurkey	50
Thomas Lurkey	"Lurkey" tbc Thomas Cumings	50
John Edmundson	"Adventure" tbc: • pt. resurveyed for Arthur Rigbey – 100 a. (f. 117) • Robert Goldsborough – 100 a. • Andrew Oram – 200 a.	400
Ralph Dawson	"Fair Play" tbc: • Thomas Studham – 50 a. • h/o George Merchat (QA) – 50 a.	100
Robert Evans	"Stamforth Point" – land sold from Thomas Howel to James Tucker who is dead & no person that does claim	100
Ralph Elston	"Blydon" tbc Charles Bridges	100
John Squires	"Warwick Point" tbc Henry Conyers (DO)	100
Thomas Brerely	"Brerelys Delight" tbc Mr. Edward Lloyd	150
47:1739:60 ...		
Robert Kemp	"Kemps Lott" tbc John Ackels for h/o William Kemp	100
William Wattson	"Wattson" tbc Rizdon Bozman	150
John Whittington	"Fisburns Neglect" –lies in His Lordships Mannor	130
James Scott	"Triangle" tbc Lewis Jones	100
William Parratt	"Strawberry Field" tbc Isaac Dobson for h/o John Kirbey	100
John Pitt	"Johns Kill" tbc: • Joseph Turner – 90 a. • Isaa Coxe in right of his wife – 90 a. • Thomas Spiger (AA) – 40 a. • William Turner – 90 a. • Thomas Turner – 90 a.	400

Joseph, James, & John Boon	"Hiccory Ridge" – taker up not known nor any person that does claim	150
John Edmundson	"Desire Addition" tbc John Edmundson	60
47:1739:61 ...		
Ralph Fishburne	"Fisburns Lott" tbc: • John Lowe for h/o Loghlin McDaniel – 100 a. • John Williams h/o Enion Williams (CE) – 50 a.	150
James Murphy	"Barns Neck Addition" – escheated by Edward Elliott & included in resurvey called "Chance" for 223 a. (f. 132)	100
James Harrison	"Dover Marsh" – lies in His Lordships Mannor	74
John Hunt	"Devine St. Andrew" tbc John Hunt	200
Hugh Sherwood	"Sherwoods Island" tbc Francis Sherwood	20
Hugh Sherwood	"Crooked Intention" tbc: • Mr. Daniell Sherwood – 80 a. • Robert Harrison – 50 a.	130
John Sharp	"Hawks Hill Hope" tbc: • Edward Speding – 50 a. • John Speding – 50 a.	100
Alexander Jordan	"Jordans Folly" – John Wrightson	100
47:1739:62 ...		
David Fairbank	"Yourk" tbc Laurance Porter	100
Henry Parrott	"White Oak Swamp" tbc James Willson, Jr.	100
Henry Parrott	"Buck Range" tbc Michaell Kirbey	50
Bryan Omely	"Omalys Range" tbc Thomas Eubanks	200
William Berry	"Poplar Neck" – taker up not known nor any person that does claim	400
Roger Price	"Lee Hall" – resurveyed for Col. Math. Ward as "Union" for 831 a.	150
Thomas Smithson	"Arcadia" tbc: • William Bush – 166 a. • John James in right of his wife – 34 a.	200
Edward Fuller	"Old Womans Folly" tbc Mrs. Frances Ungle	50
William Garey	"Knightlys Addition" tbc Mrs. Hen. Mar. Chew	50
47:1739:63 ...		
William Gary	"Garys Delight" – George Garey the heir says he cannot find the bounds but will make further inquiry	50

Cornelius Mullraine	"Cornelius Garden" tbc Robert Cutcart	50
Cornelius Mullraine	"Warepoint" – let fall by Cornelius Mullraine	50
Cornelius Mullraine	"Quillin" tbc: • Mr. Samuell Dickinson – 16½ a. • Mary Welch – 16½ a. • Susanna Welch – 16½ a.	50
Francis Morling	"Morlings Folly" tbc Thomas Winchester for h/o Isaac Martin	50
Francis Morling	"Morlings Choice" tbc Thomas Winchester for h/o Isaac Martin	50
Anthony Mayle	"Wyatts Fortune" tbc Mr. Robert Goldsborough	50
Anthony Mayle	"Goose Neck" tbc William Banning	50
47:1739:64 ...		
John Davis	"Knave Keep Out" tbc John Davis	50
Richard Royston	"Clays Addition" tbc Richard Aldern	50
Robert Knapp	"Poplar Neck" tbc James Dawson	50
Roger Price	"Prices Neck" – resurveyed for Col. Math. Ward as "Union" for 231 a. (f. 124)	200
Henry Costin	"Sarahs Lott" tbc Fra. Pickrin, Jr. in right of his wife	50
Henry Costin	"Doctors Gift" tbc John <unr>; no heirs appeared nor any person that does claim	100
William Porter	"Bellfast" tbc John Fairbank	100
Alexander Larrimore	"Bampshire" tbc Robert Larramore	50
Henry Clay	"Clays Neck" – resurveyed for Mary Wrightson for 102 a. (f. 134)	100
47:1739:65 ...		
Abraham Hurlock	"Abrahams Lott" tbc: • John James in right of his wife – 66 a. • James Harvey – 100 a. • Joseph Parrott – 34 a.	200
John Morely	"Newman" tbc Thomas Atkisson	50
John Morely & John Sharp	"Hawks Hill Addition" tbc Terrance Ferrell	100
William & Sollomon Jones	"Widows Chance" tbc Mr. Robert Loyd	50
Francis Marling	"Batchellors Branch" tbc James Horney	100
John Davis	"Personage" tbc John Davis	100
James Barber	"Sommerby" tbc Henry Oldfield in right of his wife	300
Thomas Anderson	"Bonnington" – lies in His Lordships Mannor	50
47:1739:66 ...		

John Dunn	"Dunns Range" – resurveyed for William Brown for 225 a. (f. 128)	200
John Wooters	"Buckby" tbc: • Jacob Bradberry – 200 a. • William Dudley – 50 a. • John Harrington – 150 a.	400
George Robins	"Buckingham" – Mr. George Robins the heir of Thomas Robins will disclaim, supposing it to be lost in elder surveys	300
Francis Neale	"Fairfield" – lies in QA; Francis Neal the heir will disclaim	200
Thomas Faulkner	"Faulkners Folly" tbc Mr. James Hollyday, Esq.	100
Peter Dennis	"Peters Rest" tbc Mr. Robert Goldsborough	50
Thomas Smithson	"Millread Addition" tbc: • Peter Harwood – 100 a. • Charles Skinker – 25 a. • h/o Thomas Smithson (ENG) – 25 a.	150
Edward Stevenson	"Stevenson Range" tbc: • Edm. Ferrell – 100 a. • Mr. Fra. Ungle – 180 a. • h/o Robert Register but not known nor any person will claim – 20 a.	300
47:1739:67 ...		
Bryan Omaly	"Poplar Levell" tbc Peter Harwood	100
John Rousby	"Morgans Point" tbc Charles Markland	50
Christopher St. Tee	"Christopher Lott" tbc: • George Beswicks – 100 a. • Richard Beswick – 100 a.	200
James Hall	"Edwards Hopewell" tbc Daniell Vinton	100
George Parrott	"Eagles Neck" tbc John Ervan for h/o William Dobson	100
George Robins	"Gouldsborough" tbc: • Mr. Daniell Maynadier – 187 a. • John Robinson – 100 a. • William White – 113 a.	400
George Robins	"Robins Range" tbc George Robins	300
Richard Dudley	"Dudley" tbc Samuell Broadway	200
47:1739:68 ...		
Thomas Taylor	"Kings Creek Marsh" tbc Joseph Durden	50
Robert Noble	"Nobles Addition" tbc John Swett for h/o Robert Noble	150

John Newman	"Coventry" tbc: • George Palmer – 30 a. • Edward Hardin – 40 a. • Edm. Ferrell – 60 a. • Joseph Elliott – 120 a. • Dennes Hopkins who will disclaim being taken in elder surveys – 50 a.	300
Henry Costin	"Lambeth" – included in elder surveys	200
Abraham Hurlock	"Abrahams Choice" – taker up not known nor any person that does claim	50
Samuell Crayker	"Ramah" – taker up not known nor any person that does claim; in ENG	300
John Whittington	"Fisburnes Neglect" – twice charged (f. 60)	130
George Robins	"Buckingham" tbc Mr. George Robins	450
47:1739:69 ...		
William Kirkham	"Mount Hope" – lies in QA	150
Emanuell Jenkinson	"Beginning" tbc h/o George Royston (CV)	300
William Jones	"Sandy Bile" – taker up not known nor any person that does claim; escheated by Col. Ernault Hawkins as "Cabbin Neck, Sandy Bite, & Halls Fortune" for 238 a. (f. 138)	50
James Hall	"James Folly" – Robert Grundey the last possessor of this land alleges it was included in elder surveys	50
James Hall	"James Look Out" tbc Thomas Robson	50
John Newman	"Newmans Range" tbc Edward Robins	100
John Newman	"Newmans Addition" tbc Mr. Robert Goldsborough	50
Richard Royston	"Cumberland" tbc: • William Bennett – 50 a. • Richard Aldern – 150 a.	200
47:1739:70 ...		
William Jones	"Jones's Lott" tbc Richard Dawson	50
Henry Parker	"Freshes" – resurveyed for Richard Bennett, Esq. as "Bennetts Freshes" for 423 a. (f. 137)	200
Henry Parker	"Huntingtons Addition" tbc Richard Bennett, Esq.	150
Henry Parker	"Parkers Thickett" tbc Robert Hall; resurveyed for Robert Hall	100
Henry Parker	"Neglect" – resurveyed for Richard Bennett, Esq. for 107 a. (f. 137)	100
Henry Parker	"Warwick" tbc Andrew Abbington (PG)	400

Henry Parker	"Parkers Freshes" tbc Edward Goodwin (QA)	380
Henry Parker	"Parkers Farm" tbc: • Edward Clark – 350 a. • Sarah Greenwood – 100 a.	450
John Newman	"Babbs Hill" tbc Henry Burges	100
47:1739:71 ...		
William Dixon	"Dixons Lott" tbc: • Mr. Tench Francis – 50 a. • h/o Robert Finley (ENG) – 50 a.	100
Francis Anketill	"Anketill" tbc: • Mr. Daniell Sherwood – 440 a. • lost in the resurvey – 60 a.	500
John Miller	"Millers Purchase" tbc John Carr	100
John Newman	"Bedworth" tbc: • James Barnwell – 100 a. • Lambert Shield – 100 a.	200
Richard Dudley	"Dudleys Choice" tbc: • John Leverton – 100 a. • Thomas Purnell (QA) – 100 a.	200
John Wooters	"Sybland" tbc w/o Enion Williams for his heirs	200
John Price	"Hobsons Choice" tbc Mr. Samuell Dickinson (100 a.)	700
John Wotters	"Coventry" tbc James Kendrick	250
47:1739:72 ...		
John Miller	"Hobsons Choice" tbc John Millar	150
James Clayland	"Personage Addition" tbc Mrs. Hen. Maria Chew	100
Thomas Vaughan	"Eatsoms Addition" tbc: • Richard Eaton – 180 a. • William Bennett – 60 a. • Thomas Pamphilion – 60 a.	300
Robert White	"Hogg Neck Addition" – John Rhodes the last possessor not known nor any person that does claim	50
Cuthbert Phillips	"Cudlingtons Addition" tbc James Dawson	50
Cuthbert Phillips	"Cudlingtons Encrease" tbc James Dawson	50
Thomas Smithson & John Stanley	"Gaterly Moore" tbc Edward Fish	120
47:1739:73 ...		
Bryan Omaly	"Batchellors Range Addition" tbc William Dawson	500
James Withgott	"Josephs Lott" tbc Joseph Withgott	100

John Davis	"Davies Outlett" tbc John Pitts & James Sanders	50
Henry Parker	"Duns Range Addition" – ~~resurvey for William <unr> for 252 a. [this is in error]~~ tbc Robert Stonestreet	200
John Hatten	"Hatten Garden" tbc John Harrington	50
John Hatten	"Bentley Hay" tbc John Wiles	50
Robert Colson	"Folly" tbc Rizdon Bozman	100
John Anderson	"Lostocks Addition" – disclaimed by John Camp on 3 December 1737	50
Daniell Walker	"Woodland Neck" – Mr. Robert Goldsborough who purchased the land will disclaim	100
47:1739:74 ...		
Roger Price	"Battfield" – resurveyed for Col. Math. Ward as "Union" for 831 a. (f. 124)	100
William Gaskin	"Gaskin Pasture" – taker up not known nor any person that does claim	50
Zebobell Wells	"Wells Out Lett" tbc Thomas Foster	50
Ralph Elston	"Exchange" – taken up by elder surveys upon which Elston will disclaim	100
John Hatton	"Hattons Hope" tbc William Dawson	100
William Combs	"Security" – taken by elder surveys; William Coombes disclaimed on 28 December 1736	200
William Carvin	"Scarborough" tbc: • John Dickinson – 200 a. • Christopher Burket – 200 a. • John Leeds – 200 a. • Jeremiah Jadwin (QA) – 200 a. • wanting supposed to be included in elder surveys – 600 a.	1400
Thomas Smithson	"Cumberland" tbc: • George Sprouse – 70 a. • Grundey Pemberton – 30 a.	100
47:1739:75 ...		
Alexander Larrimore	"Larramores Addition" tbc Peter Hunt	50
James Hall	"Greenland" – Mr. Robert Loyd will disclaim not knowing where it is	50
Henry Parker	"Timber Neck" tbc Richard Bennett, Esq.	100
Thomas Smithson	"Long Acre" tbc Michell Fletcher	150
John Wooters	"Dunsmore Heath" tbc Mr. George Robins	200

John Edmundson	"Heworth" tbc: • Grundey Pemberton – 205 a. • h/o (N) Johnson (ENG) – 195 a. • pt. resurveyed for John Edmondson as "Desire" for 683 a. (f. 130)	700
Thomas Hutchinson	"Lords Gift" tbc: • William Barker for h/o Richard Robinson – 100 a. • Thomas Bullen – 100 a. • Thomas Bullen on escheat – 60 a. • William Buckley – 175 a.	450
47:1739:76 ...		
William Parrott	"Strawberry Hills Addition" tbc John Rathell	50
Thomas Hutchinson	"Hutchinsons Addition" tbc Samuell Abbott	150
Edward Webb	"Bolton" tbc John Kemp	100
John Mitchell	"Mitchells Lott" tbc Richard Bennett, Esq.	200
Wallter Quinton	"Cross Haze" tbc Mr. Daniell Maynadier for Vestry of St. Peters Parish	50
Christopher Battson	"Bradford" – taker up not known nor any person that does claim	50
Christopher Battson	"Beverdam" tbc Samuell Abbott	100
James Scott	"Scotland" tbc Mr. Robert Loyd	50
Francis Chaplin	"Whitte Chapell" tbc Hezekiah Maccotter	100
47:1739:77 ...		
John Edmundson	"Clifton" tbc: • John Speding – 100 a. • Edward Speding – 100 a.	200
Miles Cooke	"Cooks Hope" – resurveyed for John Edmondson as "Edmondsons Difficulty" for 1253 a. (f. 130)	414
William Hemsley	"Pickadilly" tbc William Vickers	200
William Hemsley	"Triangle" tbc Richard Bennett, Esq.	55
William Hemsley	"Little Brittain" tbc George Garey	150
Jacob Bradbeury	"Jacobs Beginning" tbc Robert Hunter	100
William Gary	"Dirty Weeden" tbc George Garey	100
Charles Stevens	"Stevens Lott" tbc Richard Bennett, Esq.	19
Thomas Smithson	"Brafferton" tbc George Garey	100
47:1739:78 ...		
Allixson Ray	"Addition to Batchellor Branch" tbc: • Mr. Tench Francis – 33⅓ a. • James Horney – 66⅔ a.	100

Hen. Maria Loyd	"Henrietta Maria Discovery" tbc Richard Bennett, Esq.	216
Hen. Maria Loyd	"Adventure" tbc Mr. John Blake (QA)	446
William Warrilow	"Warrilows Exchange" – taker up not known nor any person that does claim	326
Walter Quinton	"Timothys Lott" tbc Mr. Daniell Maynadier	25
Robert Kemp	"Mable Addition" tbc John Ackles for h/o William Kemp (100 a.)	50
Thomas Taylor	"Addition" – taker up not known nor any person that does claim	472
John Lurky	"Lurky Hills" tbc Daniell Sherwood	100
47:1739:79 ...		
John Boram	"Borams Range" tbc John Higgins	177
Samuell Farmer	"Rogue Keep Off" – lies in His Lordship Mannor	50
Robert Sands	"Sands Lott" tbc: • Robert Sands – 103 a. • Daniell Lambdon in right of his wife – 50 a.	153
Robert Kemp	"Wolfe Harbour" tbc John Kemp	62
John King	"Swine Yard" tbc h/o John Parr (minors) & no person will pay the rent	176
Robert Sand	"Chance" tbc Robert Sands	50
Nathaniel Grace & Robert Hetherington	"Adventure" tbc: • William Hambleton – 113½ a. • Richard Harrington – 113½ a.	227
William Grace	"Fortunes Addition" tbc George Garey	52
Ambross Kinemon	"Long Point" tbc Grundey Pemberton (QA)	42
47:1739:80 ...		
William Hemsley	"Brittania" tbc: • John Nailer – 150 a. • Ferdinando Callahan – 100 a. • Thomas Keet – 200 a. • William Cole – 230 a.	600
William Hemsley	"Neglect" – included in elder surveys as alleged by h/o Thomas Edmondson	310
Daniell Walker	"Walkers Tooth" tbc Thomas Bruff	147
Edward Elliott	"Elliotts Lott" tbc Thomas Ashcraft	276
William Rich	"Rich Park" tbc Mr. Edward Oldham	569
Richard Skinner	"Skinners Vineyard" tbc Richard Skinner	7[illegible]

Robert Harrison	"Haphazard" tbc: • Robert Harrison – 50 a. • John Harrison – 50 a. • William Harrison – 20 a.	120
Richard Holms	"Buck Row" tbc Richard Holmes & Thomas Metcalfe	80
Richard Dudley	"Dudleys Inclosure" tbc Henry Clift for h/o Richard Dudley	104
47:1739:81 ...		
George Bowes	"Sybland Addition" tbc Fra. Williams for h/o Enion Williams	110
Michaell Rusell	"Addition to Huntington" tbc Perry Benson for h/o Michell Russell	80
Michaell Rusell	"Huntington" tbc Perry Benson for h/o Michell Russell	510
Hen. Maria Loyd	"Hen. Mar. Purchase" tbc Col. Ward	412
Hen. Maria Loyd	"Out Lett" tbc Mrs. Hen. Mar. Chew	220
Robert Pearson	"Bishoprick" tbc: • Samuell Chamberlain – 50 a. • Ralph Person (QA) – 50 a.	100
John King	"Kings Neglect" tbc Mrs. Hen. Maria Chew	115
John King	"Kings Forrest" tbc Mrs. Hen. Maria Chew	150
Richard Carter	"Carters Forrest" tbc: • Henry Downs (QA) – 158 a. • h/o Richard Carter (ENG) – 168 a.	326
47:1739:82 ...		
Ambross Kinnemont	"Kinnemonts Delight" tbc John Kinnemont	168
John Mullican	"Mullicans Choice" tbc: • Mary Mullican – 70 a. • Hugh Linch in right of his wife – 100 a.	170
Richard Woolman	"Woolmans Hermitage" tbc Mrs. Hen Maria Chew	164
Peter Taylor	"Rome" tbc: • Mr. Samuell Chamberlain – 100 a. • Grundey Pemberton as h/o Robert Grundey who will disclaim – 56 a.	156
William Hemsley	"James Fields" tbc Samuell Broadway	102
Robert Grundy	"Shingleys Fortune" tbc: • John Lockerman – 100 a. • William Dawson – 170 a. • Mrs. Frances Ungle – 121 a.	391
Robert Grundy	"Grundys Lott" tbc Mrs. Frances Ungle	46

Robert Grundy	"Grundys Addition" tbc Mr. Robert Goldsborough	73
47:1739:83 ...		
Ralph Fishburne	"Fisburne Land" tbc George Haddaway	104
William Dickinson	"Come Wilton" tbc Peter Harwood	200
William Dickinson	"Cross Dower Addition" – included in a resurvey by Samuell Dickinson called "Samuells Lott" (f. 130)	220
William Dickenson	"Dickensons Lott Addition" – resurveyed for Samuell Dickinson for 113 a. (f. 129)	95
Robert Kemp	"Kemps Lott Addition" tbc: • John Ackles for h/o William Kemp – 26 a. • Henry Swording – 26 a.	52
Richard Hetherington	"Hetheringtons Delight" tbc Richard Hetherington	50
Robert Register	"Durham" – Fran. Register the heir will disclaim; land being pt. of elder surveys	73
William Troth	"Acton Addition" – lies in His Lordships Mannor in TA	57
47:1739:84 ...		
William Troth	"Hackney Marsh" tbc h/o Henry Troth & natural guardian refuses to pay	50
John Paddison	"Judiths Garden" tbc: • Edward Oldham – 80 a. • John Pattison – 113 a.	193
Nicholas Lurkey	"Beggars Hall" tbc Daniell Sherwood	36
James Bampton & Thomas Taylor	"Partnership" tbc Selvester Abbot	36
John Mitchell	"Mitchells Hermitage" tbc: • Samuell Dickinson – 75 a. • James Harbert (North Carolina) – 25 a.	100
William Curtis	"Springfield Grange" – taker up not known nor any person that does claim	64
Edward Loyd	"Stock Range" tbc Mr. James Hollyday	400
John Morgan	"Morgans Neglect" tbc: • James Morgan – 120 a. • Mary Morgan for h/o John Morgan – 30 a.	150
47:1739:85 ...		
John Davis	"Addition" tbc John Davis	350
William Sharp	"Inclosure" tbc William Sharp	300

Fran. Kinnamont	"Limrick" tbc Robert Hall	70
Robert Grason, Jr.	"Roberts Fancy" tbc George Gresham	65
John Hatton	"Jane Progress" tbc: • Bartholomew Roberts – 35 a. • David Hughs – 35 a.	70
William Cooper	"Long Neglect" – resurveyed by Michaell Cummings & called "Knave Keep Out" for 180 a. (f. 127)	100
John Newman	"Newmans Folly" tbc Mark Williams	50
James Benson	"Bensons Enlargement" tbc: • Robson Dodson – 120 a. • John Bartlett – 50 a. • William Harrison – 190 a. • James Spencer – 187 a. • William Skinner – 150 a. • Nicholas Benson – 50 a.	740
47:1739:86 ...		
David Rogers	"Marys Dower" tbc William Turnor	200
Edward Clark	"Delerory" – Edward Clark h/o Edward Clark will disclaim, being included in elder surveys	100
James Standford	"Stanfords Hermitage" tbc Elizabeth Davis	250
Francis Clapin	"Newlin" tbc Thomas Bullen	140
William Skinner	"Skinners Point" tbc Philemon Skinner	50
Nicholas Lowe	"Lows Ramble" tbc Mr. Nicholas Lowe	1440
William Hemsley	"Hemsleys Arcadia" tbc: • included in resurvey by William Elbert & called "Loyd Costine" – 150 a. • John Downs (QA) – 75 a. • Edward Harding, lies in QA – 376 a. • included in resurvey for (N) Bennett, Esq. – 140 a. • George Gary – 239 a. • h/o Anthony <unr> – 100 a.	1030
George Taylor	"Taylor & Janes Discovery" tbc George Taylor	100
Anthony Cox	"Coxs Addition" tbc Mr. Samuell Chamberlain	70
47:1739:87 ...		
Charles Batson	"York" tbc: • John Hixon in right of his wife – 153 a. • Dennes Morris in right of his wife – 102 a. • John Fairbank in right of his wife – 51 a.	306
David Fairbank	"Jones Hole" tbc John Fairbank	36

Ennion Williams	"Ennions Lott" tbc John Williams (CE) son & h/o Enion Williams	151
Samuell Abbott	"Barren Ridge" – Dugles Chace who married natural guardian of the heir refuses the rent & says he knows nothing of it	100
Thomas Smith	"Lambeth Addition" tbc Peter Smith	150
William Gary	"Dirty Weden Addition" tbc George Garey	100
John Swift	"Swifts Chance" tbc Edward Eubanks	80
Isaac Saferson	"Abrahams Hermitage" tbc Isaac Safserson the heir moved to North Carolina & no person will pay	160
James Sandford	"Sandfords Folly" tbc Elizabeth Davis	45
47:1739:88 ...		
Nicholas Millburn	"Lambs Corner" tbc: • William Bennett – 23 a. • Thomas Pamphilion – 23 a. • Grundey Pemberton – 14 a.	60
Richard Fiddeman	"Fortaine" tbc Elizabeth Feddeman for h/o Phil. Fiddeman	121
William Hemsley	"Hemsleys Addition" – resurveyed for Richard Bennett, Esq. & included in "Bodwells Indian Neck" for 913 a. (f. 130)	520
John Cope	"Tranquility" – recovered by Edward Man Sherwood of the Vestry of St. Peters Parish & included in an elder survey for "Pitts Chance"	185
Francis Perkins	"Demeans Recover'd" – taker up not known nor any person that does claim	136
William Sharp	"Sharps Addition" tbc William Sharp	24
Andrew Oram	"Foxs Denn" tbc Morris Oram	56
William Aldern	"Alderns Island" tbc Richard Aldern	41
Nicholas Lowe & Thomas Erle	"Discovery" tbc Nicholas Lowe	53
47:1739:89 ...		
Richard Skinner	"Skinners Swine Yard" tbc Mr. Tench Francis & Col. Arnoult Hawkins (QA)	20
Richard Woolman	"Nameles" – alleges included in land resurveyed for Richard Woolman called "Woolmans Hermitage" (f. 81) & "Woolmans Inheritance" (f. 118)	15
Abraham Morgan	"Lizey Fortune" – William Dawson alleges this land is included in "Shregleys Fortune"	1

Edward & Richard Turner	"Beverdam Neck" tbc: • Robert Lowther – 70½ a. • Dennes Larey – 70½ a.	141
Patrick McDaniell	"Patricks Delight" – taker up not known nor any person that does claim	65
Henry Baily	"Bettys Chance" tbc Elizabeth Bailey	100
Thomas Cox	"Coxs Delight" – escheated by Mr. George Robins & included in resurvey called "First Hazard" (f. 122)	110
Samuell Abbott	"Mill Garden" – Dugles Chase who married the natural guardian of heir refuses to pay & says he knows nothing of it	35
47:1739:90 ...		
Walter Quinton	"Tatterhurst" tbc Mr. Daniell Maynadier	38
James Bramphton	"Thief Keep Out" tbc Mr. George Brinsfield	72
Jasper Hall	"Glades Addition" – Joseph Hall sold this land to Thomas Lee who is removed to VA & no person will pay the rent	71
George Bows	"Kindall" – lies in QA & sold by George Bows to Timothy Tool (QA)	273
Robert Grundy	"Grundys Inclosure" tbc Mr. Robert Lloyd	171
James Ridley	"Broad Lane" tbc: • Thomas Dudley – 103 a. • John Burges in right of his wife – 50 a.	153
Robert Grundy	"Yourkshire" tbc Mrs. Ungle	280
John Emerson	"Buckingham & Meeding" tbc Philemon Emerson	393
George Bowes	"Bowes Range" – Enion Williams who married the widow said he would disclaim this land & since his death the widow will disclaim	227
47:1739:91 ...		
George Cowley	"Intention" tbc Mr. William Ayres for h/o (N) Chaplin	100
Samuell Abbott	"Wallnutt Garden" tbc Dugles Chace for h/o Samuell Abbott	50
Thomas Hill	"Northumberland" – resurveyed for John Bartlett as "Bartletts Inheritance" for 140 a. (f. 166)	61
William Harris	"Long Negleck" tbc William Harris	35
William Godwin	"Godwins Addition" tbc Nathaniel Grace	90
William Gross	"Ashbys Addition" tbc Capt. John Carpenter (AA)	200

Thomas Hopkins	"Hopkins Point Addition" tbc: • James Hopkins – 25 a. • Edward Hopkins – 25 a. • lost by elder surveys – 50 a.	100
George Hurlock	"Addition" tbc Abednego Bodfield for h/o James Hurlock	50
47:1739:92 ...		
William Hamilton	"Hamiltons Addition" tbc William Hambleton	100
William Hemsley	"Addition" tbc Phil. Emerson	63
Allexander Moore & William Vaughan	"Moorfields Addition" tbc John Sweat	30
John Newman	"Newmans Addition" tbc Robert Goldsborough	50
Simeon Stevens	"Addition" tbc John Millar for h/o Charles Stevens	75
Richard Skinner	"Skinners Addition" tbc Richard Skinner	150
Robert Wheetson	"Adventure" tbc Thomas Richardson	70
Daniell Walker	"Daniels Addition" tbc: • Thomas Bruff – 70 a. • Richard Bennett, Esq. – 30 a.	100
John Bailey	"Bayleys Forrest" – taker up not known nor any person that does claim	135
47:1739:93 ...		
John Brown	"Browns Lott" tbc Mr. Anthony Richardson	200
Francis Bishop	"Bishops Fields" – Col. Jacob Gibson the present possessor says he will disclaim	170
Richard Carter	"Bodkin" tbc h/o Richard Carter (ENG)	15
David Fairbank	"Bradford" tbc John Fairbank	62
Richard Gurling	"Buckland Marsh" tbc Mr. Robert Loyd	50
Thomas Hutchinson	"Beverly" – same as "Beverlys Addition" below	522
Thomas Hutchinson	"Beverlys Addition" – heir lives in East Jersey; Thomas Bozman as attorney in fact for the heir had a commission from the County Court to examine evidence of the bounds but could not find any person that knows of them, so it is entirely taken by elder surveys or lost	230
George Hurlock	"Bloomsberry" tbc h/o William Kinting (QA)	200
47:1739:94 ...		
John King	"Bettys Dowry" tbc Mrs. Hen. Mar. Chew	150
Thomas Hutchinson	"Barmestone" tbc Mr. Samuell Chamberlain	106
Edmund Webb	"Boltons Addition" tbc John Kemp	50

Henry Alexander	"Alexanders Chance" tbc John Alexander	250
James Benson	"Bensons Chance" tbc Nicholas Benson	90
Henry Costin	"Costins Chance" tbc: • William Cole – 32 a. • Henry Downs (QA) – 109 a.	141
Henry Costin	"Court Road" tbc Col. Matthew Tilghman Ward	138
Francis Collins	"Collins Pasture" tbc Thomas Frampton	50
Richard Carter	"Carters Out Work" tbc h/o Richard Carter (ENG)	19
47:1739:95 ...		
Richard Carter	"Carters Sconce" tbc h/o Richard Carter (ENG)	139
Richard Carter	"Craven" tbc h/o Richard Carter (ENG)	300
John Coppin	"Coppin Copice" – resurveyed for Edward Hardin as "Hardens Endeavour" for 200 a. (f. 137)	50
Jasper Hall	"Couple Close" tbc Hannah Davis	100
John Stanley & Christopher Batson	"Chance" tbc: • Thomas Bullen – 139 a. • David Robinson – 23 a. • alleged included in elder surveys – 49 a.	200
Sollomon Thomas	"Chance" tbc William Sharp	40
Richard Bennett, Esq.	"Darlington" tbc: • Michell Fletcher – 229 a. • he will disclaim being taken by elder surveys – 51 a.	280
Thomas Hutchinson	"Hutchinsons Discovery" – Thomas Bozman attorney in fact for h/o said Thomas Hutchinson had a commission out of County Court to examine evidence to the bounds & it is included in an elder survey called "Cook Hope"	300
47:1739:96 ...		
Richard Dudley	"Dudleighs Clift" tbc Charles & Samuell Morgan	200
John Pooley & William Vaughan	"Pooleys Discovery" tbc Solomon Warner	168
Joseph Winslow	"Duxbury" – although patented to Joseph Winslow, he soon made another resurvey & called it "Boston Clift" (f. 24) which alleges to include this land	680
William Wintersall	"Devise" – Mr. Nicholas Lowe the present possessor will disclaim	440
Edward Elliott	"Elliotts Folly" tbc: • Thomas Ashcraft – 50 a. • Edward Auld – 50 a.	100
William Snelling	"Endeavour" tbc Mrs. Frances Ungle	50

Richard Carter	"Carters Forrest" tbc h/o Richard Carter (ENG)	420
Robert Frampton	"Frampton" tbc Mr. George Robins	122
Edward Fitch	"Fitchs Range" tbc Edward Fish	74
47:1739:97 ...		
Richard Feddeman	"Fiddemans Choice a/s Chance" tbc Elizabeth Feddeman for h/o Phil. Feddeman	100
Thomas Faulkner	"Faulkner Levell" tbc Margery Smallcorn	150
William Hemsley	"Farm" tbc Richard Bennett, Esq.	348
Robert Smith	"Fork" tbc John Ervan for h/o (N) Dobson (200 a.)	250
Richard Carter	"Gore" tbc h/o Richard Carter (ENG)	170
Anthony Wise	"Gore" tbc John Wise	45
George Bowes	~~"Pasco Green"~~ "Hasco Green" tbc: • Jane Turner for h/o Edward Turner – 160 a. • Samuell Dudley for h/o Richard Thompson – 50 a.	210
47:1739:98 ...		
John Cook	"Hasely" tbc Mr. Anthony Richardson	200
Thomas Hutchinson	"Hulls Addition" tbc: • Dugles Chace for h/o Samuell Abbott – 100 a. • h/o Robert Jones (PA) – 10 a.	110
Thomas Hutchinson	"Hull" tbc: • David Robinson – 70 a. • h/o Robert Jones (PA) – 130 a.	200
Nicholas Hackett	"Hacketts Fields" – resurveyed for Samuell Turbutt as "Turbutts Fields" for 168 a. (f. 120)	143
Thomas Hutchinson	"Hutchinsons Point" – Thomas Bozman attorney in fact for the heir can't find this land	72
Moses Harris	"Harris's Range" tbc w/o Samuell Wright (KI)	400
Thomas Smithson	"Holders Range" tbc h/o Col. Smithson (ENG)	73
John Kinnemont	"Hopewell" tbc John & Andrew Kinnemont	80
Thomas Smithson	"Hazard" – Francis Porter the present possessor will disclaim	70
47:1739:99 ...		
Thomas Skillington	"Hamiltons Neck" – Thomas Skillington the heir refuses to pay the rent by this resurvey as no patent ever granted but will hold by the first survey (f. 8)	256
John Newman (cnp)	"Jacob & John Pasture" tbc: • James Ratclif – 170 a.	340

	• Edward Eubanks – 50 a. • Thomas Eubanks – 120 a.	
John King	"Kings Plains" tbc Mrs. Hen. Mar. Chew	158
Christopher St. Tee	"Knave Stand Off" tbc Nathaniel St. Tee	50
John Martingdale	"Little Minories" tbc Robert Philips (SM)	200
William Scott	"Leith" tbc Woolman Gibson	40
George Bowes	"Maxfield" tbc Fra. Williams	152
Phill. Loyd	"Mersgate Addition" – included in tract of same name for 267 a. (f. 105)	69
47:1739:100 ...		
Alexander Maccoter & Daniell Glover	"Maccotters Glover Addition" – Edward Elliot the present possessor will disclaim; says he cannot find it	100
George Bowes	"Moorfields" – Ennion Williams who married the w/o George Bowes says this land belongs to William Turner	280
John Mill	"Millers Hope" tbc: • Samuell Dickinson – 11 a. • Henry Harris for h/o Simond Fisher – 121 a.	132
Alexander Moore & William Vaughan	"Moorfields" tbc John Swett	94
Thomas Smithson	"Mickle Mire" tbc: • ~~Col. Thomas Smithson (ENG) – 480 a.~~ • Mr. Henry Nicols – 230 a. • Edward Hardin – 100 a. • lost in elder surveys – 150 a.	480
Timothey Lane	"New Town" tbc Richard Bennett, Esq.	100
John Newman	"Newington" – taker up not known nor any person that does claim	100
Charles Battson	"Prospect" tbc William Anderson	125
47:1739:101 ...		
Peter Haddaway	"Point & Marsh" tbc Edward Elliott	50
Benjamin Parrott	"Parrotts Lott" tbc Edward Clark	82
George Parrott	"Poplar Levell" a/s "Parrott Levill" tbc William Turner	116
John Warren	"Poors Mans Port" – taker up not known nor any person that does claim	80
Samuell Broadaway	"Ramah" tbc Samuell Broadway	100

Moses Harris	"Rumleys Forrest" tbc: • Roger Clayland in right of his wife – 43 a. • William Madden – 107 a. • James Benney – 150 a.	300
Benjamin Parrott	"Parrotts Reserve" tbc: • Fra. Regester – 150 a. • Thomas Turner – 50 a.	200
Thomas Alcock	"Strawbridge" tbc: • Samuell Broadway – 100 a. • John Stevens – 163 a.	263
47:1739:102 ...		
Thomas Faulkner	"Faulkners Square" tbc: • Philemon Banning – 100 a. • Abedegoe Bodfield – 100 a.	200
Edmund Fish	"Staplton" tbc Joshua Grasham for h/o Robert Johnson	77
Elexander Maccotter	"Sutton Grange" tbc: • William White – 280 a. • James White – 120 a. • Mark Noble – 200 a. • wanting no person will own it – 45 a.	645
James Murphy	"Snellings Delight" tbc Cath. Barrett	150
George Sprouse	"Sprouse Fortune" – disclaimed by George Sprouse on 3 December 1736	100
Thomas Smithson	"Sydenburgh" tbc Robert Welsh	100
Richard Sweetnam	"Sweetnames Hope" tbc Richard Bennett, Esq.	120
John Stanley & Christopher Battson	"Timber Neck" tbc: • Thomas Bozman – 150 a. • pt. resurveyed for Mr. Thomas Bozman for 294 a. (f. 134)	300
47:1739:103 ...		
Richard Skinner	"Skinners Borders" tbc Richard Skinner	10[illegible]
John Newman	"Newmans Thickett" tbc h/o Richard Carter (ENG)	5[illegible]
John Theobald	"Theobalds Addition" tbc John Tibbals	2[illegible]
John Emerson	"Vincents Lott" tbc h/o John Emerson (QA)	4[illegible]
Christopher Battson	"Wilderness" tbc David Jones	7[illegible]
Elizabeth Christian	"Widdows Chance" – taker up not known nor any person that does claim	5[illegible]
David Fairbank	"Wisbick" tbc Bridget Shehawn (DO)	6[illegible]

William Winters	"Wintersell" – resurveyed for William Wintersell for 145 a. (f. 126)	200
47:1739:104 ...		
Thomas Price	"Wallop" a/s "Sallop" – resurveyed for Jane Parrott for 167 a. (f. 129)	200
Elizabeth Alexander	"Yowell" – John Alexander the last possessor will disclaim	50
Col. Thomas Smithson	"Gaterly Moore" tbc Edm. Fish	120
David Fairbank	"Fairbanks Chance" tbc John Fairbank	195
Richard Carter	"Addition" tbc h/o Richard Carter (ENG)	68
William Porter	"Fools Paradice" tbc John Hunt	38
Richard Carter	"Addition" tbc h/o Richard Carter (ENG)	21
Nicholas Lowe	"Good Luck" tbc: • John Alexander – 100 a. • Samuell Dickinson – 54 a. • Mr. Nicholas Lowe will disclaim – 26 a.	180
Ennion Williams	"Ennions Range" tbc: • Bartholomew Roberts – 50 a. • Fra. Williams for h/o Enion Williams – 170 a.	220
47:1739:105 ...		
Anthony Cox	"Coxs Chance" tbc Mr. Samuell Chamberlaine	160
Col. Edward Lloyd	"Meersgate Addition" tbc Mr. Edward Lloyd	267
Col. Edward Lloyd	"Long Neglect" tbc Mr. Edward Lloyd	133
Thomas Teat	"Teats Lott" – resurveyed for Mr. Thomas Bozman for 459 a. (f. 133) • lost in elder survey – 190 a.	333
Benjamin Parrott	"Oakin" – Aron Parrott heir of Benjamin Parrott will disclaim, being of elder surveys	100
<n/g>	"Nevington" – William Troath gave this land to William Lewis & Lewis sold it to a man (QA)	240
John Dun	"Burniston" – h/o John Dunn says he knows nothing of this land & will disclaim	170
Debor. Cornall	"Graves" – Mr. Robert Lloyd who should have the right to this land will disclaim	280
Samuell Withers	"Maidens Point Addition" tbc Mr. Henry Nichols	100
47:1739:106 ...		
Richard Howard	"Batchellors Range" tbc William Dawson	250
Simeon Stevens (cnp)	"Stevens Plain" tbc: • George Beswicks – 50 a.	200

	• Richard Beswicks – 50 a. • Daniell Baker – 50 a. • Mr. James Hollyday – 50 a.	
John Newman	"Good Chance" tbc h/o Richard Carter (ENG)	50
John Ball	"Cowallyn" tbc: • William Dudley – 200 a. • Fra. Williams for h/o Ennion Williams – 100 a.	300
Ralph Elston	"Elstons Hazard" tbc John Lurty (49 a.)	50
Samuell Withers	"Withers Range" tbc: • Mr. Henry Nichols – 50 a. • lost in elder survey – 56 a.	206
Robert Gough	"Goughstone" tbc: • Mr. Joseph Parrott – 100 a. • John Ratcliff – 100 a.	200
47:1739:107 ...		
Robert Gouldsborough	"Gouldsborough Triangle" tbc Mr. Robert Goldsborough	45
William Cathrop	"Cathrops Securety" tbc Lemon John Cathrop	205
Edward Russum	"Russums Inclosure" – Edward Russum the son & heir will disclaim, being in elder surveys	65
Samuell Abbott	"Baildon" tbc: • James Dickinson – 30 a. • included in an elder survey – 167 a.	197
George Haddaway	"Haddaway Lott" tbc: • John Lowe – 50 a. • William Webb Haddaway – 73 a. • included in an elder survey called "Grafton Mannor" – 27 a.	150
John Reedles	"Allumby Fields" tbc Maj. John Sherwood	115
William Landnum	"Winterton" tbc Daniell Lambdon	50
47:1739:108 ...		
Benjamin Ball	"Benjamins Lott" tbc John Ball	100
Richard Carter	"Carters Chance" tbc h/o Richard Carter (ENG)	74
Edward Loyd	"Inlett" tbc Mr. Edward Loyd	88
James Loyd	"Loyds Discovery" tbc Mr. Robert Loyd	96
William Dixon	"Dixons Outlett" tbc: • Mr. Tench Francis – 50 a. • Isaac Dixon – 150 a.	200
Edward Barrowclife	"Hern Island" tbc Richard Bennett, Esq.	75
William Hamilton	"Williston" tbc William Hambleton	224

Thomas Austin	"Austin" tbc: • Thomas Keild – 100 a. • William Thorp – 100 a.	200
Robert Betts	"Betts Chance" tbc: • Daniel Baker – 100 a. • Oliver Millington – 100 a.	200
47:1739:109 ...		
Stephen Tulley	"Tullys Addition" tbc: • Edward Roe (QA) – 150 a. • John Roe (QA) – 150 a.	300
Thomas Alcock	"Alcocks Choice" tbc Thomas Keild	100
John Story	"Storey Point" tbc Thomas Chears (QA)	100
Joseph Man	"Churley" – taker up not known nor any person that does claim	100
John Keld	"Hogg Island" – disclaimed by John Keild on 1 May 1736	140
David Rogers	"Moorefields Addition" tbc William Turner in right of his wife	65
47:1739:110 ...		
Henry Fox	"Mitchells Point" a/s "Rich Neck" tbc Col. Mathew Tilghman Ward	1000
Thomas Phillips	"Killam" a/s "Kilton" tbc: • Joshua Clark will disclaim – 100 a. • Edward Needles – 509 a. • Edward Man Sherwood – 229 a. • Rogger Bradberry who disclaimed on 24 December 1736 – 269 a.	1107
John Bateman	"Clayborns Island" tbc Richard Bennett, Esq.	700
James Hall	"Barren Point" – let fall on records as John Edmondson the heir refuses to pay	200
Edward Elliott	"Elliotts Addition" – John Auld son & heir to James Auld to whom this land did belong say that this land is included in a resurvey made by his father called "New Port Glasgow" for 258 a. (f. 123)	200
John Pitt	"Pitts Freshes" – taker up not known nor any person that does claim	200
John Ingram	"Hunting Hill" – taker up not known nor any person that does claim	100
47:1739:111 ...		
Thomas Alexander	"Poplar Hills" – resurveyed for Samuell Turbutt for 57 a. (f. 123)	50

Edward Winckles	"Virgins Inn" – escheated by William Hemsey by the name of "Hemsley Upon Wye Addition" for 146 a. (f. 138)	250
Leonard Daniell	"Virgins Inn Addition" – escheated by Mr. William Hemsley by the name of "Hemsley Upon Wye Addition" for 146 a. (f. 138)	100
Thomas Bradnox	"Cæder Bradnox" – included in a survey called "Loyds Insula" (QA)	300
Anthony Griffin	"Griffins Hambton" – let fall by the records	150
Roger Groce	"Groce Coat" – resurveyed for Madam Henrietta Maria Lloyd as "Henrietta Maria's Purchase" for 442 a. (f. 133)	300
Jonathan Sibery	"Wickom" – taker up not known nor any person that does claim	170
Charles Masters	"Vineyard" – included in elder surveys; no person will pay rent	250
47:1739:112 ...		
John Chafe	"Hole Haven" – let fall as appear by the records	100
Ann Stevenson	"Ann's Chance" – taker up not known nor any person that does claim	50
Henry Costin	"Lambeth" – included in "Henrietta Maria's Purchase" (f. 133)	100
William Gross	"Groces Addition" – included in "Henrietta Maria's Purchase" (f. 133)	24
Edward Roe	"Dover" – William Combs the heir to Edward Roe will disclaim	800
Henry Newman	"Willingham" – taker up not known nor any person that does claim	50
Henry Newman	"Luck Hill" – taker up not known for any person that does claim	179
George Cowley	"Yarford" – let fall by the records	600
Francis Marling	"Batchellors Branch" – included in tract of same name for 100 a. (f. 65)	50
47:1739:113 ...		
William Jones	"Batchellors Hope" tbc John Davis as "Batchelors Point" for 100 a. (f. 16)	100
William Parrott	"Marshy Point Addition" – included in "Marshy Point" an elder survey (f. 8)	100
James Hall	"James Neck" – Robert Hall the heir will disclaim	200
James Hall	"James Addition" – Robert Hall the heir will disclaim	100

Richard Peacock	"Anderbys Addition" – resurveyed for Arthur Rigby for 78 a. (f. 118)	100
James Harrison	"Dover Marsh" – lies in His Lordships Mannor in TA	150
Henry Price & Joannes Dehinnosa	"Copartnership" – lies in QA & also the possessors	373
John Eason	"Easons Lott" tbc William Sharp	50
47:1739:114 ...		
William Dixon	"Dixons Lott" – William Dixon knows nothing of this survey & therefore declined it but pays rent for another tract called "Dixons Outlett" for 200 a. (f. 108)	200
Francis Armstrong	"End of Controversey" – Francis Armstrong says this is the same charged to Isaac Dixon (f. 42)	150
Samuell Winslow	"Plain Dealing" – Samuell Winslow removed to New England & died there; no heirs appear; neverless this land is included in an elder survey called by the same name for Joseph Winslow	50
Michell Kerwick	"Kerwicks Addition" tbc Michell Kirby	49
William Dickinson	"Crooked Lane" tbc: • James Dickinson – 116 a. • wanting – 6 a.	122
Arthur Rigby	"Rigbys Discovery" tbc Arthur Rigbey	105
George Taylor	"Taylors & James Discovery" tbc George Taylor	100
William Stevens	"Stevens" – heir of the taker up is a minor & the guardian refuses to pay alleging included in elder surveys	50
47:1739:115 ...		
Mary Cook	"Widdows Lott" tbc Mr. Anthony Richardson	85
Charles Walker	"Walkers Corner" tbc Thomas Bruff	18
Richard Carter	"Carters Reserve" tbc h/o Richard Carter (ENG)	164
John Carr & Sarah his wife	"Jordans Hill" tbc Thomas Stuart in right of his wife	157
Timothy Lane	"Kinsale" tbc William Marshal	126
Edward Hamilton & John Robinson	"Partnership" tbc Mr. Daniell Maynadier for Vestry of St. Peters Parish	34
Richard Carter	"Addition" tbc: • h/o Richard Carter (ENG) – 118 a. • James Ratcliff – 52 a.	170

William Troth	"Troth Security" – John Stevens who married the natural guardian of the heir of Henry Troth refuses to pay the rent; says he knows not where the land lies	109
47:1739:116 ...		
Charles Harbott	"Harbotts Choice" tbc: • Samuell Dickinson – 14 a. • James Harbott (North Carolina) – 86 a.	100
Mathew Griffin	"Griffins Adventure" – lies in QA	220
John Carr	"Addition" – lies in His Lordships Mannor in TA	190
Phill. Loyd	"Carters Inheritance" tbc: • Mrs. Hen. Mar. Chew – 300 a. • Alice Hewet for Robert Hewet – 100 a.	400
Seth Garrett	"Westford" – taker up not known nor any person that does claim	247
Robert Morton	"Hopewell" tbc Henry Burges	50
Thomas Grundy	"Turners Point" pt. or "Morely" tbc Mr. Robert Loyd	200
Anthony Wise	"Sheephead Point" tbc John Wise	246
47:1739:117 ...		
James Spencer	"Mainsale" tbc: • Thomas Studham – 73 a. • Frances Camperson – 25 a.	98
James Spencer	"Toresale" tbc James Spencer, Sr.	12
Arthur Rigby	"Adventure" tbc: • Mr. Robert Goldsborough – 100 a. • Peter Russam – 100 a. • Andrew Oram – 200 a.	400
William & Christopher Walker	"Partnership" tbc Thomas Bruff	100
Col. Edward Loyd	"Roadway" tbc Mr. Edward Lloyd	50
Robert Bishop	"Champinham" tbc Jacob Gibson	450
<n/g>	"As Also Bendon" tbc Jacob Gibson (550 a.)	10
Aurthur Rigby	"Rigbys Folly" tbc Arthur Rigbey	4
William Farrell	"Port Junony" tbc Edward Ferrell	7
47:1739:118 ...		
William Lambdon	"William & Marys Addition" tbc: • William Lambdon – 52 a. • taken in by "Grafton Mannor" an elder survey – 100 a.	15

Isaac & Jacob Marling	"Braintrees Addition" tbc: • Thomas Winchester for h/o Isaac Marlin – 10 a. • John Wise – 50 a.	60
Robert Hopkins	"Turkey Park" tbc Robert Hopkins	329
Arthur Rigby	"Anderbys Addition" tbc Arthur Rigbey	78
Daniell Crowley	pt. "Hier Dier Loyd" tbc Thomas Browning in right of his wife	80
James Lord	"Lords Chance" tbc Rosanna Lord	100
Richard Woolman	"Woolmans Inheritance" tbc Mrs. Hen. Mar. Chew	310
Phill. Sherwood	"Sherwood Neck" tbc Risdon Bozman	268
47:1739:119 ...		
Richard Bennett & Elizabeth his wife	"Tobacco Pipe" tbc Richard Bennett, Esq.	359
Daniell Walker	pt. "Jamaico" tbc Mr. George Robins	92
Edmund Fish	"Contention" tbc Edmond Fish	130
David Airey	"Davids Ridge" tbc Jonathan Airey	125
Robert Ungle, Esq.	"Intention" tbc Mrs. Frances Ungle	50
Samuell Winslow	"Intention" – resurveyed for Mr. Robert Ungle for 50 a.	50
William Benstead	"Bensteads Adventure" – heir will disclaim being included in elder surveys	64
Benjamin Cook	"Benjamins Lott" tbc Mr. Robert Goldsborough	50
47:1739:120 ...		
John Kemp	"Kemps Lott" tbc George Haddway	38
Charles Blake	"Sayers Forrest" – lies in QA as also the possessor	2250
Francis Neale	"Cubas Addition" – in His Lordships Mannor in TA	72
John Leeds	"Long Delay" tbc John Leeds	33
Samuell Turbett	"Turbetts Fields" tbc Rachell Turbott for h/o Samuell Turbott	168
Thomas Martin	"Heard Measure" tbc Thomas Martin	94
Andrew Skinner	"Skinners Securety" tbc Richard Skinner	103
William Dickinson	"Nowells Island" tbc Samuell Dickinson	55
47:1739:121 ...		
William Dickenson	pt. "Hier Dier Loyd" tbc Samuell Dickinson	101
Marke Noble	"Poor Hill" tbc Mark Noble	37

Richard Wooters	"Richard & Marys Forrest" tbc Richard Wooters (QA)	80
Jonathan Miller	"Millers Chance" tbc John Millar	85
John Pitt & Phill. Loyd	"Partnership" tbc: • Mr. Robert Lloyd – 1200 a. • Henry Nichols – 500 a. • Jeremiah Nichols – 250 a. • h/o Benjamin Pemberton (QA) – 1050 a.	3000
John Lowe	"Grafton Mannor" tbc: • John Lowe – 245 a. • John Lambdon – 100 a. • Arnold Hawkins – 28 a. • John Lurty – 49 a. • Thomas Smith – 100 a. • Webb Haddaway – 300 a.	847
John Fisher	"Fishers Chance" tbc Mr. Samuell Dickinson	125
47:1739:122 ...		
George Robins	"First Hazard" tbc Mr. George Robins	358
Francis Armstrong	"Surprise" tbc Francis Armstrong	40
Jacob Falconar	"Falconars Hazard" tbc Jacob Falconor	60
James Myrick	"Hazard Addition" tbc James Myrick	9
James Benny	"Bennys Addition" tbc John & James Benny	60
David Robinson	"Davids Folly" tbc David Robinson	50
Hannah Oldham	"Addition" tbc Mrs. Hannah Davis	32
Walter Quinton	pt. "Willinbrow" & pt. "Gurlington" tbc William White	93
47:1739:123 ...		
Samuell Turbutt	"Poplar Hill" tbc Mrs. Rachell Turbott for h/o Samuell Turbott	57
John Ratchell	"Rathells Chance" tbc John Rathel	50
William Dobson	"Dobsons Adventure" tbc John Ervan for h/o William Dobson	35
Richard Wrougton	"Mount Miserry" tbc William Harrison (bayside)	12
William Turner	"Turner Hazard" tbc William Michel	100
Edward Turner	"Tale Tale Loss" tbc: • William Vickers – 52 a. • Mary Brown – 73 a.	125
Edward Elliott	"Maccotter & Glover" tbc Edward Elliott (355 a.)	172
John Auld	"New Port Glascow" tbc John Auld	258
47:1739:124 ...		

Capt. William Greenwood	"Gurlington" tbc William Richardson	75
William Aldern & Andrew Orem	"Hopewell" – taker up not known nor any person that does claim	200
Peter Arrington	"Pasty Neck" tbc Henry Richardson	24
Charles Bridges	"New Building" – Charles Bridges discovered this survey to foul of elder surveys; disclaims it	29
Michael Kirby	"Limbrick" tbc David Kirby	60
John Powell & Thomas Saunders	"Partnership" tbc George Dulin	65
Col. Mathew Tilghman Ward	"Union" tbc: • pt. included in resurvey for Robert Dawson called "Dawsons Composition" for 282 a. (f. 134) • Col. Mathew Tilghman Ward – 611 a.	831
47:1739:125 ...		
William Turner	"Turners Range" tbc: • William Turner – 10 a. • David Kirbey – 40 a.	50
Richard Fiddeman	"Hazard" tbc Elizabeth Fiddeman for h/o Phil. Feddeman; resurveyed for Richard Feddeman	200
Richard Barrow	"Schoolhouse Lott" – land never patented; no person will pay the rent; included in elder surveys	59
John Kersey	"Kerseys Good Luck" tbc Webb Haddaway for h/o (N) Kersey	37
Michaell Kirby	"Venture" tbc Richard Kirbey	37
Alexander Larrimore	"Larrimores Prudence" tbc Robert Larramore	87
John Cooper	"Coopers Lott" tbc Thomas Adcock	52
John Leeds	"Leeds Landing" – dissolved by the survey & no patent issued	65
47:1739:125 [!] ...		
Jon Wellan	"Wellans Good Luck" tbc John Porter, Jr.	65
William Graves	"Inlargement" tbc Nathaniel Grace, Jr.	71
Jos. Clarke	"Clarks Folly" tbc Joshua Clark	101
William Skinner	"Sarahs Garden" tbc: • William Skinner, Jr. – 13 a. ~~• William Skinner – 33 a.~~	13
William Skinner, Jr.	"Skinners Lott" tbc William Skinner, Jr.	33
William Skinner, Sr.	"Skinners Addition" tbc Philemon Skinner	23
Phill. Bannor	"Bannors Hazard" tbc Philip Banning	50

Charles Lewis	"Chance" – Charles Lewis declined this survey & never applied for a patent & his heir since declined it being foul of elder surveys	79
C. M. T. Ward	"Choptank Island" tbc C. M. T. Ward	1468
47:1739:126 ...		
John Newman	"Benjamins Lott" tbc Mr. Robert Goldsborough	50
Col. M. T. Ward	"3 Necks" tbc Col. Mathew Tilghman Ward	165
Francis Storey	"Storys Lott" tbc James Clayland	56
Peter Sides	"Lobbs Crook" tbc Richard Bennett, Esq.	677
Francis Connerly	"Hollands Addition" tbc Terence Connerly	41
Jos. Winters	"Wintersell" tbc Nicholas Lowe	145
Richard Dudley	"Dudleys Addition" tbc Henry Clift for h/o James Dudley	37
John Kirby	"Woolf Pitt Ridge" tbc Isaac Dobson for h/o John Kersey	50
Francis Armstrong	"Discovery" tbc Francis Armstrong	80
47:1739:127 ...		
Francis Neale	"Hiccory Ridge" tbc: • Francis Neal – 296 a. • lies in His Lordships Mannor – 50 a.	346
Nicholas Lurkey	"Cabbin Neck, Potters Delight, & Potters Lott" tbc John Lurty	150
William Stevens	"Williams Lott" tbc Thomas Stevens for h/o William Stevens	49
Arnold Hawkins	"Discovery" tbc Thomas Bozman	231
Rizdon Bozman	"Providence" tbc Thomas Bozman	7
Michell Cummins	"Knave Keep Out" tbc Thomas Commings	180
Thomas Hopkins	"William & James" tbc: • Thomas Hopkins – 33 a. • Edward Hopkins – 25 a.	58
William Brown	"Charlevill & Cork" tbc: • Mary Brown for life – 200 a. • Thomas Vickers – 50 a.	250
47:1739:128 ...		
William Brown	"Dunns Range" tbc: • William Vickers for his daughter Sarah – 52 a. • John Nailer in right of his wife – 100 a. • Michell Kirbey for his son Richard – 100 a.	252

John Lowe	"Piney Neck" tbc John Lowe	107
William Elbert	"Loys Costine" tbc William Elbert	659
John Kemp	"Hunt Keep Out" tbc John Kemp	28
Thomas Turner	"Turners Chance" tbc Thomas Turner (millar)	100
Edward Turner	"Turners Discovery" tbc Thomas Turner (carpenter)	97
Daniell Bryen	"Hermitage" – resurveyed for Daniel Bower	90
47:1739:129 ...		
Samuell Dickenson	"Dickensons Lott" tbc Samuell Dickenson	113
William Elston	"French Hazard" tbc John Webb for h/o William Elston	41
John Hunt	"Content" tbc John Hunt	98
Jane Parrott	"Sallop" tbc William Scott in right of his wife	167
David Robinson	"Chance" tbc David Robinson	23
David Robinson	"Robinsons Beginning" tbc David Robinson	17
John Vickers	"Vickers Lott" tbc John Vickers	52
Richard White	"Whites Grove" tbc James White	40
John Wrightson	"Wrightsons Addition" tbc John Wrightson	83
47:1739:130 ...		
George Collison	"Rehoboth Point" tbc George Collison	50
Samuell Dickinson	"Samuells Point" tbc Samuel Dickinson	600
Richard Bennett	"Bodwells Indian Neck" tbc Richard Bennett, Esq.	913
Benjamin Pemberton	"Securety" – patented to Benjamin Pemberton in his lifetime & since his death the widow refuses to pay	406
John Edmundson	"Desire" & pt. "Huart" tbc John Edmondson	603
William Hemsley	"Hemsley Upon Wye" tbc Mr. William Hemsley	1160
Perry Benson	"Neglect" tbc Mr. Perry Benson	96
John Edmundson	"Edmundsons Dificulty" tbc John Edmondson	1253
47:1739:131 ...		
Francis Sherwood	"Huckleberry Garden" tbc Francis Sherwood	125
John Carslake	"Fox Harbour" tbc Robert Goldsborough	148
Thomas Frampton	"Framptons Beginning" tbc Thomas Frampton	96
Phill. Fiddeman	"Discovery" tbc Elizabeth Fiddeman for h/o Phil. Phiddeman	56
Allumby Millington	"Nobles Meadows" tbc Elizabeth Millington for h/o Allumby Millington	229

Dennis Larey	"Partnership Hazard" tbc: • Dennes Larey – 142 a. • Anthony Richardson – 142 a.	284
John Cannaday	"Cannadays Hazard" tbc John Cannaday	29
Allumby Millington	"Betts Addition" tbc Elizabeth Millington for h/o Allumby Millington	207
47:1739:132 ...		
Edward Elliott	"Chance" tbc Edward Elliot	223
Richard Bennett	"Planters Increase" tbc Richard Bennett, Esq.	504
Perry Benson & James Valiant	"Partnership" tbc: • John Valliant – 307½ a. • Perry Benson – 307½ a. • Thomas Robson – 125 a.	740
Rizdon Bozman	"Hemerby" tbc Mr. Rizdon Bozman	273
James Ratcliffe	"Ratliff Highway" tbc James Ratclife	113
George Robins	"Jennings Hope" tbc Mr. George Robins	718
John Rattliffe	"Rattliffe Choice" tbc Edward Hardin, Jr.	109
47:1739:133 ...		
Risdon Bozman	"Tates Lott" tbc Thomas Bozman	454
David Fairbank	"Good Hap" tbc John Farbank	23
John Morgan	"Morgans Addition" tbc: • William Michell – 100 a. • James Morgan – 37 a.	137
H. M. Lloyd	"Henrietta Maria Purchase" tbc Col. Mathew T. Ward	412
Thomas Bullen	"Bullens Addition" tbc William Michell	102
Michael Kirby	"Buck Range Addition" tbc William Kirbey	55
Phill. Skinner	"Skinners Discovery" tbc Phill. Skinner	70
Richard Roberts	"Robert Addition" tbc Bartholomew Roberts	47
47:1739:134 ...		
Peter Cork & patented to Mary Cork	"Lewis" tbc Sarah Cork	290
Thomas Haddaway	"Haddaways Addition" tbc Thomas Haddaway	75
Daniell Boyer	"Hermitage" tbc Daniel Maynadier	9[illegible]
Solomon Horney	"Neglect" – belongs to a minor & no person will pay the rent	1[illegible]
Mary Wrightson	"Clays Neck" tbc Mary Wrightson (widow)	102
John Stevens	"Edmundsons Cove" tbc Thomas Stevens	17[illegible]
Risdon Bozeman	"Timber Neck" tbc Thomas Bozman	29

Robert Dawson	"Dawsons Composition" tbc Robert Dawson	282
47:1739:135 ...		
William Harrison	"Taylors Ridge" tbc William Harrison (Miles Creek)	100
Richard Bennett	"Poplar Ridge" tbc Richard Bennett, Esq.	249
Jo. Mullican	"Mullicans Chance" tbc William Mullican	100
John Wooters	"Coventry" tbc James Kendrel in right of his wife	250
Thomas Delahay	"Delahays Fortune" tbc Thomas Delehay	100
Thomas Wilkinson	"Wilkinsons Choice" tbc Mrs. Hen. Maria Chew as "Carters Inheritance" it was so called in survey by Richard Carter for 300 a. (f. 116)	150
James Scott	"Addition" – alleged to be included in resurvey of "Addition to Huntington" for 80 a.	50
Henry Doberry	"Buckingham" – this & "Keilding" (f. 136) was escheated & resurveyed for John Emerson for 393 a. (f. 90)	100
47:1739:136 ...		
William Smith	"Kelding" – this & "Bucking" (f. 135) was escheated & resurveyed for John Emerson for 393 a. (f. 90)	500
William Smith	"Coxhill" – alleged to be let fall & afterwards included in "Kellam" a/s "Kilton" granted to Thomas Philips (f. 110)	300
Henry Alexander	"Alexanders Addition" – alleged to be let fall & none will pay rent	100
Thomas Baggs	"Baggs Marsh" tbc Rachell Turbutt	50
Robert Goldsborough	pt. "Four Square" tbc Robert Goldsborough	650
John Bartlett	"Bartletts Inheritance" tbc: • Nicholas Bartlett – 110 a. • John Bartlett – 30 a.	140
Isaac Marling	"Marlings Neglect" tbc Thomas Winchester for h/o Isaac Marlen	57
47:1739:137 ...		
Edward Harding	"Hardings Endeavour" tbc Edward Harding	200
Capt. John Kemble	"Kembells Industry" tbc Richard Bennet, Esq.	283
Richard Bennett	"Bennetts Freshes" tbc James Dickinson	423
Robert Ungle, Esq. & patented to S. Chamberlain	"Four Square" tbc Mr. Samuell Chamberlain	350
Peirce Fleming	"Flemings Freshes" tbc Peirce Fleming	215
John Eason	"Edmundsons Pond" tbc William Edmondson	9

Edmund Fish	"Fishers Hazard" tbc Joshua Grason	18
Richard Bennett	"Neglect" tbc Richard Bennett, Esq.	107
47:1739:138 ...		
Thomas Langley	"Langley" – taker up not known nor any person that does claim	200
Robert Hall & patented to Benjamin Peck	"Halls Neck" tbc: • Samuell Chamberlaine – 286 a. • Nicholas Goldsborough – 100 a. • Robert Goldsborough – 100 a.	476
Ernalt Hawkins	"Cabbin Neck, Sandy Bite, & Halls Fortune" tbc Col. Arnault Hawkins	238
William Hemsley	"Hemsley Upon Wye Addition" tbc Mr. William Hemsley	146
Thomas Bullen	"Bullens Discovery" tbc Thomas Bullen	136
Edward Fottrell	"Fottrells Discovery" tbc: • Mr. Daniell Maynadier – 98 a. • Edward Fotrill (AA) – 152 a.	250
47:1739:139 ...		
Anthony Richardson	"Addition" tbc Mr. Anthony Richardson	229
Michell Fletcher	"Richmond" tbc Michell Fletcher	41
Foster Turbutt & patented to Ann Goldsborough wife of John Goldsborough	"Marshy Peak" tbc John Goldsborough	132
Foster Turbutt & patented to Ann Goldsborough wife of John Goldsborough	"Peaks Marsh" tbc John Goldsborough	318
47:1739:140 ...		
~~Ernault Hawkins~~	~~"Cabbin Neck, Sandy Bite, & Halls Fortune"~~	~~238~~
Samuell Broadaway	"Broadways Meadows" tbc Samuell Broadway	100
William Porter & patented to Jo. Hunt	"Fools Paradice" tbc John Hunt (f. 104)	38
Charles Banning	"Yorks Destruction" tbc Charles Banning	50
Kenelm Skillington	"Skillingtons Happ" tbc Kenelm Skillington	20
47:1739:141 ...		
Michell Fletcher	"Dover Marsh" tbc William Harrison	348
Peter Caulk, Jr.	"Caulks Addition" tbc Peter Caulk	236
Francis Harris	"Minors Lott" tbc Joseph Eason as pt. "Taylors Ridge" (f. 31)	100
Robert Newcom	"Harbour Rouse" tbc Robert Newcomb	136

William Harrison	"Dover" tbc William Harrison	895
Jo. Atkinson	"Atkinson Chance" tbc Thomas Atkinson	43
47:1739:142 ...		
William Barker	pt. "Lower Dover" tbc William Barker	232
William Edwards	"Mistake" tbc William Edwards	51
Samuell Dickenson	"Little Creek" tbc: • Samuell Dickin in 1st Debt Book – 150 a. • on the resurvey – 50 a.	150
Fran. Neale	pt. "Hickory Ridge" tbc Fra. Neale	137
John Reynolds	"Reynolds Point" tbc John Reynolds	148
James Dawson	"Baleys Forrest" tbc James Dawson	113
47:1739:143 ...		
John Clifts	"Clifts Addition" tbc John Clift	100
Fran. Armstrong	"Ireland" – alleged to lie in elder surveys & will disclaim	500
William Moore	"Maxwell More" tbc: • Thomas Spry – 150 a. • Thomas Hopkins – 100 a.	250
William Gaskins	"Gaskins Neck" tbc John Wrightson	50
John Stanley	"Timber Neck Addition" tbc John Clift	139
James Powell	"Powells Hazard" tbc: • James Myrick – 50 a. • Capt. John Kimball has pt. resurveyed as "Kimballs Industry" – 283 a. (f. 137)	120
47:1739:144 ...		
Ralph Dawson	"Jones's Lott Addition"	50
Thomas Bozman	"Watsons Addition"	73
Robert Newcomb	"Partnerships Destruction"	66
John Harrison	"Harrisons Security"	167
David Kirby	"Kirby's Interest"	30
Thomas Turner	"Stoppard Moore"	100
47:1739:145 ...		
Dorothey Rolls	"Dorothy's Enlargement"	45
Thomas Bozman	"Neglect"	34
Michael Fletcher	"Richmond's Addition"	282
George Robins	"Buckingham"	903
47:1739:146 ...		
William Harper	"Bite the Biter"	35

John Carslake	"Carslake's Discovery"	109
Robert Hall	"Hall's Range"	353
David Jones	"Jones's Interest"	40
Thomas Purnell	"Fragment"	20
47:1739:147 ...		
Daniel Lambden	"Bridges"	176
Robert Rolls	"Roll's Range"	237
Daniel Sherwood	"Daniel & Mary"	375
John Studham	"Studham's Chance"	18
Peter Denny	"Denny's Content"	85
47:1739:148 ...		
Richard Fiddeman	"Fiddeman's Discovery"	408
Thomas Perkins	"Perkins's Discovery"	193½
Isaac Cox	"Coxe's Hazard"	103
Robert Harwood	"Harwood's Neglect"	38
James Ratcliffe	"Maple Branch"	40
47:1739:149 ...		
John Kenneday	"Kenneday's Addition"	23
Thomas Bozman	"Tale's Lott"	449
Mathew Tilghman Ward	"Rich Neck"	577
John Carslake	"Carslakes Content"	60
William Ayres	"Ayre's Venture"	96
47:1739:150 ...		
John Arrington	"Pasty Nuke" (f. 124)	24
John Stevens	"Johns Lott"	62
David Davis	"Bite the Biter"	33
Arthur Rigby	"Rigby's Choice"	101½
Thomas Smithson	"Millroad 2nd Addition"	300

46:1744:1 ...		Acres
William Clayton	pt. "Waterton"	290
	"Wisbick"	100
	"Poplar Hill"	200
	pt. "Normanton"	767
	pt. "Bettys Dowry" – from (N) King	2
	pt. "Kings Neglect" – from (N) King	107
Rachel Finney	"Finneys Range"	225
	pt. "Waterton"	170
Philip Emerson	½ "Widdows Choice"	320
	"Harwoods Lyon"	600
	pt. "Wettstone"	150
	"Hambletons Park"	263
	"Keilding & Buckingham"	393
	"Addition"	63
Varty Sweat	½ "Newmans Lott" – for h/o C. Stevens	100
	½ "Planters Delight" – for h/o C. Stevens	100
	pt. "Nobles Chance" – for h/o C. Stevens	200
	"Stevens Addition" – for h/o C. Stevens	75
John Sweat	pt. "Planters Delight" – for h/o Robert Noble	100
	"Nobles Addition" – for h/o Robert Noble	150
	pt. "Nobles Ridge" – for h/o Robert Noble	75
Oliver Millington	pt. "Betts Chance"	100
	"Epsom"	100
Mr. James Edge	½ "Widdows Chance" a/s "Choice"	320
	"Prevention"	50
	"Whartons Glade"	50
	"Couple Close"	100
	"Addition"	32
46:1744:2 ...		
Nathaniel Saintee	"Chance"	100
	"Knave Stand Off"	50
George Grason	"Tanners Hope" a/s "Hope"	50
	"Skinners Outlett"	50
	"Roberts Infancy Fancy" – for Robert Grason	65

Mr. Robert Lloyd	"Pickborne"	200
	"Elliotts Discovery"	100
	"Adjunction"	50
	"Scottland"	50
	"Lloyds Discovery" a/s "Recovery"	96
	"Hope" – from (N) Collins	100
	pt. "Turners Point" – from (N) Turner	200
	pt. "Partnership"	1200
	"Widdows Chance"	50
	"Tallwaien"	100
	"Rumbleys Marsh"	300
	"Murry"	150
	"Partnership"	310
	"New Mill"	200
	"Addition"	100
	"Buckland Marsh"	50
	"Buckland"	250
	pt. "Gurlington"	200
	"Grundys Inclosure"	175
	pt. "Marsh Land"	265
	"Graves"	500
Richard Skinner	"Skinners Choice" a/s "Tanner's Choice"	340
	"Skinners Borders"	100
	"Skinners Vineyard"	75
	"Skinners Addition"	150
	"Skinners Security"	103
Lewis Jones	"Tryangle"	100
	"Dirty Weeden Addition"	100
46:1744:3 ...		
Mr. Perry Benson	pt. "Huntington"	150
	"Neglect"	90
	pt. "Partnership"	81
	pt. "Fishing Bay"	18[illegible]
James Clayland	"Storys Lott" – from (N) Story	50

William Trippe	⅓ "Leath" – for h/o Woolman Gibson	13½
	⅓ "Edmondton" – for h/o Woolman Gibson	100
	⅓ "Chapinham & Bendon" – for h/o Woolman Gibson	189
	"Rebeccas Garden" – for h/o Woolman Gibson	150
	⅓ "Chapinhams Addition" – for h/o Woolman Gibson	16¾
	pt. "Bryans Lott" – for h/o Woolman Gibson	12
William Garey	"Dirty Weeden"	100
	"Fortunes Addition"	52
	"Braffarton"	100
	"Fortune"	150
	"Little Brittaine"	150
	"Todd Upon Derven" – from (N) Thrould	80
Mrs. Frances Elbert	pt. "Rebeccas Garden" – from (N) Emerson	25
	"Lloyds Costine"	659
	pt. "Rebeccas Garden" – from Mr. Lloyd	25
	pt. "Grantham"	106
James Sanders & John Pitts	pt. "Hambletons Park" – from (N) Shield	137
	"Damses Outlett"	50
Jonathan Gibson	⅓ "Leath"	13½
	⅓ "Edmondton"	100
	⅓ "Chapinham & Bendon"	189
	⅓ "Chapinhams Addition"	16¾
46:1744:4 ...		
Fardinando Callaghan	pt. "Brittania" – from (N) Story & Elizabeth Williams	200
Woolman Gibson	⅓ "Leath"	13½
	⅓ "Edmondton"	200
	⅓ "Chapinham & Benden"	189
	⅓ "Chapinham Addition"	16¾
Robert Stonestreet	"Dunns Range Addition" – for Charles Walker	200
John & Andrew Kininmont (cnp)	"Fools Paradise"	50
	pt. "Bartram"	150
	"Batcheldors Hope"	50
	"Hopewell"	80
	"Scotts Lott"	100

	"Kininmonts Delight"	168
William Cole	"Hilsdon" – from (N) Cockayne	200
	"Costins Chance" – from (N) Cockayne	32
	pt. "Brittania"	230
h/o James Horney	"Batcheldors Branch"	100
	"Batcheldors Branch Addition"	100
Mr. Robert Hall	"Halls Range"	353
	pt. "Partnership" – from (N) Bruff	10
William Warner	pt. "Nobles Chance"	82
Thomas Keet	pt. "Brittania" & pt. "Stevens's Plains"	50
Samuel Kininmont	⅓ "Dundee"	133
46:1744:5 ...		
Col. Edward Lloyd	"Meersgate"	300
	"Thumby Grange"	500
	"Natts Point"	50
	"Lynton"	600
	"Grange"	150
	"Salters Marsh"	100
	"Long Neglect"	133
	"Meersgate Addition"	267
	pt. "Crouches Chance"	50
	"Inlett"	88
	"Roadway"	50
	"Addition"	100
	"Scotts Close" – from (N) Start	200
	pt. "Woolmans Hermitage"	55
	pt. "Woolmans Inheritance"	104
	"Breybys Delight" – resurveyed	150
	"Doughtys Lott" – resurveyed	50
	"Cedar Point"	48
	"Doughtys Hope" – resurveyed	50
	"Meersgate Addition"	69
	"Knightly" – resurveyed	100
	"Soldiers Delight"	100
Aaron Higgs	"Puttingham"	100
Solomon Warner	"Poolys Discovery"	168

William Shield & James Sanders	pt. "Bedworth"	100
	"Rich Farm Addition"	200
Margaret Smallcorn	"Faulkners Levell"	150
Richard Gibson	pt. "Gallaway"	54
	pt. "Bryans Lott"	12½
46:1744:6 ...		
Francis Pickering, Jr.	"Sarahs Lott"	50
Thomas Ray	pt. "Dundee"	133
John Williams	pt. "Carters Inheritance" – for h/o Robert Hervey	100
George Beswicks	pt. "Christophers Lott"	100
	pt. "Stevens Plains"	50
	pt. "Nobles Ridge"	75
Richard Beswicks	pt. "Christophers Lott"	100
	pt. "Stevens Plains"	50
Vincent Loockerman	pt. "Harrisses Lott" – for h/o Robert Besswicks	111
h/o Mr. William Hemsley	"Hemsley Upon Wye"	1160
	"Hemsley Upon Wye Addition" composed of: • "Virginia Inn" • "Virginia Inn Addition" • escheated land	146
Samuel Hopkins	pt. "William & James"	33
	pt. "Maxwell Moore"	100
Daniel Dulany, Esq.	"Timber Neck"	120
	"Bettys Dowry"	150
	"Kings Plains"	158
	"Kings Forrest"	150
	"Outlett"	220
	pt. "Woolmans Hermitage"	109
	pt. "Woolmans Inheritance"	200
	"Knightleys Addition"	50
	"Parsongs Addition"	100
46:1744:7 ...		
Richard Bennett, Esq. (cnp)	"Morgan St. Michaells"	300
	"Marron"	130
	"Clayburn's Island"	700
	"Abbington"	400
	"Poplar Neck"	100

	pt. "Whetstone"	150
	"Town Road"	50
	"Henrietta Marias Discovery"	216
	"Lobbs Creek on Resurvey"	679
	"Tobacco Pipe"	359
	pt. "Crouches Choice"	100
	"Farme"	348
	"Sweatnames Hope"	120
	pt. "Daniels Addition"	30
	"Huntington Addition"	150
	"Timber Neck"	100
	"Batchelders Delight"	100
	"Hern Island"	75
	"Bodwells Indian Neck Resurveyed"	913
	"Winkleton"	185
	"Mitchels Lott"	200
	"Tryangles"	55
	"Advantage"	500
	"New Town"	100
	"Planters Increase", "Turners Ridge", et.al. resurveyed	504
	"Stevens Lott"	19
	"Poplar Neck" – on escheat	249
	"Neglect on Resurvey"	107
	"Kimbles Industry" – from (N) Kemble	383
	"Carters Inheritance"	300
h/o Roger Clayland	"Skipton"	300
	pt. "Rumsey Forrest"	43
	pt. "Finneys Hermitage"	200
Robert Blunt (KI)	"Harrisses Range"	400
Mary Sherwood	pt. "Huntington" & pt. "Addition" – per your father's will	90
46:1744:8 ...		

h/o Thomas Russell	pt. "Huntington" & pt. "Huntington Grange" – per your fathers will	200
	pt. "Huntington"	88
h/o William Edwards	pt. "Addition" & pt. "Fishing Bay" – per will of Michael Russell	90
	"Mistake"	51
Mr. William Dawson	"Batcheldors Range"	250
	"Batcheldors Range Addition"	463
	"Hatton Hope"	100
	pt. "Shrigleys Fortune"	170
	pt. "Gallaway"	100
	pt. "Huntington" & pt. "Addition"	90
William Hadden	pt. "Ramsey Forrest" a/s "Rumley's Forrest"	107
Vincent Jones	pt. "Nobles Chance"	100
Joseph Kininmont	⅓ "Dundee"	133
Peter Harwood	"Harwoods Hill"	100
	"Poplar Levill"	100
	"Mill Road", "Mill Roads Addition", & "Mill Road 2nd Addition"	150
	"Mill Roads Addition" – from (N) Smithson	80
	"Addition" – from (N) Blake	320
	pt. "Cottingham"	150
	"Comwhitten"	200
Thomas Gully	pt. "Ashby"	150
46:1744:9 ...		
Mr. Robert Goldsborough (cnp)	pt. "Ashby"	250
	pt. "Halls Neck"	100
	"Wyatts Fortune"	50
	pt. "Plain Dealing"	200
	pt. "Grundys Addition"	73
	"Peters Rest"	50
	"Annual Pence" pt. "St. Michaell Fresh Run"	50
	"Chance"	50
	pt. "Four Square"	300
	pt. "Adventure"	100
	"Goldsboroughs Triangle"	45
	pt. "Cottinham" – from (N) Abrahams	150

	"Newnams Addition" – from (N) Crowley	50
	"Four Square" – from (N) Ungle	350
	"Benjamins Lott"	50
	"Fox Harbour"	148
Adam & Richard Eubanks	pt. "Omalys Range"	150
	"Jacob & Johns Pasture"	120
John Tibbles	pt. "Sheepshead Point"	50
	"Tibbels's Addition"	20
Thomas Robson	"Jones Look Out"	50
	pt. "Partnership" – from (N) Benson & (N) Valient	125
James Hopkins	pt. "Hopkins Point"	100
	"Hopkins's Point Addition"	25
	pt. "Partnership"	65
John Barwick	"Newmans Folly" – from (N) Williams	50
Ebednego Botfield	"Bettys Cove Addition"	50
	"Addition"	50
	pt. "Bettys Cove"	30
46:1744:10 ...		
Richard Hethrington	"Hethringtons Delight"	50
John Fellows	pt. "Abrahams Lott", pt. "Gofston", & pt. "Mill Road 2nd Addition"	65
	pt. "Abrahams Lott" – from John James, Jr.	58
Mary Atwell	pt. "Bantry"	200
John Bartlett	pt. "Bensons Enlargement"	27
	"Rockney Neck"	50
	"Rockney Neck Addition"	58
	pt. "Bartletts Inheritance"	30
Matthew Kirby	"Swamp Hole"	100
	pt. "Partnership"	65
Jacob Falconar	"Falconars Hazard"	60
James Merrick	"Hazard Addition"	[illegible]
	"Powells Hazard" – from (N) Powell	50
h/o Phillip Baning	"Bannings Hazard"	50
	"Falconars Square" – from Ed. Carslake	100
James Webb	"Rocknenook"	40
Jeffeory Horney	pt. "Cottingham" – from (N) Abrahams	50

Mr. Samuel Cockayne	pt. "Saint Michaels Fresh Run" – from his mother	401
46:1744:11 ...		
Robert Harwood for h/o Isaac Dixon	pt. "Cottingham" – from (N) Abrahams	25
	pt. "Cottingham" – from (N) Newton	50
	pt. "Carters Plains" & pt. "Carters Farm"	306
	"Bennetts Hill"	50
	"Ending Controversie"	150
	pt. "Ashby"	60
	pt. "Dixons Outlett"	150
Thomas Perkins	pt. "Carters Farm" – from your wife's mother	400
	"Perkins Discovery"	193½
John Harwood	pt. "Carters Farm"	100
Jacob Hindman	pt. "Harrington" & pt. "Kirkham"	200
John Williams	"Kemps Choice" a/s "Chance" – from (N) Wintersell	100
	pt. "London Derry" – from (N) Armstrong	1½
	"Marys Dower"	200
Morris Oram	pt. "Waistland" & "Bartletts Triangle" – from (N) Bartlett	40
	pt. "Fox Hole"	145
	pt. "Fox Harbour"	50
	"Fox Denn"	56
	"Waterford" – from (N) Vaughn & (N) Robins on 9 November 1734	100
John Potts	"Nears Carters Bridge"	15
	pt. "St. Michaels Fresh Run"	60
	"Potts Discovery"	60½
Elizabeth Eubanks	"Swifts Chance" – for h/o Edward Eubanks	80
	"Jacob & Johns Purchase" – for h/o Edward Eubanks	50
46:1744:12 ...		
John Loockerman	pt. "Kirkham" & pt. "Harrington"	420
	pt. "Shrigleys Fortune"	100
Francis Stanton	pt. "Bantry"	100
Henry Henrix	pt. "Mount Hope" – from Thomas Edmondson	35
Free School of Talbot County	pt. "Tilghmans Fortune"	100

William Thomas, Jr.	pt. "Cottingham" – from (N) Chew	140
	pt. "Cottingham" – for your wife	125
	"Morefields"	280
Henry Burges	"Bobbs Hill"	100
	"Hopewell"	50
James Rattcliffe	"Ratcliffs High Way"	113
	pt. "Jacob & Johns Pasture" – from your father	85
	pt. "Addition" – from (N) Cockayne	52
	pt. "Jacob & Johns Pasture" – from (N) Ratcliffe on 18 March 1737	85
	"Maple Branch"	40
John Neighbours	pt. "Edmondsons Freshes" – from John Price	50
Nicholas Goldsborough, Jr.	pt. "Halls Neck" – from (N) Peck	100
Joseph Hix	pt. "Ashford"	50
Francis Pickering	pt. "Ashby"	100
46:1744:13 ...		
George Palmer	pt. "Mount Hope"	100
Edward Perkins	"Newmans Range"	100
Thomas Spry	pt. "Maxwell Moor"	150
h/o William Bennett	"Eatons Addition" & "Lobbs Corner"	83
	pt. "Cumberland"	50
	"Covehall"	100
	"Fort Adventure"	50
Mr. James Tilghman	"Fosley"	250
	"Addition"	100
	"Edmonds Range"	400
	"Dixons Lott" or "Out Lett"	50
Joseph Harrington	½ "Adventure"	113½
Richard Eaton	pt. "Fox Hole"	100
	pt. "Fox Harbour"	50
	"Eatons Addition" – from (N) Grundy & (N) Ungle to Peter Anderton	18[illegible]
John Wise	"Gone"	4[illegible]
	"Sheepshead Point Resurveyed"	19[illegible]
	"Bantrees" – from (N) Marlin	5[illegible]
Benjamin Hopkins	pt. "Hopkins Point"	66¾

Peter Denny	pt. "Hopkins Point"	66¾
	"Clifton"	200
	"Dennys Content"	85
46:1744:14 ...		
James Willis	pt. "Adventure" – for h/o Peter Russam	100
Richard Aldern	pt. "Gaffords Neck"	300
	"Roystons Addition"	50
	"Alderns Island"	41
William Harrison (Irish Creek)	½ "Ashford"	50
	"Long Neglect"	35
Edmond Ferrall	pt. "Stevens Range"	100
	pt. "Coventry" – from (N) Hopkins on 6 June 1734	60
	pt. "Coventry" – from (N) Harding	40
	"Micklemire"	100
John Rattcliffe	"Gofstan" – from (N) Fellows to your wife	100
Mrs. Elizabeth Davis	pt. "Tilghmans Fortune"	83
	"Sandfords Hermitage"	250
	"Sandfords Folly"	45
	"Bite the Biter"	33
h/o James Harvey	"Abrahams Lott"	100
Thomas Winchester	"Marlins Folly" – for h/o Isaac Marlin	50
	"Marlins Chance" – for h/o Isaac Marlin	50
	"Bantry" – for h/o Isaac Marlin	500
	"Spring Close" – for h/o Isaac Marlin	100
	pt. "Bantrees" – for h/o Isaac Marlin	60
	pt. "Bantrees Addition" – for h/o Isaac Marlin	10
	"Marlins Neglect" – for h/o Isaac Marlin	57
Robert Newcomb	"Harbour Rouse Resurveyed"	130
	"Partnerships Distribution"	66
46:1744:15 ...		
John Valiant	pt. "Gaffords Neck" – from (N) Aldern	100
William Baning	"Goose Neck"	50
~~Elizabeth~~ William Skinner	"Clays Hope" – for h/o James Colson	200
Edward Harding (cnp)	pt. "Bite"	13
	pt. "Tilghmans Fortune"	19
	"Hardings Endeavour"	200

	pt. "Hemsly Arcada"	301
Arthur Rigby	"Rigbys Folly"	45
	"Anderbys Addition Resurveyed"	78
	"Anderbey"	100
	"Grafford"	100
	"Rigbys Discovery"	105
	pt. "Fox Hole"	65
	"Lamberton"	150
	"Rigbys Choice"	101½
William Ridgway	"Westland"	100
Edward Elliott	"Mecotter & Glover Resurveyed"	355
	"Chance Resurveyed"	223
	"Point & Marsh"	50
	pt. "Bensons Enlargement"	28
	"Sarahs Garden"	13
Mrs. Frances Ungle	"Room"	100
	"Golston"	50
	"Old Womans Folly"	172
Dennis Hopkins	pt. "Hopkins Point"	90
46:1744:16 ...		
Thomas Atkinson	pt. "Cottingham" – from (N) Abrahams	37
	pt. "Cottingham" – from (N) Jadkins	100
	"Newman" – from (N) Jadkins	50
Richard Hopkins	pt. "Nominy" – from (N) Forby	100
	pt. "Hopkins Point"	150
	pt. "White Phillips" – from (N) Dickinson	42
Thomas, John, & James Bartlett	pt. "Ratcliffe Mannor"	520
Andrew Oram	pt. "Adventure"	100
Samuel Harwood	"Dudleys Choice"	100
	"Subland"	200
	"Maxfield"	152
	"Syblands Addition"	110
	pt. "Coalin"	100
Thomas & James Lenard	pt. "Partnership" – from (N) Benson	120
William Price	a tract of land adjoining "St. Michaels Fresh Run"	100

Joseph Elliott	pt. "Coventry"	120
	pt. "Ratcliffs Choice"	79
Joseph Merrick	pt. "Batcheldors Range Addition"	37
Joseph Atkinson	"Atkinsons Chance"	43
John Reynolds	"Reynolds Point Resurveyed"	148
46:1744:17 ...		
George Eubanks, Jr.	pt. "Omley Range" – from Thomas Eubanks per will	50
	pt. "Harwood Neglect"	11
George Dulin	pt. "Partnership" – from George Robins	28
Mr. John Goldsborough	"Peaks Marsh on Resurvey" – 25 March 1715 patented 9 August 1736	318
	"Marshey Peak" – surveyed 17 June 1719 patented 9 August 1736	132
	pt. "Thief Keep Out"	36
Mr. Thomas Cockayne	pt. "Carters Plains"	294
John Brascope	pt. "Coventry" – from (N) Palmer	30
	pt. "Ratcliffs Choice"	36
Rebecca Durdin	"Johns Neck"	700
Richard Hall	pt. "Smiths Clifts"	372
h/o John Rathell	"Strawberry Field Addition" a/s "Halls Addition"	50
	"Ratherels Chance"	50
Samuel Chamberlain, Esq. – carried to f. 26	pt. "Hyer Dier Loyd"	858
	pt. "Halls Neck"	286
	pt. "Barmston", pt. "Coxes Addition", & pt. "Coxes Chance"	224
	"Contention"	100
46:1744:18 ...		
Samuel Brodaway	"Dudley"	200
	"Ramah"	100
	"Sams Fields"	102
	"Strawbridge"	100
	'Brodaways Meadows"	100
Edward Clark	pt. "Parkers Farm"	350
	"Parrotts Lott"	82
Joshua Clark	"Clarks Folly"	101
	pt. "Johns Neck"	118

Jonathan Airey	pt. "Roeclift"	118
	"Davids Ridge"	125
John Nailer	pt. "Duns Range"	100
	"Morefields" – from (N) Sweat	30
	pt. "Morefields"	10
William Michaell	"Turners Hazard" & "Bullens Addition" – from (N) Bullen	171
	pt. "Morgans Addition", pt. "Morgans Neglect", & pt. "Ramsey Forrest"	101
h/o John Loveday	"Middle Spring" – from (N) Trotter	150
Robert Lowther	"Beverdam Neck" – from (N) Skinner	70½
John Tomlinson	pt. "Roeclift" – from (N) Nedles	50
Samuel Morgan	pt. "Dudleys Clifts"	92
46:1744:19 ...		
h/o Caleb Clark	pt. "Parkers Range" – from (N) Jadwin	56
	"High Field" – from (N) Webb	100
	pt. "Hampton" & pt. "Parkers Range"	200
	"Highfield Addition"	150
	pt. "Parkers Range" & part from (N) Jadwin	2
Aaron Parrott	pt. "Kingstown" – from (N) Wilson	51½
	pt. "Johns Neck"	264
Henry Oldfield	"Summerly" – from (N) Russam	250
James Morgan	pt. "Morgans Neglect" & "Morgans Addition"	120
Michael Kerwick	"Buck Range"	50
	"Buck Range Addition"	55
	pt. "Duns Range" – per your son	100
	"Bowes Range"	227
Richard Kerwick	"Venture"	37
	½ "Dudleys Demesens"	50
Charles Morgan	pt. "Chesnut Bay"	95
	pt. "Dudleys Clifts"	92
Samuel Dudley	pt. "Advantage" – from (N) Powell	18
	"Beverneck" – from Thomas Dudley per will	100
	pt. "Smiths Clifts" – for h/o Richard Tompson per will	94
	pt. "Hasco Green" – from Thomas Dudley	50
William Warring	pt. "Hampton" – from (N) Jadwin	200

46:1744:20 ...		
Sarah Morgan wife of Capt. Edward Morgan	"Holme Hill" – from (N) Cemey	62
	pt. "Smiths Clifts"	258
Isaac Dobson	"Woolfe Pitt Ridge" – for h/o John Kirby	50
	"Strawberry Fields" – for h/o John Kirby	100
	pt. "Turners Discovery" – for h/o John Kirby	30
David Kirby	pt. "Turners Range"	40
	"Limbrick" – from your father	60
	"Kirbys Interest"	30
Frances Camperson	pt. "Hampton" & pt. "Parkers Range"	100
William Frampton	pt. "Rich Range"	50
	pt. "Rich Range"	50
John Walker	pt. "Rich Farme" – on Kings Creek from (N) Berry	100
Robert Hunter	"Jacobs Begining"	50
	pt. "Dudleys Dennesen"	40
	pt. "Jacobs Begining" – from (N) Sweeny	50
Thomas Hutchinson	pt. "Johns Neck"	19
	pt. "Bugby" – from (N) Bradbury	200
Thomas Frampton	"Framptons Begining"	96
	"Collins Pasture"	50
h/o Allemby Millington	"Nobles Meadows on Resurvey"	229
	"Betts Addition"	207
46:1744:21 ...		
John Cannady	"Cannadys Hazard"	29
	"Cannadys Addition"	23
Joseph Turner	pt. "Johns Hill"	90
	pt. "Johns Hill"	90
	"Turners Discovery"	67
Isaac Cox	pt. "Johns Hill"	90
	"Coxes Hazard"	103
Henry Buckingham	pt. "Midle Spring"	100
William Scott	"Salop Resurveyed"	67
Jonathan Tyler	pt. "Kingstown" – from (N) Southerby to your father on 18 June 1684	100
William Thorpe	pt. "Austin" – from (N) Lary	50
	pt. "Austin" – from (N) Kelld	50

h/o John Burges	"Beverneck"	141
	"Beverneck" & pt. "Brand Land"	150
James Kendrick	"Coventry"	250
Thomas Thompson	pt. "Smiths Clifts"	94
Thomas Vickars	pt. "Charlevale"	50
	"Moorefield" – from (N) Sweat	84
Jane Turner	"Hases Green" – from (N) Paris	160
	"Sought Out" – from (N) Lasswell	100
46:1744:22 ...		
William Vickars	pt. "Dunns Range" – for your daughter Sarah	50
	"Pickadilla" a/s "Paddington" – from (N) Hemsley	200
Mr. Edward Nedels	⅓ "Pitts Range"	200
	⅓ "Killen"	369
	pt. "Killen" – from (N) Sherwood	140
	pt. "Johns Neck"	4
	½ "Exchange"	100
	pt. "Roeclifts" – for h/o (N) Grosier	50
James Wilson, Jr.	pt. "Middle Spring"	50
	pt. "White Oak Swamp"	100
James Berry	pt. "White Marsh" pt. "Pitts Will"	760
Thomas Dudley	pt. "Broad Laine"	103
William Dudley	"Dudley Demesene"	115
	pt. "Bugby" – from (N) Bradbury	50
	pt. "Callin" – from (N) Bull	200
John Herrington	pt. "Bugby"	150
Francis Regester	"Parrotts Reserve" – from (N) Parrott	150
Thomas Kelld	pt. "Austin"	100
	"Alcocks Choice"	100
Isaac Dobson, Jr.	pt. "Dobsons Advantage"	28
	"Egles Neck"	100
	"Worgans Reserve"	200
46:1744:23 ...		
George Sprouce	pt. "Cumberland" & pt. "Chance Help" – from (N) Chance	157
Dennis Larey	pt. "Partners Hazard" – from (N) Cook	142
	"Beaver Dam Neck" – from (N) Mountague	70½

Edward Slater guardian to h/o John Sprignall	tract of land b/o Phillip Morgan pt. "Chesnutt Bay"	100
h/o Thomas Turner (miller)	"Turners Chance"	100
William Kirby	"Kirbys Addition" – from your father	49
Thomas Purnall	pt. "Hampton"	8
	pt. "Rich Range"	218
	pt. "Teltates Loss" – for h/o John Vickars	125
	"Vickers Lott" – for h/o John Vickars	52
	pt. "Charlevail & Cork"	200
Joseph Darden	"Kings Creek Marsh" – from James Tayler	50
	pt. "Bless Land" – from James Tayler	100
	"Kingsberry" – from James Tayler	130
	pt. "Turkey Neck" – from (N) Cemey	100
William Robins	pt. "Smiths Clifts" – from (N) Wootters	201
	pt. "Holm Hill" – from (N) Wootters	34
	pt. "Holm Hill"	400
	pt. "Rich Range Addition"	14
	"Fragment"	20
46:1744:24 ...		
Mr. Grundy Pemberton	"Smiths Clifts"	232
	"Elms Addition" & "Lobbs Corner"	14
	pt. "Cumberland"	30
	pt. "Hueath"	205
Mr. Robert Goldsborough, Jr.	pt. "Rich Range"	140
	pt. "Rich Range Addition"	86
Andrew Bandey	pt. "Kingstown"	100
Henry Clift	"Dudleys Inclosier" – for h/o James Dudley	104
	pt. "Dudleys Addition" – for h/o James Dudley	37
Sarah Greenwood w/o Bartholomew Greenwood	pt. "Parkers Farm"	100
John Regester	"Kingberrys Addition"	100
John Baynard	pt. "Hampton" & pt. "Parkers Range"	1300
Daniel Ward	pt. "Summerly" – for your wife from (N) Oldfield & wife	50
James Parrott (cnp)	"Abbington"	100
	pt. "Buckrow"	150
	pt. "Cattlin Plains"	10

	"Walnut Garden"	50
	"Hulls Addition"	100
46:1744:25 ...		
William Martin	"Mitcham's Hall" – for h/o Loftus Boudle	300
Elizabeth Bush	pt. "Arcadia"	166
Thomas Ford	pt. "Partlitt"	72
	pt. "Gressell" & pt. "Otwell" – from (N) Turbutt	28
Mr. Nicholas Goldsborough	pt. "Hyer Dyer Lloyd"	400
	"Otwell"	500
	"Addition"	80
	pt. "Gressell"	122
	pt. "Parlett" – from (N) Ford	28
	pt. "Marshey Point"	157
Kenelm & Elizabeth Skillington	pt. "Turners Point"	200
	"Skillingtons Happ"	20
James Ferrall	"Hawks Hill Addition" – for h/o Terrance Ferrall	100
John Loyd	"Piney Point Advantage" – for h/o Michael Meginny	150
William Skinner, Jr.	"Skinners Lott"	33
	pt. "Bensons Enlargement" – from (N) Parrott on 6 November 1735	150
Ferrell Gallagher	pt. "Tilghmans Fortune" – for h/o John Botfield	88
46:1744:26 ...		
William Marshall	"Kings Sale" – from (N) Lane	126
Pearce Flemmon	"Flemons Freshes on Resurvey"	215
Solomon Sharp	pt. "Nomeny"	302
	"Chance"	40
Samuel Sharp	pt. "Nomeny"	200
	"Dicks Marsh"	200
	pt. "Discovery"	56
	pt. "Little Bristoll"	980
	pt. "Scarbrough"	200
Samuel Chamberlaine, Esq. – brought from f. 17 & continued onto f. 56 (cnp)	~~<unr>~~	~~<unr>~~
	~~<unr>~~	~~<unr>~~
	~~<unr>~~	~~<unr>~~
	~~pt. "<unr> Neck"~~	~~124~~

	~~<unr>~~	~~106~~
	~~"Cox Addition"~~	~~70~~
	~~"Cox Choice"~~	~~350~~
	~~<unr>~~	~~<unr>~~
	~~"Goldston"~~	~~50~~
	~~<unr>~~	~~100~~
	~~pt. "Hyer Dyer Lloyd"~~	~~300~~
	½ "Bishoprick" – from (N) Pearson	50
	pt. "Four Square on Resurvey"	350
	~~pt. "Halfs Neck" – from Daniel Peck on 22 July 1734~~	
	"Cabbin Neck"	50
	all that lot or pt. of a lot of land situate in Oxford No. 4 – from (N) Aldern & (N) Bullen	<n/g>
	pt. "Bishoprick"	50
46:1744:27 ...		
h/o Michael Fletcher	"Darlington" – from (N) Green	110
	"Long Acre"	150
	"Sharps Choice" a/s "Chance" – from (N) Wintersell	200
	pt. "Richmond"	37
	"Richmonds Addition"	282
John Frith	pt. "London Derry"	1½
h/o Charles Markland	pt. "Plembenamen" or "Morgans Point"	50
James Millard	pt. "Canterbury Mannor"	130
Thomas Browning h/o Robert Lowrey	pt. "Hyer Dyer Loyd" – surveyed for Daniel Crowley	80
	pt. "Hyer Dyer Loyd" – surveyed for Daniel Crowley	75
	pt. "Lostock"	184½
Phillip Jenkins	pt. "Edmondsons Freshes"	300
	pt. "Chesnutt Bay"	205
	pt. "Dudleys Clifts"	16
James Barnes	"Boones Hope" – for h/o Clement Sails	100
Gabriel Saile	"Rich Range"	300
	"Dolph"	100
46:1744:28 ...		

Dr. William Sharp	"Moorfields"	100
	"Adventure"	100
	"Easons Neck"	100
	"Fancy"	50
	"Conjunction"	25
	"Rattlesnake Point"	150
	"Mount Pleasure"	500
	"Easons Lott"	50
	"Sharps Addition"	24
	"Inclosure"	300
	pt. "Little Bristoll"	320
Francis Parrott	"Lords Chance"	100
Joseph Parrott	pt. "Abrahams Lott", pt. "Milroad 2nd Addition", & pt. "Gouldston" – from (N) Fellows	230
William Harrison (Miles Creek)	pt. "Taylors Ridge"	100
Richard Giles	"Swamptick"	100
	pt. "Shore Ditch"	75
Nicholas Glen	pt. "Cooks Hope"	200
Adam Brown	pt. "Hyer Dyer Loyd"	100
	pt. "Parkers Point" & pt. "Enlargement"	75
Mr. Edward Oldham	"Combsberry" – from (N) Rich	100
	"Piney Point" a/s "Judith Garden" – from (N) Rich	50
	pt. "Judiths Garden" – from (N) Pattinson	80
	"Rich Park" – from (N) Rich	569
	pt. "Nether Foston" – from (N) Rich	50
46:1744:28 [!] ...		
Col. John Sherwood	"Allembys Fields"	115
h/o John Clifts	pt. "Taylors Ridge" – from (N) Harrison	100
	"Timber Necks Addition" – from (N) Swallow	139
Henry Delehay	pt. "Hyer Dyer Loyd" – for h/o William Combes	125
Mr. Nicholas Lowe (cnp)	pt. "Anderton"	500
	"Andertons Addition"	200
	"Jacks Point"	100
	pt. "Lowes Rambles"	109[illegible]
	"Wintersell" – from (N) Winters	14[illegible]

	pt. "Nominy" – from (N) Cook	148
Joshua Hopkins	pt. "London Derry"	103
h/o Jeoffery Cox	"Spring Close"	50
Ralph Elston	pt. "Edmondsons Freshes" & pt. "Howarth"	110
	"French Hazard"	41
	"Stapleton"	77
	"Fish Hazard"	18
	"Fish Range"	74
	"Contention"	130
William Edmondson (DO)	pt. "Hyer Dyer Loyd"	112
	pt. "Hyer Dyer Loyd" – from (N) Eason	170
	pt. "Hyer Dyer Loyd" – from (N) Evans	100
	pt. "Hyer Dyer Loyd" – on escheat	9
46:1744:29 ...		
Col. Thomas Bozman	"Cardiff" – from (N) Alexander	100
	"Discovery"	231
	"Providence"	7
	pt. "Timber Neck"	150
	"Browns Park"	119
	"Tates Lott on Resurvey"	449
	"Timber Neck on Resurvey"	294
	"Piney Point" – for h/o Jonathan Taylor	150
	"Piney Point Advantage" – from (N) Alexander	125
	"East Ottwell"	400
	"Bullen" ~~& "Bullens Addition"~~	350
	"Timothys Lott"	300
Phillip Martin	"Bullens Chance"	350
	pt. "Conjunction"	25
Thomas Martin	pt. "Hyer Dyer Loyd"	200
	"Hard Measure Resurveyed"	94
	"Ottwell" – from (N) Parrott on 21 May 1735	100
	"Fancey Close" – from (N) Parrott on 21 May 1735	50
	pt. "Hyer Dyer Loyd"	58
~~James Walker~~	~~"Enfield"~~	~~200~~
Thomas Skillington	"Hambletons Neck"	300
Joseph Eason	pt. "Hyer Dyer Loyd" – for h/o Francis Harrison	75

John Coward	"Plenhemmon" – from (N) Rousby	600
John Pattison	pt. "Judiths Garden"	63
	pt. "Anderton"	100
46:1744:30 ...		
Francis Armstrong	"Surprize"	40
	"Discovery"	20
	"Huntington Grange"	100
	"Cornelius's Cool Spring"	100
	pt. "London Derry"	382
h/o Edward Man Sherwood	"Exchange" – from (N) Nedels	100
	pt. "High Fields" – from (N) Russam	50
	⅓ "Pitts Range"	200
	pt. "Killam"	229
John Love	pt. "Hatton"	63
Thomas Bowdle	pt. "Hyer Dyer Loyd" – from (N) Bowdle	142
John Jones (tanner)	pt. "Chance Help" & "Cumberland" – from Richard Chance on 26 May 1736	80
Mrs. Henrietta Maria Robins	"First Hazard" – for h/o Mr. George Robins	358
	"Jobs Content" – for h/o Mr. George Robins	1000
	pt. "Cooks Hope" – for h/o Mr. George Robins	214
	pt. "Hulls Neck" – for h/o Mr. George Robins	300
	"Dunsmore Heath" – for h/o Mr. George Robins	200
	"Framtom" a/s "Frampton" – for h/o Mr. George Robins	122
	"Jenings Hope" – for h/o Mr. George Robins	718
	pt. "Marshey Point" – for h/o Mr. George Robins	300
	pt. "Tilghmans Fortune" – for h/o Mr. George Robins	445
	"Turkey Park" – for h/o Mr. George Robins	329
	pt. "Rattcliffe Manner" – for h/o Mr. George Robins	150
	pt. "Discovery" – for h/o Mr. George Robins	60
	pt. "Canterburys Mannor" – for h/o Mr. George Robins	100
	pt. "Desier & Hewerth" – for h/o Mr. George Robins	250
	"Buckingham" – for h/o Mr. George Robins	903

46:1744:31 ...		
Thomas Skinner	pt. "Marshey Point"	100
Thomas Martin, Jr.	pt. "Wilderness" a/s pt. "Hyer Dier Loyd"	100
	"Richneck"	300
	pt. "Shrodick"	25
George Parratt	"Fork" – for h/o (N) Dobson	250
William Anderson	"Prospect"	125
	"Knaps Lott"	150
John Dickinson	pt. "Roadley"	150
	pt. "Scarbrough" – from (N) Harrison to your wife per will (QA)	200
h/o Daniell Powell	pt. "Boston Clift"	550
John Carr	"Millars Purchase"	100
	pt. "Lowes Rambles"	114
h/o Thomas Steuard	"Jordans Hill Resurveyed"	175
	½ "Upper Range"	50
Richard Barnett	"Poor Hill"	37
	pt. "Sutton Grange"	100
	pt. "Sutton Grange" – from Thomas Noble	100
46:1744:32 ...		
James Barnwell	pt. "Bedworth" – from (N) Shield	100
	pt. "Mount Hope" – as heir to Elizabeth Cathrop	50
	pt. "Mount Hope" – from (N) Mills	27
	pt. "Bedworth" & pt. "Rich Farm Addition"	70
Mr. Thomas Bullen	"Newlin" – from (N) Brown	140
	"Lords Gift" – from (N) Brown	100
	"Bullens Discovery"	136
	"Turbutts Fields"	168
	"Poplar Hill"	57
	pt. "Marsh Land"	165
	pt. "Lords Gift" – from (N) Robinson	100
h/o James Dickinson (cnp)	"Hatton" – from (N) Dickinson	322
	"Crooked Lane" – from (N) Stapleford	116
	"Frankford St. Michael" – from Samuel Dickinson	616
	pt. "Hatton" – from (N) Thomas	112
	pt. "Baldon" – from (N) Goslin	300

	"Bennetts Freshes"	425
Rev. Daniel Maynadier	pt. "Goldsborough" – from (N) Quinton	187
	"Tatterhust" – from (N) Quinton	38
	"Jamacoe"	50
	pt. "Marshland"	70
	"Timothys Lott"	25
	"Hermitage" – from (N) Boyer	90
	"Partnership"	34
	"Cross Haise"	50
	pt. "Fottrells Discovery"	93
William Ayers	pt. "Studds Point" – from (N) Corkrin	100
	"Intention" – from (N) Dickinson	100
	pt. "Roadley"	80
	pt. "Hills Neck"	50
	"Ayers Venture"	96
46:1744:33 ...		
h/o Mrs. Rachel Turbutt	pt. "Blessland" & "Baggs Marsh" – from (N) Baggs	300
	pt. "Blessland" & "Baggs Marsh" – from (N) Baggs	160
	"Hogsdon"	100
John Ferrall	pt. "Mount Hope" – ~~from (N) Edmondson~~	53
	pt. "Hawks Hill Addition" – ~~from (N) Edmondson~~	50
David Robinson	pt. "Hull"	70
	"Davids Folly"	50
	"Chance"	23
Sarah Seeny	pt. "Sutton", pt. "Suttons Addition", & pt. "Partnership" – from (N) Abbott	219
	pt. "Sutton" & "Suttons Addition" – from Silvester Abbott on 6 August 1735	54
h/o William Fooks	pt. "Hogg Range" – from (N) Barnett	47
	pt. "Turkey Neck" – from (N) Taylor on 28 February 1735	16
Jeremiah Nicols	pt. "Partnership"	250
	pt. "Bettys Chance"	100
	pt. "Stevens Plains"	50
	pt. "Richmond"	4
h/o Mr. Anthony Richardson (cnp)	"Hasley"	200
	"Widdows Lott"	85

	"Partners Hazard" – from (N) Cook	142
	"Browns Lott" – from (N) Hopper	200
	pt. "Mount Hope"	50
	land adjoining to "Pitts Mill" – formerly Thomas Barrett	28
	pt. "Worgans Reserve"	300
	"Addition in Lordships Mannor"	229
	"Parkers Parke"	500
	pt. "Dobsons Advantage"	7
	pt. "Turkey Neck"	125
46:1744:34 ...		
William Mackey	"Holmsby"	200
	pt. "Bullen"	60
	pt. "Broad Oake" – from (N) Chaplain	175
William Richardson	"Gurlington" – from (N) Gaskin	75
William Barker	pt. "Lower Dover" – in His Lordships Mannor	232
William Wilson	pt. "Midle Spring"	100
John & James Barnett	pt. "Bullen"	100
	pt. "Bullen" – from (N) Macotter	50
Jonathan Neall	pt. "Hickory Ridge" – from (N) Neall	50
Robert Cuthcert for h/o Thomas Kirk	"Cornelius's Garden" – for h/o (N) Mulrain	50
John Hixon	pt. "York"	153
	"Yorks Destruction"	50
	pt. "York" – for h/o (N) Morris	102
William White	pt. "Sutton Grange"	280
	"Killingsworth"	50
	pt. "Willingborough" & pt. "Gurlington Resurveyed"	93
	pt. "Goldsborough"	113
h/o James White	pt. "Double Ridge"	120
	"Whites Gore"	40
	pt. "Sutton Grange"	120
46:1744:35 ...		
William Taylor	pt. "Middle Spring"	50
	pt. "Turkey Neck"	243
Peter Shannahan	"Chance"	100

Richard Cooper	"Woolsey Mannor" – for h/o George Sailes	1000
Sarah Webb	pt. "Roadley" – to your husband from (N) Berry	150
James Cockrin	pt. "Hogg Hole"	142
	pt. "Discovery"	347
John Shaw	pt. "Hulls Neck" – from (N) Abbott	150
John Holt	pt. "Broad Oak" – from (N) Mackey	25
Henry Harris	pt. "Millars Hope" – for h/o Simon Fisher	121
Edward Brenny	pt. "Parkers Point" & pt. "Enlargement"	75
	pt. "Parkers Point" & pt. "Enlargement" – from (N) Marsh	75
Elizabeth Jenkins	pt. "Patricks Ridge"	560
Thomas Barnett	pt. "Patricks Ridge"	100
46:1744:36 ...		
James Chaplin	pt. "Broad Oake"	300
	"Enfield"	200
Thomas Stevens	pt. "Compton"	80
	"Williams Lott"	49
	pt. "Cattlin Plains" ~~tbe Elizabeth Stevens~~	250
	"Dudley Choice"	100
	pt. "Strawbridge"	163
	pt. "Cattlin Plains"	160
	pt. "Bushrow"	34¾
	pt. "Dawsons Fortune"	34¾
	pt. "Edmondsons Cove"	116
	pt. "Compton"	14
	pt. "Coxes Addition"	7
	"Johns Lott"	6
Tristram Thomas	pt. "Ridley"	20
	pt. "Sutton"	5
	pt. "Thief Keep Out"	3
John Glover	pt. "Mount Hope"	7
	½ "Upper Range"	5
Thomas Metcalfe	pt. "Sutton"	25
	"Suttons Addition"	5
	"Buckrowe"	8
John Price (Dover)	pt. "Hatfields" & "Hatfields Addition"	2

Francis Neall	pt. "Hickory Ridge"	296
	pt. "Hickory Ridge" – in the Mannor	137
46:1744:37 ...		
Samuell Dickinson	"Cross a Door"	400
	"Samuells Lott"	600
	"Dickinsons Lott Addition Resurveyed"	113
	"Powells Island"	58
	pt. "Wales" – from (N) Alexander	46
	pt. "Lowes Good Luck" – from (N) Lowe	54
	pt. "Compton" – from (N) Stevens	13
	pt. "Mount Hope"	350
	pt. "Double Ridge"	50
	pt. "Nominy" – from (N) Sharp	350
	pt. "Reedly" – from (N) Hudson	200
	"Hobsons Choice" – from (N) Price	100
	pt. "Canterburys Manner" – from (N) Troth	350
	"Little Creek" – from (N) Sanders	200
	"Evans Point" – from (N) Sanders	300
	pt. "Hier Dier Loyd"	101
	"Dickinsons Lott"	216
	pt. "White Philips"	150
	⅔ pt. "Salem", "Quillen", pt. "Stepney", & "Cornelius Garden"	134
	"Hunting Hills"	100
	"Fishers Choice Resurveyed" – from (N) Fisher	125
	pt. "Michnells Hermitage", "Millers Hope", & pt. "Harberts Choice" – from James Harbert on 7 May 1734 (f. 76)	100
	pt. "Darlington"	119
	pt. "Hopsons Choice"	129
	"Millers Choice"	85
Daniel Powell	"Rigbys Marsh"	300
h/o William Thomas	pt. "Double Ridge"	150
	pt. "Double Ridge" – from (N) Lowe	80
Mrs. Elizabeth Harrison (cnp)	"Dover Resurveyed"	395
	"Dover Marsh"	348
	"Rockclift"	170

	"Poplar Levell"	116
46:1744:38 ...		
Lemon John Catrop	"Cathrops Security"	205
	pt. "Mount Hope" – from (N) Wiles	67
Morrice Giddens	"New Scottland"	700
Thomas Powell	pt. "Bever Neck"	259
	pt. "Advantage"	42
	pt. "Rockclift"	100
Hezekiah Macotter	pt. "White Phillips"	37½
	pt. "Studs Point"	50
	pt. "Hulls Neck"	40
John Higgins	"Boaranes Range"	177
	pt. "Lowes Rambles"	18
Elizabeth Stevens	pt. "Compton"	7
	pt. "Edmondsons Cove"	58
	pt. "Dawsons Fortune"	16¼
	pt. "Catlin Plains"	80
	"Acton"	300
	pt. "Bushrow"	16¼
Thomas Delehay	"Delehays Fortune on Resurvey" pt. "Taylors Ridge"	100
Samuel Abbott	"Beverdam"	100
	"Hutchinsons Addition"	50
	"Miners Lott"	100
Edward Neall	pt. "Mount Hope"	50
46:1744:39 ...		
Walter Jenkins	pt. "Patricks Ridge"	240
William Ardery	pt. "Mount Hope" – for h/o Joseph Barrow	50
	pt. "Lowe's Rambles" – for his own heirs	200
Thomas Elsby	pt. "Parkers Point" & pt. "Enlargement"	75
William Mullican	pt. "Taylors Ridge"	100
Samuel Mullican	pt. "Patricks Plains" & pt. "Casons Choice"	175
Hugh Lynch	pt. "Mullikins Choice"	100
Patrick Mullikin (cnp)	pt. "Patricks Plains" & pt. "Casons Choice"	175
	pt. "Taylors Ridge" – for your wife Mary Lord	100
	"Sodenbrough" – for h/o (N) Welsh	100

	"Plansly" – for h/o (N) Welsh	100
David Jones	"Wilderness" – from (N) Harding	75
	"Jones Interest"	40
Edward Hargaton	pt. "Patricks Ridge"	100
46:1744:40 ...		
Henry Withgott	"Cromwell"	100
	"Josephs Lott"	100
William Adams	pt. "Hatfield" & pt. "Hatfields Addition" – from John Price & Richard Dove on 20 November 1734	50
Terrance Connolly	"Hollands Addition"	41
	"Kingston"	400
	pt. "Mullikins Choice"	70
William Carey	pt. "Partnership" – from (N) Abbott	18
	pt. "Sutton" & pt. "Suttons Addition" – from (N) Abbott	115
William Arrington	pt. "Studs Point" – for h/o John Danolin married the coheirs of James Trayman	50
John Camper	pt. "Lostock"	50
	pt. "Lewis"	145
John Hunt	"Content"	98
	"Fools Parradice"	38
	"Divine St. Andrew"	200
Thomas Lurty	"Barkins Point"	100
	"Lanchasshire"	50
46:1744:41 ...		
Elizabeth Collison	"Rehobeth"	50
	"Rehobeth Point"	50
George W. Haddaway	pt. "Lostock"	172
Peter Caulk	pt. "Lostock"	100
	"Corks Addition"	236
	"Kerseys Good Luck"	37
John Auld	"Newport Glascoe"	22½
Thomas Adcock	"Coopers Lott"	52
John Porter	"Friths Neck" – from (N) Valliant	50
Robert Dawson	"Dawsons Composition on Resurvey"	282
Lawrance Porter	"York" – from (N) Fairbank	100
John Pooter	"Union" – from (N) Sandsberry	50

46:1744:42 ...		
Edward Hopkins	pt. "Devonport & Beach", "Elliotts Lott", & "Stopper" – from (N) Ashcroft & wife on 30 July 1737	100
Mr. William Goldsborough	pt. "Hyer Dyer Loyd"	342
Nicholas Benson	"Bogg Hole"	50
	"Bensons Choice"	90
	pt. "Bensons Enlargement"	45
Philip Skinner	pt. "Enlargement"	50
	"Skinners Point"	50
	"Skinners Addition"	23
	"Skinners Discovery"	70
John Hughes	pt. "Devenport & Beach"	12
	pt. "James Progress"	35
	"Chance"	100
	"Taylors & James Discovery"	100
Bartholomew Roberts	"Punions Range" – to your father from (N) Williams	50
	"Roberts Addition"	47
Robert Dodson	pt. "Bensons Enlargement"	114½
46:1744:43 ...		
John Fairbank	pt. "York"	51
	"Bellfast"	100
	"Campers Neck"	100
	"Jones Hole"	36
	"Fairbanks Choice"	195
	"Fairly"	100
	"Good Happ"	23
	pt. "Bradford"	6
Nicholas Bartlett	pt. "Bartletts Inheritance"	110
Maj. Risdon Bozman	"Watson & Partnership" – from (N) Knowles	150
	"Hemersby on Resurvey"	273
	"Sherwoods Neck"	268
	"Folly"	100
	"Neglect"	34
	"Watson's Addition"	73

Feddeman Rolle	resurvey of pt." Lancaster", pt. "Addition", "Feddemans Chance", "Fortune", "Hazard", "Warrington", & "Discovery"	237
	"Dorothys Enlargement"	45
	resurvey of "Cabbin Neck, Sandy Bite, & Halls Fortune"	238
	pt. "Grafton Manner"	28
John Harrison	pt. "Lostock"	172
	pt. "Miles End" – for h/o William Cooper	75
	"Harrisons Security"	167
46:1744:44 ...		
Daniel Lambden	pt. "Sands Lott"	50
	"Bridges on Resurvey"	176
William Bandy	"Adventure" – from (N) Willen	70
John Harrington	"Hatten Garden"	50
William Webb Haddaway	"Rich Neck" pt. "Grafton Mannor"	150
	"Haddaways Lott" pt. "Grafton Mannor"	73
	"Merchants Folly"	150
	"Miles End"	250
Joseph Hopkins	"Rays Point"	150
	"Enlargement"	50
	pt. "Snelings Delight"	150
Joseph Dawson	pt. "Lostock"	150
William Lambden	pt. "William & Marys Addition"	52
	"Summerton"	200
	"Winterton"	50
46:1744:45 ...		
Thomas Smith (schoolmaster)	pt. "Goose Neck" & pt. "Grafton Manner" – from (N) Lambden	100
John Lambden	pt. "Grafton Mannor"	100
Thomas Cummings	"Knave Keep Out"	180
	"Lurty" – from (N) Lurty	50
John Porter, Jr.	"Wellings Good Luck"	65
John Ball	"Long Point"	50
	"Long Neck"	180
	"Benjamins Lott"	100
Henry Swording	pt. "Kemps Lott Addition"	26

William Harrison (bayside)	"Poplar Neck"	58
	"Mount Missery Addition"	12
	pt. "Mount Missery"	25
	pt. "Prouse Point" & pt. "Haphazard"	12
	pt. "Bensons Enlargement"	190
Thomas Haddaway	"Haddaways Addition"	75
46:1744:46 ...		
James Caulk	pt. "Lewis"	145
John Wiles	"Bantly Hay"	50
Mr. Daniel Sherwood	"Lurkeys Hill"	100
	"Beggars Hall"	36
	"Anstell"	440
	"Cabbin Neck", "Potters Lott", & "Potters Delight"	150
	pt. "Bradford"	56
John Lowe	pt. "Grafton Mannor Resurveyed"	245
	"Piney Neck"	107
	"Haddaways Lott"	50
	pt. "Fishburns Lott"	100
	pt. "Ratcliffe Mannor"	150
h/o Mr. James Dawson	"Crommell" – from (N) Hawkins	300
	"Cudlington"	400
	"Cudlingtons Addition"	50
	"Cudlingtons Increase"	50
	"Poplar Neck"	50
	"Baylys Forrest"	113
Robert Harrison	pt. "Haphazard"	50
	pt. "Crooked Intention"	50
Charles Bridges	"Bloyden"	10[illegible]
46:1744:47 ...		
Richard Feddeman	"Feddemans Discovery"	40[illegible]
Robert Larrymore h/o Alexander Larrymore	"Larrymores Neck"	10[illegible]
	"Bampshire"	5[illegible]
h/o William Hambleton (cnp)	~~"Wettstone"~~ "Williston"	22[illegible]
	"Mortenham"	20[illegible]
	"Hambletons Addition"	10[illegible]
	"Cambridge"	10[illegible]

	pt. "Adventure" – from (N) Grace	113½
Francis Porter	pt. "Hemersby"	100
h/o Francis Sherwood	"Sherwoods Island"	20
	"Middle Neck"	100
	½ "Mount Missery"	50
	"Huckleberry Garden"	125
John Leeds	"Wades Point"	400
	pt. "Hatton"	410
	"Long Delay"	34
	pt. "Scarbrough"	200
	pt. "Hatton"	90
Robert Sands	pt. "Sands Lott"	103
	pt. "Chance"	25
46:1744:48 ...		
John Kemp	"Bolten"	100
	"Boltens Addition"	50
	"Woolfe Harbour"	62
	"Hunt Keep Out"	28
h/o James Spencer, Jr.	pt. "Bensons Enlargement"	187
	"Fox Harbour"	50
	pt. "Edwards Hopewell"	45
Rev. Henry Nicols	"Micklemire"	230
	pt. "Maiden Point", "Maiden Point Addition", "Witherses Range", & "Little Neck" – from (N) Benson	300
	pt. "Gallaway"	96
	pt. "Partnership"	500
	"Bolden"	225
	pt. "Bite"	15
	"Forked Neck" – for the Vestry	50
	pt. "Hopkins's Point" – from Denis Hopkins	86
	pt. "Bryans Lott"	12
Daniel Vinton	"Edwards Hopewell"	55
h/o Edmund Fish, Jr.	"Garterlymore" – from your father	120
Susannah Slaughter	pt. "Middle Spring" – by will of your husband William Parrott, made 8 May 1720	50
46:1744:49 ...		

Charles Spencer	½ "Mainsaile"	49
	½ "Fairplay"	25
	"James's Progress"	35
	pt. "Newport Glassgo"	36½
Joseph Harrison	pt. "Crooked Protection"	80
William Kemp	"Mable"	100
	"Mables Addition"	50
	"Kemps Lott"	100
	pt. "Kemps Lott Addition"	26
John Hopkins	pt. "Beach", "Elliotts Lott", "Elliotts Folly", & "Harley" – from (N) Ashcroft on 29 July 1735	100
Thomas Ashcroft, Jr.	pt. "Devenport", "Beach", & "Elliotts Lott" – from (N) Ashcroft on 29 July 1737	380
h/o Thomas Studham	½ "Fairplay" – from (N) Bartlet & (N) Spencer	25
	pt. "Mainsail" – from Charles Spencer	49
Henry Richardson	"Pasty Neck"	24
William Edmondson	"Addition" – from (N) Clayton	200
46:1744:50 ...		
James Benny	pt. "Morgans Neglect", pt. "Rumsey Forrest", pt. "Morgans Addition – for h/o Hugh Morgan	106
	pt. "Rumsey Forrest"	786
	pt. "Faulkners Square"	100
Mrs. Mary Davis	"Hope Chance"	50
	"Knave Keep Out"	50
	"Parsonage"	100
	"Batchellors Point"	100
	"Addition"	350
John Davis	pt. "Ashby"	147
	pt. "Bettys Cove"	2[illegible]
Capt. Thomas Bruff	"Daniells Addition"	7[illegible]
	pt. "Walkers Tooth"	4[illegible]
	pt. "Daniels Rest"	3[illegible]
Mr. Richard Bruff	pt. "Walkers Tooth"	10[illegible]
	pt. "Daniels Rest"	1[illegible]
	"Partnership"	9[illegible]
	"Walkers Corner"	1[illegible]
	"Millington"	

Mr. Richard Lloyd	"Faulkners Folly"	100
	"New Design Betttys Branch"	325
	"Stock Range"	200
	<n/g> – another tract of (N) Woolman	150
46:1744:51 ...		
James Hollyday, Esq.	pt. "Brittania" & pt. "Stevens's Plains"	150
John Carslake	½ "Newmans Lott"	100
	"Bartram"	50
	"Wobbly"	300
	"Sarahs Neck"	50
	"Carslakes Discovery"	509
	"Carslakes Content"	60
	pt. "Nobles Chance"	18
William Benny	pt. "Rumsey Forrest", pt. "Bennys Addition", & pt. "Bennys Thickett"	78¾
John Benny	pt. "Rumsey Forrest", pt. "Bennys Thicket", & pt. "Bennys Addition"	78¾
Robert Harwood	"Lloyds Addition"	120
	pt. "Addition"	80
	pt. "Harwoods Neglect"	27
Ralph Dawson	pt. "Elstons Hazard"	49
	"Jones Lott Addition"	50
	"Jones Lott"	50
Thomas Wilson	pt. "Kingsberry"	70
46:1744:52 ...		
h/o John Lenard	pt. "William & James"	25
	pt. "Hopkins's Point Addition"	25
Edward Starkey	"Bite the Biter" – for h/o William Harper	35
John Studham	"Studhams Chance"	18
Capt. Thomas Bullen	"Lurkey" – for h/o John Wrightson	250
	pt. "Galloway" – for h/o John Wrightson	54
	pt. "Bryan Lott" – for h/o John Wrightson	12
	"Wrighson Addition" – for h/o John Wrightson	83
David Fitzpatrick	pt. "Adventure"	100
John Robinson (cnp)	"Robinsons Begining"	17
	"Long Point"	250

	pt. "Goldsborough"	87
Abner Parratt	pt. "Jamaicoe"	100
Catherine Barratt	pt. "Hopkins's Point"	66½
Mrs. Margaret Ward	"Rich Neck Resurveyed"	577
	"Henrietta Marias Purchase"	412
	"Cart Road"	138
46:1744:53 ...		
Mr. Matthew Tilghman	pt. "Union"	611
	"Choptank Island"	1468
	"Three Necks"	165
	"Wells Outlett"	50
Henry Henrix, Jr.	pt. "Partnership" – from (N) Dulin	37
Thomas Matthews	pt. "Bedwart" & pt. "Rich Farm Addition" – from (N) Shield	83
	pt. "Bloomsbury"	44
John Thornton	"Morefields Addition"	65
Edmond Marsh	pt. "White Phillips"	87½
Christopher Spry	pt. "Partnership" – from (N) Benson	54
Samuel Bartlett	pt. "Ratcliffe Mannor"	100
Francis Wrightson	"Jordans Folly"	100
	"Clays Neck"	102
	"Gaskins Point"	50
46:1744:54 ...		
George Nix	pt. "Middle Spring"	150
Rowland Haddaway	"Fishbourns Landing"	104
Solomon Robinson, Jr.	pt. "Chance"	129
William Parrott	pt. "Canterburys Mannor"	105
Samuel Prichard	pt. "Hutchinsons Addition" – for h/o Thomas Abbott	100
Mrs. Margaret Edmondson	pt. "Edmondsons Difficulty" a/s "Cooks Hope"	350
	pt. "Desier Hewarth"	117½
	pt. "Edmondsons Difficulty"	301
	pt. "Desires Addition"	20
	pt. "Enlargement"	33⅓
	pt. "Jacks Cove"	16¾
	pt. "Tilghmans Fortune"	175¾

William Nayler	pt. "Brittania"	150
46:1744:55 ...		
Pollard Edmondson	pt. "Desire & Hewarth"	235
	pt. "Edmondsons Difficulty"	602
	pt. "Desires Addition"	40
	pt. "Enlargement"	76
	pt. "Jacks Cove"	34¼
	pt. "Tilghmans Fortune"	349
Isaiah Parrott	pt. "Canterberrys Mannor"	315
James Harrison	pt. "Poplar Neck"	42
	pt. "Prous Point", "Haphazard", & "Faresaile"	38
George Brinsfield	"Middle Neck"	200
Robert Porter	pt. "Hemersby"	100
John Mears	"White Phillips"	100
Mrs. Elizabeth Pemberton	pt. "Partnership" (QA)	670
46:1744:56 ...		
Samuel Chamberlain, Esq. (from f. 26)	pt. "Plain Dealing"	100
	"Endeavour"	50
	"Grundys Lott"	46
	"Stephens's Range"	186
	pt. "Hopkins's Point"	7¼
	"Hookland"	100
	"Northumberland"	61
	pt. "Arcadia" & pt. "Abrahams Lott"	100
	"Rest Content"	100
	"Goodwins Addition"	90
	"Enlargement"	71
	pt. "Chance"	46
	pt. "Elmis Addition" & pt. "Lobbs Corner"	83
	"Clays Addition"	50
	pt. "Cumberland"	150
	pt. "Tilghmans Fortune"	75
William Alexander	"Irish Freshes" – for h/o John Alexander	50
	"Alexanders Chance" – for h/o John Alexander	250
	pt. "Wales" – for h/o John Alexander	54
	"Lowes Good Luck" – for h/o John Alexander	100

Charles Gannon	pt. "Bloomsbury"	44
Thomas Barnet, Jr.	pt. "Hoghole"	142
Phebe Turner	pt. "Johns Hill"	90
46:1744:57 ...		
James Walker	pt. "Jamaco"	92
Elizabeth Fedeman	pt. "Londonderry" – for h/o Philip Fedeman	3
Peter Hunt	"Larimors Addition"	50
Richard Mansfield	"Wisbick"	60

48:1748:1 ...		**Acres**
Thomas Lane	pt. "Waterton"	290
	"Poplar Hill"	200
	pt. "Normanton"	767
	pt. "Bettys Dowry"	2
	pt. "Kings Neglect"	107
William Finey	"Fineys Range"	225
	pt. "Waterton"	170
Philip Emerson	½ "Widows Choice"	320
	"Harwoods Lyon"	600
	pt. "Wettstone"	150
	"Hambletons Park"	263
	"Keilding & Buckinham"	393
	"Addition"	63
George Noble	pt. "Planters Delight"	100
	"Nobles Addition"	150
	pt. "Nobles Ridge"	75
Oliver Millington	pt. "Betts Chance"	100
	"Epsom"	100
48:1748:2 ...		
James Edge	"Prevention"	50
	"Whartons Glade"	50
	"Couple Close"	100
	"Addition"	32
	"Scraps"	60
Nathaniel Santee	"Chance"	100
	"Knave Stand Off"	50
Mesech Bodfield	"Tanners Hope"	50
	"Roberts Infancy"	65
	"Grasons Discovery" – resurveyed 3 October 1742	106½
	½ "Parsonage Addition"	50
	½ "Kings Plains"	79
	½ "Kings Forrest"	75
48:1748:3 ...		
Robert Loyd (cnp)	"Pick Borne"	200
	"Elliots Discovery"	100

	"Adjunction"	50
	"Scotland"	50
	"Loyds Discovery"	96
	"Hope" – from (N) Collins	100
	pt. "Partnership"	1200
	"Widows Chance"	50
	"Tallisawn"	100
	"Rumbleys Marsh"	300
	"Murray"	150
	"Partnership"	310
	"New Mill"	200
	"Addition"	100
	"Buckland Marsh"	50
	"Buckland"	250
	pt. "Gurlington"	100
	"Grundys Inclosure"	171
	pt. "Markland" a/s "Marsh Land"	265
Richard Skinner	"Tanners Choice"	340
	"Skinners Borders"	100
	"Skinners Vineyard"	75
	"Skinners Addition"	150
	"Skinners Security"	103
h/o Lewis Jones	"Tryangle"	100
	~~"Dirty Weeden Addition"~~	~~158~~
48:1748:4 ...		
Perry Benson	pt. "Huntington"	150
	"Neglect"	96
	pt. "Partnership"	321
	pt. "Fishing Bay"	188
William Trippe	⅓ "Leath"	13½
	⅓ "Edmondton"	100
	⅓ "Champenham & Bendon"	189
	"Rebecca's Garden"	150
	⅓ "Champenham Addition"	16¾
	pt. "Bryans Lott"	12½

William Garey	"Dirty Weeden"	100
	"Fortunes Addition"	52
	"Little Brittain"	150
	"Todd Upon Dirvin"	80
Mrs. Francis Elbert	pt. "Rebecca's Garden"	25
	"Loyds Costine"	659
	pt. "Rebecca's Garden" – from Mr. (N) Loyd	25
	pt. "Grantham"	106
James Sanders & John Pitts	pt. "Hambletons Park"	137
	"Damses Outlett"	50
Ferdinando Callaghan	pt. "Brittania" – from Mary & Elizabeth Williams	100
48:1748:5 ...		
Jonathan Gibson	⅓ "Leath"	13½
	⅓ "Edmondton"	100
	⅓ "Champenham & Bendon"	189
	⅓ "Champenham Addition"	16¾
Woolman Gibson	⅓ "Leath"	13½
	⅓ "Edmondton"	100
	⅓ "Champenham & Bendon"	189
	⅓ "Champenham Addition"	16¾
Robert Stonestreet	"Tilbury" – a resurvey of "Duns Range Addition" 19 September 1744	376
John & Andrew Kinnimont	"Fools Paradise"	50
	pt. "Bartram"	150
	"Bachelors Hope"	50
	"Hopewell"	80
	"Scotts Lott"	100
	"Kenemonts Delight"	168
William Cole	"Hilsdon"	200
	"Costins Chance"	32
	pt. "Brittania"	230
James Horney	"Batchelors Branch"	100
	"Batchelors Branch Addition" a/s "Addition to Batchelors Branch"	100
48:1748:6 ...		

Robert Hall	"Halls Range"	353
	pt. "Partnership"	10
William Warner	pt. "Nobles Chance"	82
Thomas Keet	~~pt. "Brittania" &~~ pt. "Stevens's Plains"	50
Col. Edward Lloyd	"Meersgate"	300
	"Thimbrys Grange"	500
	"Natts Points"	50
	"Lynton"	600
	"Grange"	150
	"Walters Marsh"	100
	"Long Neglect"	133
	"Meersgate Addition"	267
	pt. "Crouches Chance"	50
	"Inlett"	88
	"Roadway"	50
	"Addition"	100
	"Scots Close" – from (N) Stuart	200
	pt. "Woolmans Hermitage"	55
	pt. "Woolmans Inheritance"	104
	"Soldiers Delight"	100
	"Loyds Addition to Brerely" – resurveyed 1 July 1745	380
	"Bennetts Kind Caution" – resurveyed 12 May 1743	322¾
	½ "Kings Plains"	79
	½ "Kings Forrest"	75
	"Outlett"	220
	"Knightlys Addition"	50
	"Personage Addition" – omit	50
	½ "Timberr Neck"	60
48:1748:7 ...		
Samuel Kinnimont	⅓ "Dundee"	133
Aaron Higgs	"Pattingham"	10[illegible]
	"Skips Springs"	5[illegible]
	"Skinners Swineyard"	20[illegible]

William Shield & James Sanders	~~pt. "Bedworth"~~	~~100~~
	~~pt. "Rich Farm"~~	~~200~~
	pt. "Rich Farm" & pt. "Bedworth"	97
Isaac Faulkenor	"Faulkenors Level"	150
Richard Gibson	pt. "Gallaway"	64
	pt. "Bryans Lott"	12½
	½ "Timber Neck"	60
	½ "Bettys Dowry"	75
	pt. "Addition"	50
Francis Pickrin, Jr.	"Sarahs Lott"	50
Thomas Ray	pt. "Dundee"	133
	pt. "Addition" – for son of William Edmonson	100
John Williams	pt. "Carters Inheritance"	100
48:1748:8 ...		
George Beswicks	pt. "Christophers Lott Resurveyed"	286¼
	pt. "Stevens Plains"	50
	pt. "Nobles Ridge" – omit	75
Richard Beswicks	pt. "Christophers Lott"	100
	pt. "Stevens Plains"	50
Vincent Lockerman	pt. "Harrises Lot"	111
Mr. William Hemsley	"Hemsly Upon Wye"	1160
	"Hemsley Upon Wye Addition"	146
Samuel Hopkins	pt. "William & James"	33
	pt. "Maxwell Moore"	100
	"Elm"	90
Daniel Dulany, Esq.	pt. "Woolmans Hermitage"	109
	pt. "Woolmans Inheritance"	206
48:1748:9 ...		
Richard Bennett, Esq. (cnp)	"Morgans Saint Michaels"	300
	"Marron"	130
	"Claybourne Island"	700
	½ "Abbington"	100
	pt. "Whettstone"	150
	"Town Road"	50
	"Henrietta Maria's Discovery"	216
	"Lobbs Crook on Resurvey"	679

	pt. "Crouches Choice"	100
	"Farme"	348
	"Swettnams Hope"	120
	"Batchelors Delight"	100
	"Hern Island"	75
	"Bodwells Indian Neck Resurveyed"	913
	"Winkleton"	185
	"Mitchels Lott"	200
	"Tryangles"	55
	"Advantage"	500
	"New Town"	100
	"Planters Increase, Turners Ridge, et.al. Resurveyed"	504
	"Poplar Neck" – on escheat	249
	"Neglect" – on resurvey	107
	"Kimballs Industry"	383
	"Carters Inheritance"	300
	"Tobacco Pipe & Hackers Oldfield" – surveyed 19 January 1742	745
	"Elizabeth Ventur" – resurveyed 1 October 1740	1191
48:1748:10 ...		
Joseph Atkinson	"Skipton"	300
	pt. "Fineys Hermitage"	200
	"Atkinsons Chance"	43
Robert Blunt (KI)	"Harrises Range"	400
Elizabeth Edwards	"Mistake"	51
	pt. "Huntington"	180
	pt. "Huntington Grange"	2
Mary Davis	pt. "Huntington"	130
	"Hope Chance"	5
	"Knave Keep Out"	5
	"Parsonage"	10
	"Bachelors Point"	10
	"Addition"	35
	pt. "Addition"	8
	pt. "Fishing Bay" – from "Addition to Huntington"	1

Mr. William Dawson	"Batchelors Range"	250
	"Batchelors Range Addition"	463
	"Hatton Hope"	100
	pt. "Shigleys Fortune"	170
	pt. "Gallaway"	100
	pt. "Huntington" & pt. "Addition"	90
William Haddin	pt. "Ramsey Forrest"	107
48:1748:11 ...		
Vincent Jones	pt. "Nobles Choice" a/s "Chance"	89
Joseph Kinnemont	⅓ "Dundee"	133
Thomas Gully	pt. "Ashby"	150
Peter Harwood	"Harwoods Hill"	100
	"Poplar Levell"	100
	"Mill Road" & "Mill Road Addition"	150
	"Mill Road Addition" – from (N) Smithson	80
	"Addition" – from (N) Blake	320
	pt. "Cottingham"	150
	"Cornwhiton"	200
Adam & Richard Eubanks	pt. "Omelys Range"	150
	"Jacob & Johns Pasture"	120
h/o John Tibbles – the same as to Peter Caulk (f. 48)	pt. "Sheepshead Point"	50
	"Tibbles Addition"	20
Thomas Robson	"Jones Lookout"	50
	pt. "Partnership"	125
James Hopkins	pt. "Hopkins Point"	100
	"Hopkins Point Addition"	25
	pt. "Partnership"	65
48:1748:12 ...		
John Barwick	"Newmans Folly" – from (N) Williams	50
	"Story Lott" – from (N) Story	56
	"Discovery"	331
Abednego Bodfield	"Bettys Cove Addition"	50
	"Addition"	50
	pt. "Bettys Cove"	30
Jane Hetherington	"Hethringtons Delight"	50
Samuel Attwell	pt. "Bantry"	200

John Bartlett	"Rockney Nook Addition"	50
Matthew Kirby	"Swamp Hole"	100
Jacob Faulkener	"Faulkenors Hazard"	60
James Merrick	"Hazard Addition"	9
	"Powells Hazard" – from (N) Powell	50
Philip Banning	"Faulkenors Square"	50
48:1748:13 ...		
James Webb	"Rockne Nook"	25
Isaac Dixon	pt. "Cottingham" – from (N) Abrahams	25
	pt. "Cottingham" – from (N) Newton	50
	"Bennits Hill"	50
	"Ending Controversie"	150
	pt. "Ashby"	60
	pt. "Dixons Outlett"	150
Samuel Cockayne	pt. "Saint Michaels Fresh Run"	401
Thomas Pirkins	~~pt. "Controversy"~~ pt. "Carters Farm"	400
	"Perkins Discovery"	193½
Mary Harwood	pt. "Carters Farm"	100
Jacob Hindman	pt. "Harington" & pt. "Kirkham"	200
	pt. "Kirkham"	273
Morris Oram	pt. "Waistland" & "Bartlett Tryangle"	40
	pt. "Fox Hole"	145
	pt. "Fox Harbour"	50
	"Fox Den"	56
	"Waterford"	100
48:1748:14 ...		
John Potts	<n/g> – near Carters Bridge "St. Mich Fresh Run"	15
	pt. "Saint Michaels Fresh Run"	60
	"Potts Discovery"	60½
Elizabeth Eubanks	"Swifts Chance"	80
	"Jacob & Johns Pasture"	50
John Lockerman	pt. "Kirkham" & pt. "Harrington"	147
Francis Stanton	pt. "Bantry"	100
Henry Henrix	pt. "Mount Hope"	35
Free School of Talbot County	pt. "Tilghmans Fortune"	100

William Thomas	pt. "Cottinham" – from (N) Chew	140
	pt. "Cottinham" – for your wife	125
	"Morefields"	280
	pt. "Cottingham" – from (N) Horney	50
	pt. "Anderton"	100
Henry Burges	"Bobbs Hill"	100
	"Hopewell"	50
48:1748:15 ...		
James Ratcliffe	"Ratcliffe Highway"	113
	pt. "Jacob & Johns Pasture"	85
	pt. "Addition" – from (N) Cockayne	52
	pt. "Jacob & Johns Pasture"	85
	"Maple Branch"	40
John Neighbours	pt. "Edmondsons Freshes"	50
Nicholas Goldsborough, Jr.	pt. "Halls Neck" – from (N) Peck	100
	pt. "Halls Neck" – from your father	100
	"Conjunction Resurvey"	279
Joseph Hix	pt. "Ashford"	100
Francis Pickerin	pt. "Ashby"	100
Edward Perkins	"Newmans Range"	100
Thomas Spry	pt. "Maxwell Moore"	150
Anthony Lecompt	"Eatons Addition" & "Lobbs Corner"	83
	pt. "Cumberland"	50
	"Eatons Addition" – from (N) Eaton	68
	"Anthony Enlargement"	108
48:1748:16 ...		
Mr. James Tilghman	"Fosly"	250
	"Addition"	100
	"Edmunds Range"	400
	"Dixons Lott" a/s "Outlett"	50
	"Sharps Chance"	100
Joseph Arington	½ "Adventure"	113½
Richard Eaton	pt. "Fox Hole"	100
	pt. "Fox Harbour"	50
	"Etons Addition"	112

Peter Denny	pt. "Hopkins Point"	66¾
	"Clifton"	200
	"Denny Content"	85
James Millis	pt. "Adventure"	100
Richard Aldern	pt. "Yaffords Neck"	300
	"Roystone Addition"	150
	"Alderns Island"	41
William Harrison (Irish Creek)	½ "Ashford"	50
	"Long Neglect"	35
48:1748:17 ...		
Edmund Ferril	pt. "Stevens Range"	100
	pt. "Coventry" – from (N) Hopkins	60
	pt. "Coventry" – from (N) Hardin	40
	"Micklemier"	100
John Ratcliffe	"Gofston" – from (N) Fellows	100
Mrs. Elizabeth Davis	pt. "Tilghmans Fortune"	83
	"Sandfords Hermitage"	250
	"Sandfords Folly"	46
	"Bite the Biter"	35
	pt. "Ashby"	55
~~James Harvey~~	~~pt. "Hopkins Point"~~	~~66¾~~
James Harvey	"Abrahams Lott"	100
Thomas Winchester	"Marlins Folly"	50
	"Marlins Chance"	50
	"Bantry"	500
	"Spring Close"	100
	pt. "Bantry"	60
	pt. "Bantry's Addition"	10
	"Marlins Neglect"	57
	"Widows Chance"	320
Robert Newcomb	"Harbour Rouse Resurveyed"	130
	"Partnership Destruction"	66
48:1748:18 ...		
John Valiant	pt. "Yaffords Neck"	100
William Skinner	"Clays Hope"	200

Edward Harding	pt. "Bite"	13
	pt. "Tilghmans Fortune"	19
	"Hardins Endeavour"	200
Arthur Rigby	"Rigbys Folly"	45
	"Anderbys Addition"	78
	"Anderby"	100
	"Crafford"	100
	"Rigbys Discovery"	105
	pt. "Fox Hole"	65
	"Lamberton"	150
	"Rigbys Choice"	101½
	"Lambertons Addition" a/s "Lambeth Addition"	150
William Riggaway	"Westland"	100
Edward Elliot, Jr.	"Mecotter & Glover"	355
	"Point & Marsh"	50
Mrs. Frances Ungle	pt. "Room"	100
	"Gobston"	50
	"Old Womans Folly"	172
48:1748:19 ...		
Thomas Atkinson	pt. "Cottingham" – from (N) Abrahams	37
	pt. "Cottingham" – from (N) Jadwins	100
	"Newman" – from (N) Jadwins	50
Richard Hopkins	pt. "Nomine" – from (N) Firby	100
	pt. "Hopkins Point"	150
	pt. "White Philips" – from (N) Dickenson	42
Edward Elliot, Sr.	"Chance Resurveyed"	233
	pt. "Bensons Enlargement"	28¼
	"Sarah's Garden"	13
Thomas, John, & James Bartlett	pt. "Ratcliffe Mannor"	520
Andrew Orem	pt. "Adventure"	100
Samuel Harwood	"Sybland"	200
	"Maxfield"	52
	"Sybland Addition"	110
	pt. "Coalin"	100
Dennis Hopkins	pt. "Hopkins Point"	90

William Price	<n/g> – a tract of land adjoining "St. Michaels Fresh Run"	100
48:1748:20 ...		
Joseph Elliott	pt. "Coventry"	120
	pt. "Ratcliffe Choice"	79
Joseph Merrick	pt. "Batchelors Range Addition"	37
A. Andrew Henecy's wife h/o John Renolds	"Renolds Point"	98
George Eubanks	pt. "Omyly's Range"	50
	pt. "Harwoods Neglect"	11
Mr. John Goldsborough	"Peaks Marsh"	318
	"Marshy Peak"	132
	pt. "Four Square"	650
	"Goldsboroughs Tryangle"	45
	pt. "Thief Keep Out"	30
	pt. "Adventure"	100
	"Hogston"	100
Mr. Thomas Cockayne	pt. "Carters Plains"	294
John Braseron	pt. "Coventry" – from (N) Palmer	30
	pt. "Ratclife Choice"	30
Thomas Baynard	pt. "Smiths Clifts"	360
John Rathrell	"Straw Berry Field Addition"	50
	"Rathrell Chance"	50
48:1748:21 ...		
Samuel Broadway	"Ramah"	100
	"Sam's Field"	102
	"Strawbridge"	100
	"Broadways Meadows"	100
Edward Clarke	pt. "Parkers Farm"	350
	"Parrotts Lott"	82
	"Egg Point"	40
Joshua Clark	"Clarks Folly"	101
	pt. "Johns Neck"	118
Jonathan Airey	pt. "Roeclift"	118
	"Davids Ridge"	125

John Nailer	pt. "Duns Range"	100
	"Morefields Addition" – from (N) Swett	30
	pt. "Morefields"	10
William Michael	"Turners Hazard" & "Bullens Addition"	171
	pt. "Morgans Addition", pt. "Morgans Neglect", & pt. "Ramsay Forrest"	101
Sarah Loveday	"Middle Spring" – from (N) Trotter	150
Robert Lowther	"Beverdam Neck" – from (N) Skinner	70½
48:1748:22 ...		
John Tomlinson	pt. "Roeclift"	50
Rebecca Clarke	pt. "Parkers Range" – from (N) Jadwin	58
	"Highfield" – from (N) Webb	100
	pt. "Hampton" & pt. "Parkers Range"	200
	"Berry Range"	130
	"Highfield Addition"	150
Samuel Morgan	pt. "Dudlys Clift"	92
Aaron Parrott	pt. "Kingstown" – from (N) Wilson	51½
	pt. "Johns Neck"	264
John Small	"Summerly" – from (N) Russam for h/o Henry Oldfield	250
Ann Morgan	pt. "Morgans Neglect" & "Morgans Addition" – for h/o James Morgan	120
Michael Kirby	"Buck Range"	50
	"Buck Range Addition"	55
	pt. "Duns Range" – for your son	100
	"Bows Range Resurveyed"	205
	pt. "Duns Range"	50
Richard Kerwick	"Venture"	37
	½ "Dudlys Domains"	50
	"Kirbys Outlett"	47
48:1748:23 ...		
Charles Morgan	pt. "Chesnutt Bay"	95
	pt. "Dudlys Clifts"	92
Samuel Dudly	pt. "Advantage" – from (N) Powell	18
	"Bever Neck" – from Thomas Dudly	100
	pt. "Smiths Clifts"	94
	pt. "Hases Green" – from Thomas Dudly	50

William Warring	pt. "Hampton" – from (N) Jadwin	200
Sarah Morgan	"Holme Hill" – from (N) Corney	62
	pt. "Smiths Clifts"	258
Isaac Dopson	"Woolf Pitt Ridge"	33
	"Straw Berry Fields"	100
David Kirby	pt. "Turners Range"	40
	"Limbrick" – from your father	60
	"Kirbys Interest"	30
Frances Camperson	pt. "Hampton" & pt. "Parkers Range"	100
	"Frances Delight"	46
William Frampton	pt. "Rich Range"	50
	pt. "Rich Range" [!]	50
48:1748:24 ...		
John Walker	<n/g> a/s "Rich Farm" – on Kings Creek from (N) Berry	100
Robert Hunter	"Jacob Beginning"	50
	pt. "Dudlys Demains"	40
	pt. "Jacobs Beginning" – from (N) Sweney	60
Thomas Hutchinson	pt. "Johns Neck"	19
	pt. "Bugby" – from (N) Bradbury	200
Jacob Lockerman	"Nobles Meadows on Resurvey"	229
	"Betts Addition"	207
John Kannaday	"Cannadays Hazard"	29
	"Cannadays Addition"	23
Joseph Turner	pt. "Johns Hill"	180
	pt. "Turners Discovery"	92¼
Isaac Cox	pt. "Johns Hill"	90
	"Coxes Hazard"	103
Jonathan Tyler	pt. "Kingstown"	100
William Thorpe	pt. "Austen" – from (N) Larey	50
	pt. "Austen" – from (N) Keld	50
48:1748:25 ...		
James Kindret	"Coventry"	250
Thomas Thompson	pt. "Smiths Clifts"	94
Thomas Vickers	pt. "Charlevale"	50
	"Morefields" – from (N) Swett	84

William Vickers	"Piccadilla Resurveyed"	150½
Mr. Edward Needles	⅓ "Pitts Range"	200
	⅓ "Killim"	369
	pt. "Killim" – from (N) Sherwood	140
	pt. "Johns Neck"	4
	½ "Exchange"	100
	pt. "Roeclift"	50
James Wilson	pt. "Middle Spring"	50
	pt. "White Oak Swamp"	100
James Berry	pt. "White Marsh" pt. "Pitts Mill"	760
Thomas Dudly	pt. "Broad Laine"	103
	"Beaver Neck" – from h/o (N) Bachelor	141
John Herrington	pt. "Bugby"	150
48:1748:26 ...		
Francis Register	"Parrotts Reserve" – from (N) Parrott	150
Hannah Dopson	pt. "Dopsons Advantage"	28
	"Wargens Reserve"	200
George Sprouse	pt. "Cumberland" & pt. "Chance Help"	157
Dennis Larey	pt. "Partners Hazard" – from (N) Cook	142
	"Bever Dam Neck"	70½
Edward Slaughter	<n/g> pt. "Chesnut Bay" – bought of Philip Morgan	100
Thomas Turner	"Turners Chance"	100
Michael Kirby, Jr.	"Kirbys Addition"	49
Thomas Purnell	pt. "Hampton"	8
	pt. "Rich Range"	218
Joseph Durdin	"Kings Creek Marsh"	50
	pt. "Blissland"	100
	"Kingsberry"	130
	pt. "Turkey Neck"	100
	pt. "Hog Range"	47
	pt. "Turkey Neck"	16
48:1748:27 ...		
Mr. William Robins (cnp)	pt. "Smiths Clifts"	201
	pt. "Holm Hill"	34
	pt. "Holm Hill"	400

	pt. "Rich Range Addition"	14
	"Fragment"	13½
Mr. Grundy Pemberton	"Smiths Clifts"	232
	"Plins Addition" & "Lobbs Corner"	14
	pt. "Cumberland"	30
	pt. "Heworth"	205
Mr. Robert Goldsborough, Jr.	pt. "Rich Range"	140
	pt. "Rich Range Addition"	86
	pt. "Fragment"	6½
	"Peters Rest"	50
	"Annuel Peace" "St Michaels Fresh Run"	50
	"Chance"	50
	pt. "Cottingham"	150
	"Newmans Addition"	50
	"Benjamins Lott"	50
	"Fox Harbour"	148
	pt. "Ashby"	250
Andrew Bandy	pt. "Kingstown"	100
Henry Clift	"Dudlys Inclosure" – for h/o (N) Dudley	104
	pt. "Dudlys Addition" – for h/o (N) Dudley	37
Sarah Greenwood (widow)	pt. "Parkers Farm"	100
48:1748:28 ...		
John Register	"Kingsberry Addition"	100
John Baynard	pt. "Hampton" pt. "Parkers Range"	130
Daniel Ward	pt. "Summerly"	50
Isaac Williams	pt. "Maxfield"	100
	pt. "Dudlys Choice"	50
William Williams	pt. "Dudlys Choice"	50
Peter Commerford	½ "Johns Neck"	350
	"Solap" – for h/o (N) Parrott	167
	"Neglect"	126
Capt. Thomas Porter	½ "Johns Neck"	350
	½ "Boston Clift"	266
James Broadway	"Dudly"	200
James Dudly	"Dudlys Demeans"	115
Abner Dudly	pt. "Collyn"	200

John Plowman	pt. "Austin" – from (N) Keld	100
48:1748:29 ...		
Simon Keld	pt. "Alcoks Choice" – from (N) Keld	50
John Keld	pt. "Alcocks Choice" – from (N) Kield	50
William Brown Vickers	"Telltale's Loss"	125
	"Vickers Lott"	52
	pt. "Charlevale" & "Cork"	200
Anthony Booth	pt. "Bloomsberry"	100
Charles Gannon	pt. "Bloomberry"	44
Thomas Matthews	pt. "Bloomsberry"	44
Daniel Bradford	pt. "Johns Hill"	90
	"Roeclift"	50
Thomas Barrow	pt. "Ashby" & pt. "Bettys Cove"	92
James Parrott	"Abbington"	100
	pt. "Buckrow"	150
	pt. "Catlins Plains"	10
	"Walnutt Garden"	50
	"Hulls Addition"	100
William Martin	"Mitchams Hall"	300
	"Martins Purchase"	5¼
48:1748:30 ...		
Richard Bush	pt. "Arcadia"	166
Elijah Skillington	pt. "Turners Point"	100
Mr. Nicholas Goldsborough	pt. "Hyer Dier Loyd"	100
	"Ottwell"	500
	"Addition"	80
	pt. "Gressell"	122
	pt. "Partlett" – from (N) Ford	28
	pt. "Marshy Point"	157
	pt. "Partlett" – from (N) Ford	72
	pt. "Gressell" & pt. "Ottwell" – from (N) Ford	28
Kenelm Skillington	pt. "Turners Point"	100
	"Skillingtons Hap"	20
John Loyd	"Piney Point Advantage"	150
William Skinner, Jr.	"Skinners Lott"	33
	pt. "Bensons Enlargement"	150

Ferril Gallaher	pt. "Tilghmans Fortue"	88
William Marshall	"Kingsale" – from (N) Lane	126
Pearce Flemon	"Flemons Freshes on Resurvey"	215
48:1748:31 ...		
Solomon Sharp	pt. "Nomini"	302
	"Chance"	40
Samuel Sharp	pt. "Nomini"	200
	"Dicks Marsh"	200
	pt. "Discovery"	56
	pt. "Little Bristol"	986
	pt. "Scarborough"	200
Mrs. Rachel Taylor	"Piney Point"	150
	"Piney Point Advantage" – from (N) Alexander	100
	"East Ottwell"	400
	"Bullen" & "Bullens Addition"	356
	"Timothys Lott"	300
Michael Fletcher	"Darlington" – from (N) Green	110
	"Long Acre"	150
	"Sharps Choice" – from (N) Wintersill	200
	pt. "Richmond"	36
	"Richmonds Addition"	282
Mary Markland	pt. "Plemhemmon" or "Morgans Point"	50
James Millard	pt. "Canterberry Mannor"	130
	pt. "Canterberry Mannor" – from (N) Parrott	40
Thomas Browning	pt. "Hyer Dier Loyd"	80
	pt. "Hyer Dier Loyd" – from (N) Dawsey	75
48:1748:32 ...		
Mr. Samuel Chamberlaine (cnp)	pt. "Hyer Dier Loyd"	928
	pt. "Halls Neck"	286
	~~pt. "Coxes Addition"~~	~~73~~
	"Baronston"	106
	"Coxes Chance"	160
	"Contention"	100
	"Bishoprick"	100
	pt. "Four Square"	350
	"Gore"	45

	"Sheepshead Point"	196
	pt. "Bantry" a/s "Baintrees Addition"	50
	pt. "Plain Dealing"	100
	"Endeavour"	50
	"Grindys Lott"	46
	"Cabbin Neck"	50
	"Stephens Range"	186
	pt. "Hopkins Point"	7¼
	"Hookland"	100
	pt. "Yorkshire"	155
	pt. "Arcadia" pt. "Abrams Lott"	100
	"Rest Content"	100
	"Goodwins Addition"	90
	"Intention"	50
	"Rooking Nook" a/s "Rockey Nook"	75
	"Inlargement"	71
	pt. "Chance"	40
	pt. "Elm" & "Lobbs Corner"	83
	"Clays Addition"	50
	pt. "Cumberland"	100
	pt. "London Derry"	250
	pt. "Tilghmans Fortune"	75
	"Goose Neck"	50
	pt. "Abrams Lott" & "Mill Road Addition"	123
	pt. "Bensons Enlargment" – from (N) Bartlett	27
	pt. "Bartletts Inheritance"	30
	"Northumberland" – from Thomas Hill	61
48:1748:33 ...		
John Cooly	pt. "Lostock" – for h/o John Lowry	184½
Philip Jenkins	pt. "Edmondsons Freshes"	300
	pt. "Chesnutt Bay"	205
	pt. "Dudlys Clift"	16
James Barnes	"Boons Hope"	100
Gabriel Sailes	"Rich Range"	300
	"Dolp" a/s "Dolph"	100

Dr. William Sharp	"Morefields"	100
	"Adventure"	100
	"Easons Neck"	100
	"Fancy"	50
	"Conjunction"	25
	"Rattle Snake Point"	150
	"Mount Pleasure"	500
	"Easons Lott"	50
	"Sharps Addition"	24
	"Inclosure"	300
	pt. "Little Bristol"	320
Francis Parrott	"Lords Chance"	100
Joseph Parrott	pt. "Abrahams Lott", pt. "Millroad 2nd Addition", & pt. "Gouldston" – from (N) Fellows	230
William Harrison (Miles Creek)	pt. "Taylors Ridge"	100
48:1748:34 ...		
Nicholas Glen	pt. "Cooks Hope"	200
Adam Brown	pt. "Hier Dier Loyd"	100
	pt. "Parkers Point" pt. "Enlargement"	75
Mr. Edward Oldham	"Comsberry" – from (N) Rich	100
	"Piney Rum" a/s "Judith Garden" – from (N) Rich	130
	"Rich Park" – from (N) Rich	569
	pt. "Nether Foster" – from (N) Rich	50
	"Jacks Point"	100
	"Oldhams Discovery"	115½
Thomas Bozman	"Cardiffe" – from (N) Alexander	100
	"Providence"	7
	pt. "Timber Neck"	150
	"Browns Park"	119
	"Tates Lott on Resurvey"	459
	"Timber Neck on Resurvey"	294
	pt. "Desire & Heworth"	10
	pt. "Smiths Clifts"	12
Philip Martin	"Bullens Chance"	350
	pt. "Conjunction"	25

Thomas Martin, Sr.	pt. "Hyer Dier Loyd"	200
	"Hard Measure Resurveyed"	94
	"Attwell" – from (N) Parrott	100
	"Tawny Close" – from (N) Parrott	50
	pt. "Hier Dier Loyd"	58
	pt. "Hier Dier" – from (N) Bowdle	38
48:1748:35 ...		
Thomas Skillington	"Hambletons Neck"	300
Joseph Eason	pt. "Hier Dier Loyd"	75
John Coward	"Plenhemmon" – from (N) Rousby	600
John Pattison	pt. "Judiths Garden"	63
John Sherwood	"Allenbys Fields Resurvey"	124¾
Henry Clift	pt. "Taylors Ridge" a/s "Clifts Addition" – from (N) Harrison	100
	"Timber Necks Addition"	139
Henry Dallahay	pt. "Hier Dier Loyd"	125
Nicholas Lowe, Jr.	pt. "Anderton"	100
Joshua Hopkins	pt. "London Derry"	103
John Cox	"Spring Close"	50
48:1748:36 ...		
Ralp Elston	pt. "Edmondsons Freshes" pt. "Heworth"	110
	"French Hazard"	41
	"Stapleton"	77
	"Fish Hazard"	18
	"Fish Range" a/s "Fitches Range"	74
	"Contention"	120
w/o William Edmondson (DO)	pt. "Hyer Dier Loyd"	112
	pt. "Hier Dier Loyd" – from (N) Eason	170
	pt. "Hier Dier Loyd" – from (N) Evans	100
	pt. "Hier Dier Loyd" – on escheat	10
Francis Armstrong	"Surprize"	40
	"Discovery"	20
	"Huntington Grange"	100
	"Cornelius Cole Spring"	100
	pt. "London Derry"	132

Edward Sherwood	"Exchange" – from (N) Needles	100
	pt. "Highfields" – from (N) Russam	50
	⅓ "Pitts Range"	200
	pt. "Kellam"	229
John Love	pt. "Hatten"	63
Thomas Bowdle	pt. "Hier Dier Loyd"	104
John Jones (tanner)	pt. "Chance Help" & "Cumberland"	80
	pt. "Heworth" – from (N) Davis	40
48:1748:37 ...		
Mrs. Henrietta Maria Robins	"First Hazard"	358
	"Jobs Content"	1000
	pt. "Cooks Hope"	214
	pt. "Hulls Neck"	300
	"Jenings Hope"	718
	pt. "Marshy Point"	300
	pt. "Tilghmans Fortune"	445
	"Turkey Neck" a/s "Turkey Parks"	329
	pt. "Ratcliffe Mannor"	150
	pt. "Discovery"	60
	pt. "Canterberry Mannor"	100
	pt. "Desire & Heworth"	240
	"Buckinham"	903
	pt. "Turners Point"	200
	"Graves"	100
Thomas Skinner	pt. "Marshy Point"	100
Thomas Martin, Jr.	pt. "Wilderness" a/s pt. "Hyer Dier Loyd"	100
	"Rich Neck"	300
	pt. "Shrodick"	25
Jonathan Dopson	"Fork"	250
William Anderson	"Prospect"	125
	"Knaps Lott"	50
John Dickenson	pt. "Roadly"	150
	pt. "Scarborough" – from (N) Harrison	200
48:1748:38 ...		
John Carr (cnp)	"Millars Purchase"	100
	pt. "Lowes Rambles"	114

	"Gatherly Moore"	120
Richard Barnett	"Poor Hill"	37
	pt. "Sutton Grange"	100
	pt. "Sutton Grange"	100
James Barnwell	pt. "Bedworth"	100
	pt. "Mount Hope"	50
	pt. "Mount Hope" – from (N) Mills & (N) Bedworth	97
	pt. "Rich Farm Addition"	
Mr. Thomas Bullen	"Newellyn" – from (N) Brown	140
	pt. "Lords Gift" – form (N) Brown	100
	"Bullens Discovery"	136
	"Turbotts Fields"	168
	pt. "Marshland"	165
	pt. "Lords Gift" – from (N) Robinson	100
William Dickenson	"Hatton" – from (N) Dickenson	322
	"Brooked Lane" – from (N) Stapleford	116
	"Frankford Saint Michaels"	616
	pt. "Hatton" – from (N) Thomas	112
	pt. "Bildon"	30
	"Bernetts Freshes"	125
	pt. "Hatton"	25
Rev. Thomas Bacon	"Partnership"	34
	"Cross Haze"	50
48:1748:39 ...		
Mr. Daniel Maynidier	pt. "Goldsborough"	187
	"Tatter Hust"	38
	"Jamaico"	50
	pt. "Marshland"	70
	"Timothys Lott"	25
	"Hermitage"	90
	pt. "Fotrils Discovery"	93
William Ayres (cnp)	pt. "Studs Point"	100
	"Intention"	100
	pt. "Roadly"	80
	pt. "Hulls Neck"	50

	"Ayres Venture"	96
Richard Turbutt	pt. "Blessland" & "Baggs Marsh"	300
	pt. "Blessland" & "Baggs Marsh"	160
John Ferril	pt. "Mount Hope"	53
	pt. "Hawks Hill Addition"	50
	pt. "Mount Hope" – from (N) Cathrop	5½
David Robinson	pt. "Hull"	70
	"Davids Folly"	50
	"Chance"	23
Sarah Scenia	pt. "Sutton", pt. "Sutton Addition", & pt. "Partnership"	219
	pt. "Sutton" & pt. "Sutton Addition"	7
48:1748:40 ...		
Jeremiah Nicols	pt. "Partnership"	250
	pt. "Bettys Chance"	100
	pt. "Stevens Plains"	50
	pt. "Richmond"	4
Mr. Anthony Bacon	"Hasley"	200
	"Widows Lott"	85
	"Partners Hazard" – from (N) Cook	142
	"Browns Lott"	200
	pt. "Mount Hope"	50
	<n/g> – land adjoining to "Pitts Mills"	20
	pt. "Worgans Reserve"	300
	"Addition" – in His Lordships Mannor	229
	"Parkers Park"	500
	pt. "Dopsons Advantage"	7
	pt. "Turky Neck"	125
Thomas Barnett, Jr.	pt. "Hogg Hole"	142
William Mackey	"Holmby"	200
	pt. "Bulling"	66
	pt. "Broad Oak" – from (N) Chaplain	175
William Richardson	"Gurlington"	75
William Barker	pt. "Lower Dover" – in His Lordships Mannor	302
William Wilson	pt. "Middle Spring"	100
	pt. "Kingsberry"	70

48:1748:41 ...		
John & James Barnett	pt. "Bullen"	150
Jonathan Neal	pt. "Hiccory Ridge"	50
Robert Cutcart	"Cornelius Garden"	50
John Hixon	"Poplar Hill" – from (N) Bullen	57
	pt. "Hopkins Choice" – should be "Hopkins Chance"	21
	pt. "York"	153
William White	pt. "Sutton Grange"	287
	"Killingsworth"	50
Thomas Jenkins	pt. "Double Ridge"	120
	"Whites Gore"	40
	pt. "Sutton Grange"	120
William Taylor	pt. "Middle Spring"	25
	pt. "Turkey Neck"	243
Peter Shanahan	"Chance"	100
Sarah Webb	pt. "Roadly"	150
48:1748:42 ...		
James Corkerin	pt. "Hogg Hole"	142
	pt. "Discovery"	147
John Shaw	pt. "Hulls Neck"	150
John Hoult	pt. "Broad Oak"	25
Thomas Ayres	pt. "Millars Hope"	121
Edward Brenny	pt. "Parkers Point" & pt. "Inlargement"	75
	pt. "Parkers Point" & pt. "Inlargement" [!]	75
Elizabeth Jenkins	pt. "Patricks Ridge"	560
Thomas Barnett, Sr.	pt. "Patricks Ridge"	100
	"Swamptick"	100
	pt. "Sure Ditch"	75
James Chaplain	pt. "Broad Oak"	300
	"Enfield"	200
Thomas Stevens (cnp)	pt. "Compton"	80
	"Williams Lott"	49
	"Dudlys Choice"	100
	pt. "Catlins Plains"	166
	pt. "Buckroe"	34¼

	pt. "Dawsons Fortune"	34¼
	pt. "Edmondsons Cove"	116
	pt. "Compton"	14
	pt. "Coxes Addition"	70
48:1748:43 ...		
William Alexander	"Irish Freshes"	50
	"Alexander Chance"	250
	pt. "Wales"	54
	"Lowes Good Luck"	100
Trustram Thomas	pt. "Reedly"	200
	pt. "Sutton"	50
	pt. "Thief Keep Out"	36
	pt. "Sutton" & pt. "Sutton Addition"	47
	"Double Ridge"	150
	pt. "Double Ridge" – from (N) Lowe	80
John Glover	pt. "Mount Hope"	75
	½ "Upper Range"	50
Thomas Metcalfe	pt. "Sutton"	250
	"Suttons Addition"	50
	"Buckroe"	80
Mrs. Elizabeth Harrison	"Dover Resurveyed"	895
	"Dover Marsh"	348
	pt. "Roeclift"	170
	"Poplar Level"	116
Daniel Powell	"Rigbys Marsh"	300
Lemon John Cathrop	"Cathrops Security"	205
	pt. "Mount Hope"	61½
	pt. "Bugby"	50
48:1748:44 ...		
Mr. Samuel Dickenson (cnp)	"Cross Dower"	400
	"Samuels Lott"	600
	"Dickensons Lott Addition"	113
	"Powells Island"	55
	pt. "Wales"	46
	pt. "Lowes Good Luck"	54
	pt. "Compton"	10

	pt. "Mount Hope"	250
	pt. "Double Ridge"	50
	pt. "Nomine"	350
	pt. "Reedly"	200
	"Hobsons Choice"	100
	pt. "Canterberry Mannor"	250
	"Little Creek"	200
	"Coans Point"	300
	pt. "Hier Dier Loyd"	101
	"Dickensons Lott"	216
	pt. "White Philips"	150
	pt. "Salem", "Quillen", pt. "Stepney", & pt. "Cornelius Garden"	134
	pt. "Michaels Hermitage", pt. "Millers Hope", & pt. "Harbour Choice"	100
	pt. "Darington"	119
	pt. "Hopsons Choice"	120
	"Millers Chance"	85
	"Hunting Hills Resurveyed" – called "Fishers Chance"	125
48:1748:45 ...		
Morris Giddins	"New Scotland"	700
Thomas Powell	pt. "Bever Neck"	259
	pt. "Advantage"	42
	pt. "Roeclift"	100
	pt. "Broad Lane" & pt. "Bever Neck"	150
Hezekiah Maccotter	pt. "White Philips"	37½
John Higgins	"Boarams Ranger"	177
	pt. "Lowes Rambles"	28
Elizabeth Stevens	⅓ "Compton"	6¾
	⅓ "Edmonsons Cove"	58
	⅓ "Dawsons Fortune"	16¼
	⅓ "Buckroe"	16¼
	⅓ "Catlains Plaines"	80
Thomas Dellahay	"Dellahays Fortune" pt. "Taylors Ridge"	100
Samuel Abbott (cnp)	"Beverdam"	100
	"Huchinsons Addition"	50

	"Manor Lott"	100
Edward Neale	pt. "Manor Hope"	50
	pt. "Nanticoke Mannor"	171
	pt. "Mount Hope" – from (N) Ragon & wife	29
48:1748:46 ...		
Walter Jenkins	pt. "Patricks Ridge"	240
William Ardery	pt. "Mount Hope"	50
	pt. "Lowes Rambles"	200
Thomas Elsby	pt. "Parkers Point" & pt. "Enlargment"	75
William Mullican	pt. "Taylors Ridge" a/s "Mullicans Chance"	100
	pt. "York" – from (N) Hixon	150
	"Yorks Destruction"	50
Samuel Mullican	pt. "Patricks Plains"	90
	"Mullicans Delight"	63
Hugh Lynch	pt. "Mullicans Chance"	100
Patrick Mullikin	pt. "Patricks Plains"	210
	pt. "Taylors Ridge"	100
	"Sedenborough"	100
	"Plansly"	100
David Jones	"Wilderness" – from (N) Hardin	75
	"Jones Interest"	40
	pt. "Naps Lott"	100
Edward Hargoton	pt. "Patricks Ridge"	100
48:1748:47 ...		
Henry Harris	"Cornwell"	100
	"Joseph's Lott"	100
William Adams	pt. "Hatfield" pt. "Hatfield Addition"	50
Terence Connerly	"Hollands Addition"	41
	"Kingstown"	400
	pt. "Mullicans Choice"	70
William Carey	pt. "Partnership"	18
	pt. "Sutton" & pt. "Sutton's Addition"	115
William Arington	pt. "Studs Point"	50
John Hunt	"Content"	98
	"Fools Paradise"	38
	"Divine Saint Andrew"	200

Thomas Lurty	"Parkers Point"	100
	"Lancashire"	50
George Haddaway	pt. "Lostock"	102
John Satchel	pt. "Discovery" – from (N) Corkrin	200
48:1748:48 ...		
Peter Caulk	"Corks Addition Resurveyed" pt. "Lostock"	236
	pt. "Ashby" pt. "Bettys Cove"	37
	pt. "Sheepshead Point"	50
	"Tibbles Addition"	20
John Auld	"Newport Glasgow"	221½
Thomas Adcock	"Coopers Lott"	52
John Porter	"Friths Neck"	50
Robert Dawson	"Dawsons Composition"	282
Lawrence Porter	"York" – from (N) Fairbank	100
John Poor	"Union" – from (N) Sandsberry	50
Edward Hopkins	pt. "Devint Port, Beach, Elliots Lott, & Stopper"	100
Mr. William Goldsborough	pt. "Hyer Dier Loyd"	342
Nicholas Benson	"Bogg Hole"	50
	"Bensons Chance"	90
	pt. "Bensons Enlargment"	43
48:1748:49 ...		
Philimon Skinner	pt. "Enlargement"	50
	"Skinners Point"	50
	"Skinners Addition"	23
	"Skinners Discovery"	70
William Matthews	⅓ "Woolsey Mannor"	333⅓
William Edmonson	pt. "Woolsey Mannor"	666⅔
John Hughs	pt. "Devint Port & Beach"	12
	pt. "James Progress"	35
	"Chance"	100
	"Taylors & James Discovery"	100
Bartholomew Roberts	"Ennions Range"	50
	"Roberts Addition"	47
John Fairbank (cnp)	"Belfast"	100
	"Camper Neck" a/s "Camphier's Neck"	100
	"Jones Hole"	36

	"Fairbank Chance"	195
	"Fairly"	100
	"Good Hap"	23
	pt. "Bradford"	6
Charles Gorsage	pt. "Bensons Enlargement"	114½
48:1748:50 ...		
Mr. Risdon Bozman	"Wattson & Partnership"	150
	"Hemersby"	270
	"Sherwoods Neck"	268
	"Folly"	100
	"Neglect"	34
	"Wattsons Addition"	73
	pt. "Lewis" – from (N) Camper	145
	"Gaskins Point"	50
	"Lurky"	250
	pt. "Gallaway"	54
	pt. "Bryans Lott"	12½
	"Wrightsons Addition"	83
Mrs. Margarett Lowe	pt. "Anderton"	400
	pt. "Lower Rambles"	1008
	"Andertons Addition"	100
Fedemon Roles	pt. "Lancashire" & pt. "Addition, Feddemans Chance, Fortune Hazard, Warington, & Discovery" – resurveyed	237
	"Dorythys Enlargement"	45
	"Cabin Neck, Sandy Bite, & Halls Fortune" – resurveyed"	238
	pt. "Grafton Mannor"	28
	"Hoopers Insell"	200
William Cooper	pt. "Lostock"	172
	"Harrisons Security"	167
48:1748:51 ...		
Daniel Lambdon	pt. "Sands Lott"	50
	"Bridges on Resurvey"	176
William Stevans	pt. "Catlins Plains"	250
	pt. "Catlins Plains"	160
William Bandy	"Adventure"	70

John Herrington	"Hatton Garden"	50
Webb Haddaway	"Rich Neck" pt. "Grafton Mannor"	150
	"Haddaways Lott" pt. "Grafton Mannor"	73
	"Merchants Folly"	150
	"Miles End"	250
Henry Lowe	"Wintersill"	145
	pt. "Anderton"	100
Joseph Hopkins	"Rays Point"	150
	"Enlargment"	50
	pt. "Delight Snellings"	150
Joseph Dawson	pt. "Lostock"	150
William Lambdon	pt. "William & Marys Addition"	52
	"Summerton"	200
	"Winterton"	50
48:1748:52 ...		
Thomas Smith	pt. "Goose Neck" & pt. "Grafton Mannor"	100
John Porter, Jr.	"Willings Good Luck"	60
John Ball	"Long Point"	50
	"Long Neck"	180
	"Benjamin Lott"	100
Henry Swording	pt. "Kemps Lott Addition"	26
William Harrison	"Poplar Neck"	58
	"Mount Misery Addition"	12
	pt. "Mount Misery"	25
	pt. "Prouse Point" & pt. "Hap Hazard"	12
	pt. "Bensons Enlargement"	190
Thomas Haddaway	"Haddaways Addition"	75
James Corke	pt. "Lewis"	145
John Wiles	"Bantly Hay"	33¼
Daniel Sherwood	"Anketell"	440
	"Cabbin Neck, Potters Lott, & Potters Delight"	150
	"Bradford"	56
48:1748:53 ...		
John Lowe (cnp)	pt. "Grafton Mannor"	245
	"Piney Neck"	107
	"Haddaways Lott"	50

	pt. "Fishburns Lott"	100
	pt. "Ratcliffe Mannor"	150
John Sanders	pt. "Sutton Grange"	93
Solomon Neale	pt. "Hiccory Ridge"	137
Mrs. Mary Dawson	"Crummall" – from (N) Hawkins	300
	"Cudlington"	400
	"Cudlington Addition"	50
	"Cudlington Increase"	50
	"Poplar Neck"	50
	"Bayles Forrest"	113
Robert Harrison	pt. "Hap Hazard"	50
	pt. "Crooked Intention"	50
Daniel Bridges	"Bloydon"	100
Thomas Bunton	pt. "Dover"	123
Richard Fidemon	"Fidemons Discovery"	408
Robert Larrimore	"Larrimores Neck"	100
	"Bampshier"	50
48:1748:54 ...		
Philemon Hambleton	"Mortenham"	200
	"Hambletons Addition"	100
	"Cambridge"	100
	pt. "Adventure" – from (N) Grace	113½
Francis Porter	pt. "Hemersby"	100
John Sherwood	"Sherwoods Island"	20
	"Middle Neck"	100
	½ "Mount Misery"	50
	"Huckleberry Garden"	125
John Leeds	"Wades Point"	400
	pt. "Hatton"	410
	"Long Delay"	34
	pt. "Scarborough"	200
	pt. "Hatton"	90
Robert Sands	pt. "Sands Lott"	103
	"Chance"	25
Edward Collison	pt. "Rehoboth" & pt. "Rehoboths Point"	33⅓
George Collison	pt. "Rehoboth" & pt. "Rehoboths Point"	33⅓

48:1748:55 ...		
John Kemp	"Bolten"	100
	"Bolton Addition"	50
	"Woolf Harbour"	62
	"Hunt Keep Out"	28
James Spencer, Jr.	pt. "Bensons Enlargement"	187
	"Fox Harbour"	50
	pt. "Edwards Hope Well"	45
Rev. Henry Nicols	"Micklemore"	230
	pt. "Maiden Point"	150
	"Maiden Point Addition"	100
	pt. "Witherses Range"	50
	pt. "Gallaway"	90
	pt. "Partnership"	500
	"Holden"	225
	pt. "Bite"	15
	"Forked Neck" – for the Vestry	50
	pt. "Hopkins Point"	86
	pt. "Bryans Lott"	12
Daniel Vinton	"Edwards Hopewell"	55
Susannah Slaughter	pt. "Middle Spring"	50
Charles Spencer	½ "Mansail"	48
	½ "Fairplay"	25
	"Janes Progress"	35
	pt. "Newport Glassgo"	36½
	pt. "Ennions Range"	96¾
48:1748:56 ...		
Joseph Harrison	pt. "Crooked Prolention"	80
	"Josephs Lott"	31
William Kemp	"Mable"	100
	"Mable's Addition"	50
	"Kemps Lott"	100
	pt. "Kemps Lott Addition"	26

John Hopkins	pt. "Beach, Elliots Lott, Elliots Folly, & Harsley" – from (N) Ashcraft	100
	"Jordins Folly"	100
	"Clays Neck"	102
Thomas Ashcraft	pt. "Devent Port, Beach, & Elliots Lott" – from (N) Ashcraft	380
John Studhams	pt. "Fairplay"	25
	pt. "Mainsail"	49
	"Studhams Chance"	18
Henry Richardson	"Pasty Neck"	24
James Benny	pt. "Morgans Neglect", pt. "Ramsey Forrest", & pt. "Morgans Addition"	106
	pt. "Ramsey Forrest"	78⅓
	pt. "Faulkenors Square"	100
	pt. "Ramsey Forrest"	43
48:1748:57 ...		
Mr. Thomas Bruff	"Daniels Addition"	70
	pt. "Walkers Tooth"	47
	pt. "Daniels Rest"	38
Mr. Richard Bruffe	pt. "Walkers Tooth"	100
	pt. "Daniels Rest"	12
	"Partnership"	96
	"Walkers Corner"	18
	"Millington"	50
Mr. Richard Loyd	"Tolkenors Folly"	100
	"New Desire Bettys Branch"	325
	"Stock Range"	400
	"Grany"	100
	<n/g> – another tract of (N) Woolman	150
Mrs. Sarah Hollyday	pt. "Brittania" & pt. "Stevens Plains"	150
John Carslake	½ "Newmans Lott"	100
	"Bartram"	50
	"Carslake Discovery"	109
	"Carslake Content"	60
	pt. "Nobles Chance"	29
William Benny	pt. "Ramsey Forrest", pt. "Bennys Thickett", & pt. "Bennys Addition"	78⅓

John Benny	pt. "Ramsey Forrest", pt. "Bennys Thickett", & pt. "Benny Addition"	78⅓
48:1748:58 ...		
Robert Harwood	"Loyd Addition"	120
	pt. "Addition"	80
	pt. "Harwoods Neglect"	27
	pt. "Carters Plains"	206
Mrs. Margarett Ward	"Henrietta Maria's Purchase"	412
	"Court Road"	138
Mr. Mathew Tilghman	pt. "Union"	611
	"Choptank Island"	1468
	"Three Necks"	165
	"Williams Outlett"	50
	"Rich Neck"	577
Henry Henrix, Jr.	pt. "Partnership" – from (N) Dulin	37
William Collison	pt. "Rehoboth" & pt. "Rehoboths Point"	33⅓
Thomas Matthews (Kings Creek)	pt. "Bedworth" & pt. "Rich Farm Addition"	83
John Thornton	"Morefields Addition"	65
Edmund Marsh	pt. "Studs Point"	50
	"Hulls Neck"	40
Christopher Spry	pt. "Partnership" – from (N) Benson	54
48:1748:59 ...		
Roland Haddaway	"Fishburns Landing" – from (N) Haddaway	104
Samuel Bartlett	pt. "Ratcliffe Mannor"	100
George Nix	pt. "Middle Spring"	150
George Haddaway, Jr.	pt. "Lostock"	170
William Parrott	pt. "Canterberry Mannor"	105
	pt. "Canterberry Mannor" – from Isaiah Parrott	65
Samuel Prichard	pt. "Hutchinson Addition"	100
Mrs. Margarett Edmondson (cnp)	pt. "Edmondsons Difficulty" a/s "Cooks Hope"	350
	pt. "Desire & Heworth"	117½
	pt. "Edmonsons Difficulty"	301
	pt. "Desire Addition"	20
	pt. "Enlargement"	33⅓
	pt. "Jacks Cove"	16¾

	pt. "Tilghmans Fortune"	175¾
Mr. Polard Edmonson	pt. "Desire & Heworth"	235
	pt. "Edmonsons Difficulty"	602
	pt. "Desire Addition"	40
	pt. "Enlargment"	76
	pt. "Jacks Cove"	34¼
	pt. "Tilghmans Fortune"	349
48:1748:60 ...		
Isaiah Parrott	pt. "Canterberry Mannor"	210
James Harrison	pt. "Poplar Neck"	42
	pt. "Prous Point, Hap Hazard, & Foresail"	38
George Brinsfield	"Middle Neck"	200
Robert Porter	pt. "Hemersby"	100
John Mears	"White Philips"	100
Laurence Caulk	pt. "Lostock" – from (N) Camper	50
Henry Pollock	"Bannings Hazard" – for h/o Phil. Baning	50
	pt. "Faulkenors Square" – for h/o Phil. Baning	50
John Lockerman	pt. "Shrigleys Fortune"	100
John Bennett	"Covehall"	100
	"Fort Adventure"	50
David Fizpatrick	pt. "Adventure"	100
	"Dirty Weeden Addition"	100
	pt. "Tryangle"	50
48:1748:61 ...		
Benjamin Cooper	pt. "Miles End"	75
Thomas Comings	pt. "Knave Keep Out"	75
Nicholas Comings	pt. "Knave Keep Out"	75
William Comings	"Lurty"	50
Thomas Wiles	pt. "Bantly Hay"	16¾
John Hambleton	"Wellingston"	224
Terty Sweat	½ "Newmans Lott"	100
	½ "Planters Delight"	100
	pt. "Nobles Chance"	100
	"Stevens Addition"	7[illegible]
James Ferril	"Hawks Kill"	100
James Walker	"Jamaica"	9[illegible]

Philip Walker	"Jordins Hill"	157
	½ "Upper Range"	50
Catherine Barwood	pt. "Hopkins Point"	66½
48:1748:62 ...		
Ralp Dawson	"Elstons Hazard"	49
	"Jones Lott Addition"	50
	"Jones Lott"	50
	"Rest Content"	45
Peter Hunt	pt. "Larrimores Neck" a/s "Larrimores Prudence"	87
Quakers Meeting	pt. "London Derry"	3
Edward Starkey	"Bite the Biter"	35
Stanly Robinson	pt. "Goldsborough"	87
Abner Parrott	pt. "Jamaica"	100
John Robinson	pt. "Long Point"	150
	"Robinsons Beginning"	17
Richard Mansfield	"Wisbitch"	60
	"Up Holand"	50
Nathaniel Conner	"Fortune" – from (N) Garey	150
	"Braferton"	100
Hugh Spencer	pt. "Matthew Circumvented"	150
48:1748:63 ...		
Daniel Berry	pt. "Chance"	129
Gilbert Barrow	"Orford"	338
Francis Karsey	"Webbly"	300
	"Sarahs Neck"	50
Edmund Blades	pt. "Matthew Circumvented"	184
Abner Turner	"Hasco Green"	160
Jacob Gore	"Duns Moor Heath"	200
	"Frantom"	122
Thomas Loveday	½ "Swineyard"	88
	pt. "Middle Spring"	100
Sarah Bartlett	pt. "Partnership"	120
	pt. "Reynolds Point"	50
	pt. "Williams & James"	25
	pt. "Hopkins Point Addition"	25
Richard Robinson	pt. "Long Point"	100

48:1748:64 ...		
John Sylvester	"Horse Point"	21
Daniel Dickenson	pt. "Boston Clift"	260
Elizabeth Clayland	pt. "Turners Discovery"	30
	pt. "Woolf Pitt Ridge"	17¾
James Barnwell, Jr.	pt. "Rich Farm Addition"	50
Mr. William Troth	"Acton"	300
Dr. Edward Knott	"Poolys Discovery"	168
Benjamin Hopkins	pt. "Hopkins Point"	66¾
Thomas Frampton	"Framptons Beginning"	96
	"Collins Pasture"	50
John Price (Dover)	pt. "Hatfield" & pt. "Addition"	25
Francis Neal, Jr.	pt. "Hiccory Ridge"	296
John Lambdon	pt. "Grafton Mannor"	100
48:1748:65 ...		
Thomas Sherwood	"Daniel & Mary Resurveyed" composed of: • "Lurky Hills" • "Beggars Hall" • pt. "Addition" • pt. "Fortune"	375

49:1756:1 ...		**Acres**
Samuel Abbott	pt. "Hutchinsons Addition"	50
	"Beaverdam"	100
	pt. "Buckrow"	40
	"Minors Lott"	100
	pt. "Sutton" – surveyed for (N) Skinner; for h/o (N) Homes	125
	pt. "Suttons Addition" – for h/o (N) Homes	25
John Atkinson	"Cottingham" – by Francis Baker for ⅔rds	100
	"Skipton" – for your wife; by Francis Baker for ⅔rds	300
	pt. "Finneys Hermitage" – for your wife	200
	"Newman"	50
	"Atkinsons Chance"	43
Thomas Atkinson	"Cottingham"	37
William Alexander	"Wales" tbc Henry Alexander	54
	"Irish Freshes" tbc Henry Alexander	50
	"Alexanders Chance" tbc Henry Alexander	250
	pt. "Good Luck" tbc Henry Alexander – surveyed for (N) Low	100
	pt. "<t> Advantage"	28
	pt. "<t> Reserve" – for his wife	200
Jonathan Airey (QA)	pt. "Rochcliffe"	118
	"Davids Ridge"	125
William Ayres	pt. "Studds Point"	100
	"Ayres's Venture"	96
Elizabeth w/o Richard Aldren	"Yaffords Neck"	300
	"Roystons Addition"	150
	"Aldrens Island"	41
49:1756:2 ...		
Thomas Ashcroft	pt. "Beach & Elliotts Lott"	180
	"Davenporth"	114¾
Mary w/o William Addams	pt. "Hattfield" & pt. "Hattfields Addition"	75
	pt. "Hattfield" & pt. "Hattfields Addition"	5
	"Addams Right"	70
Samuel Attwell	pt. "Bantry"	200

John Arrington	pt. "Adventure"	113½
	"Hethringtons Delight" a/s "Arringtons Delight"	50
John Anthony (KEDE)	"Morgans Neglect" & "Morgans Addition" – for his son Morgan Anthony	24
Thomas Ayres	pt. "Millers Hope"	121
William Anderson	pt. "Prospect"	19
John Auld	pt. "Newport Glascow"	221½
	"Elliots Folly" – alleged in older survey; denied	50
49:1756:3 ...		
Thomas Adcock	pt. "Coopers Lott" – dead; land not be be found	26½
John Auld, Jr.	"Auds Security"	47
	pt. "Grantham" – for his wife	106
Nathaniel Ashcomb (CV)	"Campton" – alleged neglected & lost	300
h/o Francis Armstrong	"Holland" – will disclaim	200
	"Westmoreland" – will disclaim	200
William Aldren & h/o Andrew Oram	"Hopewell" – supposed lost	200
h/o Francis Alexander	"Ireland" – alleged will disclaim	500
h/o Andrew Abbington (PG)	"Warwick"	400
49:1756:4 ...		
h/o John Alexander	"Youell" – alleged he will disclaim	50
Thomas Browning	pt. "Hir Dyer Lloyd"	75
	pt. "Hyer Dyer Lloyd on Resurvey"	80
Thomas Bowdle	pt. "Hir Dier Lloyd" – denies has any such land	43
Anne Bowdle w/o Loftus Bowdle	pt. "Hir Dier Lloyd"	61
	pt. "Hard Measure"	37
John Berry	pt. "Roadley" – for h/o John Dickinson	168
	"Dickinsons Field" – for h/o John Dickinson	18¾
Jacob Bromwell	pt. "Anderton"	100
	"Cove Hall"	100
	"Fort Venture"	50
	"Wintersell"	200
Lambert Booker	pt. "Tilghmans Fortune"	88
	pt. "St. Michals Fresh Run"	100
49:1756:5 ...		

Phebe Barnett	pt. "Shore Ditch"	75
	"Swamp Tick"	100
John Barnett	pt. "Cattlin Plains"	100
Jo. Barnett	pt. "Rattcliffe Manor"	270
James Barnett	pt. "Rattcliffe Manor"	250
	pt. "Bullen" – denied	150
Katharine Barnett	pt. "Hopkins Point" tbc Vinton Barwood as heir-at-law	66⅔
Anne w/o William Brooks who married Daniel Powell	"Dickes Marsh"	200
	pt. "Little Bristoll"	400
	"Little Bristoll" – for h/o Solomon Birkhead	580
	pt. "Nominy"	200
	pt. "Discovery"	56
w/o Adam Brown	¼ "Parkers Point"	30
	¼ "Enlargement"	45
Thomas Barrow & James Barrow for their wives	pt. "Ashby"	48
	pt. "Bettys Cove"	13⅓
49:1756:6 ...		
George Brinsfield guardian to William Arrington	pt. "Studs Point" tbc James Brinsfield	50
	pt. "Middle Neck" tbc: • James Brinsfield – ⅔ • Ann Harrington (Middle Neck) – ⅓	100
	pt. "Middle Neck" – for himself	100
John Ball	pt. "Long Point"	25
	pt. "Long Neck"	90
	pt. "Benjamins Lott"	50
John Blades	pt. "Matthew Circumvented"	169½
Anne Barnes	pt. "Boones Hope" – dead; no heirs to be found	26⅔
Mr. John Bozman (cnp)	pt. "Piney Point Advantage" – denies; says belongs to h/o Michael Meginey	100
	"Caerdiffe"	100
	pt. "Timber Neck"	150
	"Providence"	7
	pt. "Desire" & pt. "Hurt" tbc h/o George Robins	10
	pt. "Timber Neck"	64
	"Tates Lott"	449
	"Browns Park"	119

	"Bozmans Addition"	393¾
	"Teats Lott" – alleged in "Piney Point" & "Piney Points Advantage"	190
49:1756:7 ...		
Rachell Barnett	"Hogg Hole" tbc James Connoly	142
	"Patricks Ridge" a/s "Powicks Ridge" tbc James Barnet	100
	"Discovery" tbc James Barnet	140⅓
Anthony Bacon	pt. "Worgans Reserve" – for h/o Anthony Richardson	300
	pt. "Turkey Neck" – denied	125
	pt. "Mount Hope" – for h/o Anthony Richardson	50
	"Perkins Park" – denied 400 a.; for h/o Anthony Richardson	500
	"Browns Lott" – for h/o Anthony Richardson	200
	"Hasely" – for h/o Anthony Richardson	200
	pt. "Mill Land" – for h/o Anthony Richardson	20
	"Widows Lott" – for h/o Anthony Richardson	85
	"Benjamins Lott" – denied	50
	pt. "Dobsons Advantage" – for h/o Anthony Richardson	7
	pt. "Partnership Hazard" – for h/o Anthony Richardson	142
	"Addition" – denied 129 a.; for h/o Anthony Richardson	229
James Benson	pt. "Huntington Grange"	80
	"Neglect" tbc William Dawson (73¾ a.)	96
	pt. "Mistake"	25½
	"Fishing Bay"	126¾
Richard Barrow for his wife • ½ of lands tbc said Barrow • ½ of lands tbc Phill. Horney	⅓ "Batchlors Hope"	16⅔
	⅓ "Bartram"	50
	⅓ "Fools Parradise"	16⅔
	⅓ "Scotts Lott"	33⅓
	pt. "Kinniments Delight" & ⅓ "Hopewell"	26⅔
	"School House Lott on Tostpone" for himself	59
49:1756:8 ...		
Nicholas Benson (cnp)	pt. "Hoggs Hole"	50
	pt. "Bensons Enlargement"	4[illegible]

	pt. "Bensons Chance"	89
Obednigo Bodfield	pt. "Bettys Cove"	30
	"Bettys Addition" a/s "Bettys Cove Addition"	50
	"Addition" – surveyed for (N) Hurlock	50
Samuel Bowman	"St. Johns Neck"	350
James Barnwell, Jr.	pt. "Mount Hope"	50
	pt. "Rich Farm Addition"	50
	pt. "Partnership"	42
James Barnwell	pt. "Mount Hope"	27
	pt. "Bedworth"	150
	pt. "Rich Farm Addition"	20
Matthew Lewis Barnett	pt. "Kingston"	133⅓
	pt. "Millingtons Choice" – in right of his wife	70
	pt. "Hollands Addition"	13⅔
Sarah Berry	pt. "White Marshes"	760
	pt. "Rich Farm"	50
49:1756:9 ...		
w/o Gilbert Barrow	pt. "Rich Farm"	50
	pt. "Mill Land"	40
	"Oxford"	338
Andrew Bandy	pt. "Kingston"	100
Thomas Bruffe	pt. "Daniels Rest"	38
	pt. "Walkers Tooth"	47
	pt. "Inclosure"	150
	pt. "Daniels Addition"	70
Richard Bruffe	pt. "Daniels Rest"	12
	pt. "Walkers Tooth"	100
	"Walkers Corner"	18
	pt. "Partnership"	96
Daniel Bridges	"Blydon"	100
w/o Daniel Bradford (DO)	pt. "Johns Hill"	90
w/o William Bush	pt. "Arcadia"	166
49:1756:10 ...		
Mr. Rizdon Bozman (cnp)	pt. "Kemps Lott"	150
	"Wattson" a/s "Watson & Partnership"	150
	"Folly"	100

	pt. "Kemps Lott Addition"	26
	"Sherwoods Neck"	268
	"Hemersly"	273
	pt. "Lewis"	145
	"Gaskins Neck" a/s "Gaskins Point"	50
	"Wattson Addition"	73
	"Neglect"	34
	"Moor & Cassott"	34
Richard Beswick	pt. "Christophers Lott"	100
	pt. "Stevens Plains"	50
John Brascrop	pt. "Coventry" – sold to Sarah Botfield w/o Zadock who denied	30
	pt. "Rattcliffe Choice" – taken away by James Barnwell by elder survey	30
husband of w/o Zadock Bodfield	pt. "Coventry" tbc: • James Robinson as guardian to h/o (N) Botfield – ⅔ • Isaac Nicks who married w/o Zadock Botfield – ⅓	125
	pt. "Rattcliffs Choice" tbc Isaac Nicks who married w/o Zadock Botfield	79
Samuel Broadway	"Jams Fields"	102
	"Ramah"	100
	pt. "Strawbridge" tbc Thomas Stevens	100
	"Broadways Meadow"	100
49:1756:11 ...		
Rev. Thomas Bacon	"Cross Haze"	50
	pt. "Hull" – for County School	70
	"Partnership"	34
	"Davids Folly"	50
	"Chance" – for the Charrity School	23
James Benny	pt. "Morgans Neglect"	14
	pt. "Morgans Addition"	46
	pt. "Rumleys Forrest"	78⅓
	pt. "Falkenars Square"	100
	"Good Luck"	60
	"Duck Pond"	50

Abraham Bromwell	pt. "Bensons Enlargement"	1
	pt. "Bensons Enlargement" – for Charles Gorsage	114½
	pt. "Bensons Chance"	1
Sarah Bartlett	pt. "Hopkins Point Addition" – overcharged in "William & James"	25
	pt. "William & James"	25
	pt. "Partnership"	120
	pt. "Reynolds Point" – overcharged	50
John Bonnett	"Moorfields Addition" – for his wife	30
	pt. "Moorfields" – for his wife	10
	pt. "Duns Range" – for his wife	100
Anthony Booth	pt. "Bloomsbery" – for his wife	100
49:1756:12 ...		
William Bandy	"Adventure" – for h/o Thomas Richardson	70
Daniel Berry	pt. "Chance" – taken away by John Bozman in elder survey	129
Thomas Benny	pt. "Rumleys Forrest", pt. "Bennys Thickett" & pt. "Bennys Addition" – pt. "Rumleys Forrest" (6⅓ a.) & "Bennys Addition" (32 a.) sold to James Benny	78⅔
Sarah Benny	pt. "Rumly Forrest", pt. "Bennys Addition", & pt. "Bennys Thickett" – for h/o William Benny	78⅓
Sarah Beswick	pt. "Stevens Plains"	50
	"Christophers Lott"	286¼
	"Sarahs Addition"	50
Henry Burgess	"Hopewell"	50
	pt. "Discovery"	10
John Barwick	"Storeys Lott" tbc Henry Henricks	56
	pt. "Discovery"	9
	"Discovery Addition"	10
49:1756:13 ...		
Mr. John Bracco	"Poplar Ridge" – for Anne Bell (minor)	249
h/o Nicholas Bartlett (minors)	pt. "Bartletts Inheritance"	110
h/o Henry Baily	"Bettys Chance" – alleged in "Marshy Point"	100
	"Marshy Point" – alleged in "Turners Point"	143
h/o James Barber	pt. "Holden Addition"	50
h/o Roger Bradberry	pt. "Pitts Range" – will disclaim	200

John Blake (QA)	"Adventure" – will disclaim	446
	"Upper Range" – will disclaim	200
h/o Charles Bridges	"Newbuilding" – will disclaim	29
h/o Nicholas Bartlett	pt. "Bartletts Inheritance"	110
h/o Richard Burden (RI)	"Larramores Lott"	50
49:1756:14 ...		
h/o William Buckley (SM)	"Lords Gift"	175
h/o Christopher Battson	"Bradford" – escheatable	50
John Barnes	"Barnes's Chance" – escheatable	100
Robert Bryon	"Hattfield Addition" – escheatable	62
William Brett	"Jamaica Addition" – escheatable	50
h/o James Bishop	pt. "Chance" – escheatable	48
h/o John Barker	pt. "Lower Dover" – alleged in His Lordships Manor	200
h/o John Burke	"Old Indian Cabbin"	50
Benjamin Cooper	pt. "Mile End"	65
	pt. "Mile End"	10
49:1756:15 ...		
Samuel Chamberlaine, Esq. (cnp)	pt. "Hir Dier Lloyd"	928
	pt. "Tilghmans Fortune"	75
	pt. "Hopkins Point"	7¼
	pt. "Plain Dealing"	100
	"Cabbin Neck"	50
	"Hook Land"	100
	pt. "Rocky Hook"	75
	pt. "London Derry" tbc James Lloyd Chamberlaine	250
	"Gouldstone" – denied	50
	"Rest Content"	100
	"Contention"	100
	pt. "Arcadia" – denied	34
	"Goose Neck"	50
	"Clays Addition"	50
	"Abrams Lott" – denied	100
	"Stevensons Range"	186
	pt. "Cumberland"	100
	"Bishoprick"	100

	pt. "Rome"	100
	pt. "Shriglys Fortune"	121
	"Grundys Lott"	46
	"Marys Dower"	200
	"Morgans Neglect" & pt. "Morgans Addition" – should be charged 36 a. more	101
	pt. "Bensons Enlargement" – denied 7 a.	27
	"Yorkshire"	155
	"Godwine Addition"	90
	"Barmiston" – denied	106
	"Endeavour"	50
	"Gore"	45
	pt. "Shepshead Point"	196
	pt. "Braintrees Addition"	50
	"Intention"	50
	"Turners Hazard"	100
	"Hopewell" – denied	200
	"Inlargement"	71
	pt. "Chance" – surveyed for (N) Elliott	40
	"Bullens Addition"	102
	pt. "Bartletts Inheritance"	30
	"Four Square"	350
	pt. "Halls Neck"	286
	"Grundys Lott Resurveyed"	55
	pt. "Arcadia" & pt. "Abrams Lott"	100
	pt. "Abrams Lott" & pt. "Millroad Addition" – denied 90 a.	123
	"Rockey Neck Addition" – on escheat	39¼
	pt. "Cumberland" – alleged in water	50
49:1756:16 ...		
James Chaplain	pt. "Roadley"	80
	pt. "Broad Oak"	300
	"Enfield"	200
	"Intention"	100
Capt. John Coward	"Plinkimmon"	600

John Caulke	pt. "Lostock"	50
	"Sheepshead Point" tbc Thomas Tibbles	50
	"Caulks Addition"	236
William Cooper (big)	pt. "Lostock" tbc Col. Edward Lloyd	172
	pt. "Bentley Hay" tbc William Cooper (the little)	16⅔
	"Harrissons Security"	167
John Cooley	pt. "Lostock"	184½
Francis Chaplain for his wife	½ "Parkers Point" tbc William Stevens guardian to Edward Briney	60
	½ "Enlargement" tbc William Stevens guardian to Edward Briney	90
Peter Cox	pt. "Marsh Land" – for h/o Thomas Bullen	165
	pt. "Lords Gift" – for h/o Thomas Bullen	200
	"Newlin" – for h/o Thomas Bullen	140
	"Turbutts Fields" – for h/o Thomas Bullen	168
	"Bullens Discovery" – for h/o Thomas Bullen	136
49:1756:17 ...		
Powell Cox	pt. "Nominy" – for h/o Solomon Sharp	302
	pt. "Knaps Lott" – for h/o Solomon Sharp	50
	pt. "Boston Clift" – for himself	260
Samuel Cockayne	pt. "St. Michaels Fresh Run"	386
Henry Corckrin	pt. "Hogg Hole"	142
	pt. "Discovery"	147
h/o John Carslake	pt. "Bartram"	50
	pt. "Newnames Lott"	100
	pt. "Nobles Chance"	29
	"Carslakes Discovery"	109
Rebecca Clark (widow)	pt. "Hampton" & pt. "Parkers Range"	200
	pt. "Parkers Range"	58
	"Highfield Addition"	150
	pt. "Highfield"	100
	"Berrys Range"	130
Frances Camperson	pt. "Hampton"	50
	pt. "Rich Range"	50
	"Frances Delight"	48
William Cooper (little man)	pt. "Haphazard" tbc William Cooper (big)	100

49:1756:18 ...		
Peter Cumerford	pt. "St. Johns Neck"	350
	"Sallop" – for h/o (N) Parrott	167
Col. Thomas Chamberlaine	pt. "Rocky Nook" & "Rocky Nook Addition"	158
	pt. "Ealoms Addition"	60
	"Lobbs Corner"	23
Lemon John Cathrop	pt. "Mount Hope"	61½
	pt. "Buckby"	50
	pt. "Cathrops Security"	192
h/o Terence Connerly	⅔ "Kingston" tbc Mathew Lewis Barnet guardian to h/o (N) Connerly	266⅔
	"Hollands Addition" tbc Mathew Lewis Barnet guardian to h/o (N) Connerly	27⅓
Joshua Clark	pt. "Johns Neck"	118
	"Clarks Folly"	101
	"Killam" – alleged in "Johns Neck"; denied	100
John Cox	"Spring Close"	50
	"Coxes Venture"	38
h/o Sarah Cockayne	pt. "Carters Plains"	294
49:1756:19 ...		
William Cummings	"Lurkey"	50
w/o John Cuthcart	"Cornelius's Garden"	50
Edward Clark	pt. "Parkers Farm"	350
	"Deleroy" – denied	100
	"Parrotts Lott"	82
	"Pigg Point"	40
	"Parkers Farm Addition"	42
William Carr	"Millers Purchase"	100
	pt. "Lowes Rambles"	114
Ferdinando Callaghane	pt. "Brittania" tbc James Callahan (heir)	100
William Cole	pt. "Brittania", pt. "Hilldon", & pt. "Costine Chance"	162
William Cary	pt. "Sutton" & pt. "Sutton Addition" – denied	100
	pt. "Partnership"	18
Anne Corkrine (widow)	pt. "Discovery"	70⅓
49:1756:20 ...		
Philemon Chew	"Claybourns Island"	700

Thomas Cumings	pt. "Knave Keep Out" – 15 a. denied as per patent	90
Nicholas Cumings	pt. "Knave Keep Out" – 15 a. denied as per patent	90
Foster Cunliffe, Esq. (Liverpool)	"Hunt Keep Out"	28
Edward Collisson	pt. "Rehoboth Point"	33⅓
William Collisson	pt. "Rehoboth Point"	16⅔
James Caulk	pt. "Lewis"	145
John Clift	"Clifts Addition" a/s "Taylors Ridge"	100
	pt. "Timber Neck"	89
49:1756:21 ...		
h/o Richard Carter (ENG) – heirs have said that Mr. James Tilghman has purchased some of the lands & as such can be found in his account	pt. "St. Michals Fresh Run"	624
	pt. "Addition"	16
	"Carters Preserve"	200
	"Carters Farme"	250
	"Carters Range"	200
	"Carters Outwork"	19
	"Carters Forrest"	420
	"Carters Chance"	74
	"Carters Reserve"	164
	"Carters Sconce"	139
	pt. "Finneys Hermitage"	200
	"Good Chance"	50
	"Newnames Thickett"	50
	"Bodkin"	15
	"Gore"	170
h/o John Chambers – arrears paid by John Goldsborough	"Chambers Adventure"	132¾
	"Bedsteads Adventure" – said would disclaim	64
Edward Combs	"Nether Foster" – alleged in pt. "Hir Dir Lloyd"; not to be found	150
devisees of John Carpenter (AA)	"Ashbys Addition" – not to be found	200
	"Newnames Fields"	50
Doughlass Chace	"Barren Ridge" – for h/o (N) Holt; alleged cannot be found	100
	"Mill Garden" – for h/o (N) Holt; alleged cannot be found	35
Robert Curtice (VA)	"Boone Hill"	250
49:1756:22 ...		

Henry Conyers (DO)	"Maidstone"	250
	"Warwick Point"	100
Samuel Cracker (ENG)	"Ramah"	300
h/o William Curtice	pt. "Dixons Lott"	50
	"Springfield Grange"	64
Elizabeth Christian	"Widows Chance" – escheatable	50
h/o William Combs	"Galston" – says would disclaim	50
Impey Dawson	"Cromwell" – resurveyed with "Poplar Neck" for 476¾ a.	300
	"Poplar Neck" – resurveyed with "Cromwell" for 476¾ a.	50
Thomas Dawson	"Cudlington"	400
	"Cudlingtons Addition"	50
	"Cudlingtons Inheritance"	50
Henry Delahay	pt. "Hir Dier Lloyd"	125
49:1756:23	...	
Samuel Dickinson (cnp)	pt. "Harberts Choice"	14
	"Little Creek"	200
	"Samuels Lott"	600
	"Dickensons Lott"	113
	"Cross Dover"	400
	pt. "Roadley"	182
	pt. "Canterbury Manor"	250
	"Ewens Point"	300
	pt. "Wales"	46
	pt. "Salem, Stepney, & Quillen"	134
	pt. "Nominy"	350
	pt. "Edmondsons Cove" – from Thomas Stevens	<n/g>
	"White Phillips"	150
	pt. "Mount Hope"	250
	pt. "Compton"	13
	"Hobsons Choice"	100
	pt. "Hobsons Choice" – another	129
	pt. "Darlington"	119
	"Dickensons Lott"	206
	pt. "Millers Hope"	11

	"Mitchells Hermitage" – from (N) Thomas	50
	"Mitchells Hermitage" – from (N) Harbert	75
	pt. "Good Luck" – surveyed for (N) Lowe	54
	pt. "Crooked Lane" tbc old William Dickinson	6
	"Powells Island"	55
	pt. "Hier Dier Lloyd on Resurvey"	101
	"Millers Chance"	85
	"Fishers Chance"	125
	"Bennington" – alleged in His Lordships Manor	50
	pt. "Mount Hope"	119
	"Security" – patented 15 June 1728	406
	"Chance" – charged rightly above	125
49:1756:24 ...		
James Dickinson	"East Ottwell"	400
	pt. "Bullen"	350
	"Piney Point" – for his wife	150
	"Timothys Lott" – for his wife	300
Joseph Dawson	pt. "Lostock"	150
Elizabeth Davis	pt. "Tilghmans Fortune"	83
	pt. "Ashby"	49
	pt. "Betty's Cove"	6⅔
	"Standfords Hermitage"	250
	"Standfords Folly"	45
	"Bite the Biter"	33
Isaac Dixon	pt. "Cottingham"	75
	pt. "Ashby"	60
	"Bennetts Hill"	50
	"Ending of Controversie"	150
	pt. "Dixons Outlett"	150
John Dickinson	pt. "Rockciffe" – for h/o William Harrisson	170
	"Poplar Levell" a/s "Parrotts Levell" – for h/o William Harrisson	116
	"Dover Marsh" – for h/o William Harrisson	348
	"Dover" – for h/o William Harrisson	771½
	pt. "Lower Dover" – for h/o William Harrisson	241

Samuel Dickinson or w/o John Cuthcart	pt. "Salem, Stepney, & Quillen"	16
49:1756:25 ...		
Thomas Dudley	pt. "Broad Lane"	103
	"Brads Lanes Addition"	41¼
	pt. "Beaver Neck" – for h/o husband of Deborah Dudley	106
	pt. "Advantage" – for h/o husband of Deborah Dudley	18
	pt. "Beaver Neck" – for h/o (N) Batchelor	141
Samuel Dunning (Dover on Delaware)	pt. "Beaver Neck"	100
	pt. "Broade Lane"	50
Joseph Durding	pt. "Bless Land"	100
	pt. "Turkey Neck"	116
	pt. "Kingsberry"	130
	"Kings Creek Marsh"	50
	pt. "Kingsberry Addition"	37
Cornelius Daily	pt. "London Derry"	132
	"Cornelius's Cool Spring"	100
	"Surprize"	40
	pt. "Discovery"	20
h/o William Dudley	pt. "Smiths Clifts"	138
Peter Denny	pt. "Heworth"	23
	"Clifton"	200
	pt. "Hickory Ridge"	12
	pt. "Dennys Content"	73
49:1756:26 ...		
William Dawson (QA)	pt. "Gallaway"	100
	pt. "Batchelors Range Addition"	463
	pt. "Shrigleys Fortune" – arrears paid by John Lookerman, Jr.	270
	"Batchelors Range"	250
	pt. "Huntington" & pt. "Huntington Addition"	90
	pt. "Huntington"	150
	"Lizey Fortune" – alleged in "Shrigleys Fortune"	16
	"Choetank" – says cannot find	100
	"Thief Keep Out" – says cannot find	50

John Dixon	pt. "Carters Plains"	206
	"Neglect"	126
h/o William Dixon	"Dixons Lott" – alleged in "Dixons Outlett"	200
Ralph Dawson	"Jones's Lott"	50
	pt. "Grafton Manor" a/s "Elstons Hazard"	49
	"Jones's Lott Addition"	50
	"Rest Content"	45
Thomas Dudley, Jr.	"Dudleys Inclosure"	104
	"Dudleys Addition"	37
Mrs. Henrietta Maria Dulany	pt. "Woolmans Hermitage"	109
	pt. "Woolmans Inheritance"	206
Jo. Denny	"Wisbick"	60
49:1756:27 ...		
Abner Dudley (QA)	pt. "Cowallyn" – arrears paid by Mr. John Bozman	200
Sarah w/o Robert Dawson	"Dawsons Composition"	282
Thomas Dillahay	"Dillahays Fortune"	100
Peter Davis a/s Petter Davidson	pt. "Dover" – for his wife	123½
George Dawson	"Baylys Forrest"	113
Daniel Dickenson	pt. "Boston Clift"	260
James Dudley	pt. "Dudleys Demesne"	115
Jonathan Dobson	"Fork"	250
John Dixon (taylor)	"Dixons Discovery" – taken by elder survey	20¼
h/o old William Dickinson	"Crooked Lane" – alleged in "Frankford St. Michaels"; not to be found	6
49:1756:28 ...		
h/o William Dudley	pt. "Smiths Clifts" – alleged in older surveys	138
h/o James Davis (PA)	pt. "Heworth"	22
h/o Anne Darby (ENG)	"Pitts" or "Pitts Chance"	400
John Dunn	"Burinston" – escheatable	170
John Drywood	"Drywoods Chance"	10
w/o William Edmondson	pt. "Hir Dier Lloyd" tbc Powel Cox	39
	"Edmondsons Pond"	[illegible]
Pollard Edmondson (cnp)	pt. "Tilghmans Fortune"	349½
	pt. "Enlargement"	7
	pt. "Desire Addition" – conveyed to George Robins	4

	pt. "Desire" & pt. "Huart" tbc William Hanson (143½ a.)	235⅓
	pt. "Edmondsons Difficulty"	602
	"Jacks Cove"	33⅓
	"Freshes" – cannot find & will disclaim	300
49:1756:29 ...		
Margaret Edmondson (widow)	pt. "Tilghmans Fortune"	174⅔
	pt. "Enlargement"	33⅓
	pt. "Desire Addition"	20
	pt. "Desire" & pt. "Huart"	117⅔
	pt. "Edmondsons Difficulty"	651
	pt. "Jacks Cove"	16⅔
Elizabeth Ellsby (widow)	¼ "Parkers Point"	30
	¼ "Enlargement"	45
Mr. James Edge	pt. "Yaffords Neck"	100
	"Prevention"	50
	"Whartons Glade"	50
	pt. "Bensons Enlargement"	150
	"Glades Addition"	71
	"Couple Close"	100
	"Addition"	32
	"Seraps"	60
	"Skinners Lott"	33
devises of Phillip Emerson	½ "Widows Choice" a/s pt. "Widows Lott"	320
	pt. "Whisstone"	150
	pt. "Hammeltons Park"	263
	"Buckingham & Kelding"	393
	"Addition" – surveyed for (N) Hemsley	63
Elizabeth Edwards	pt. "Huntington"	20
	pt. "Mistake"	25½
	pt. "Huntington"	180
James Evans	pt. "Chesnutt Bay"	100
49:1756:30 ...		
Elizabeth Ewbanks	pt. "Mount Hope"	35
	"Hattons Hope"	100
	pt. "Discovery"	75

w/o Richard Eaton	pt. "Fox Hole"	100
	pt. "Fox Harbour"	50
	pt. "Eatons Addition"	112
William Elbert (QA)	pt. "Rebeccas Garden"	50
	pt. "Lloyd Coston"	240
Tammy Elston (widow)	pt. "Omalys Range"	150
	"Fitchs Range" a/s "Fishers Range" tbc Joshua Gresham	74
	pt. "Jacob & Johns Pasture"	120
	"Stapleton" tbc Joshua Gresham	77
	"Contention" tbc Joshua Gresham	130
	"Brooke Hall" – alleged in "Anketil" tbc Joshua Gresham	100
	"Ellston" – alleged in "Anketil" tbc Joshua Gresham	50
	"Addition" – alleged to be let fall; tbc Joshua Gresham	100
George Ewbanks	pt. "Omalys Range"	50
	pt. "Harwoods Neglect"	11
Adam Ewbanks	"Falconars Levell"	150
h/o Ralph Ellston	"Exchange" – alleged in "Anketil"	100
	"Long Neck" – in older surveys	20
49:1756:31 ...		
Edward Elliott, Jr.	"Point & Marsh"	50
	"Macotter & Glover" – 272 a. included in "Elliots Purchase"	355
Edward Ewbanks	"Coxes Hazard" – for his wife	103
Edward Elliott	"Elliotts Purchase"	361
h/o William Elbert or devises of Jeremiah Greshingham	pt. "Grantham" – resurveyed in "Lloyds Costin" tbc Jeremiah Gressingham	94
h/o John Edmondson	"Norwick" – alleged in "North York"	200
	"Barren Point" – alleged cannot be found	200
	"Edmondsons Fresh Run" – alleged cannot be found	400
	"North York" – will disclaim	200
	"Neglect" – cannot find bounds	310
h/o Thomas Edmondson	"James's Reserve" – alleged cannot find bounds	300
	"Adjunction" – alleged cannot find bounds	50

h/o James Elvert	"Edmondsons Cove" – escheatable	100
	"Edmondsons Lower Cove" – escheatable	100
49:1756:32 ...		
William Eldridge	"Eldridge Point" – escheatable	100
Col. William Fitzhugh	"Marron" – for h/o John Rousby	130
	"Hern Island" – for h/o John Rousby	75
	"Morgans St. Michaels" – for h/o John Rousby	300
John Fairbanks	"Camphiers Neck"	100
	"Fairly"	100
	"Bellfast"	100
	"Joanes Hole"	36
	"Fairbanks Chance"	195
	"Good Hap"	23
	"Tobacco Pipe"	9¾
John Ferrell	pt. "Mount Hope"	80
	pt. "Hawks Hill Addition"	50
	pt. "Cathrops Security"	13
Thomas Frampton, Jr.	pt. "Rich Range" – per deed of William Whitby, only 50 a.	100
Michael Fletcher	pt. "Sharps Chance"	79
	"Long Acre"	150
	pt. "Darlington" – denied	14
	pt. "Darlington" – alleged in "Mount Hope"; denied	51
David Jones Fitzpatrick	pt. "Tryangle"	56
	"Dirty Weeden Addition"	100
	pt. "Adventure"	100
49:1756:33 ...		
h/o James Ferrell	pt. "Hawks Hill Addition" tbc John Ferrell	100
Edm. Ferrell	pt. "Coventry"	100
	pt. "Mickle More"	100
	"Portumney"	179½
	pt. "Cathrops Security"	13
Richard Farbrother	pt. "Sutton Grange" tbc James Chaplain (33 a.)	200
Thomas Frampton (cnp)	"Framptons Beginning"	96
	"Collins Pasture"	50

	"Framptons Chance"	34¾
Abraham Falconar	"Neighbours Keep Out"	46
h/o Robert Finley	pt. "Mount Hope"	200
	pt. "Rich Farm"	200
	½ "Dixons Lott"	50
h/o Edward Fottrel	pt. "Fottrels Discovery" – escheatable	157
49:1756:34 ...		
Col. William Goldsborough	pt. "Hir Dier Lloyd" – for h/o George Robins	342
	pt. "Turners Point" – for h/o George Robins	200
	"Graves" – for h/o George Robins	100
	pt. "Marshy Point" – for h/o George Robins	300
	pt. "Canterbury Manor" – for h/o George Robins	100
	"Job's Content" – for h/o George Robins	1000
	pt. "Hulls Neck" – for h/o George Robins	300
	pt. "Cookes Hope" – for h/o George Robins	214
	"Firsts Hazard" – for h/o George Robins	358
	"Discovery" – for h/o George Robins	60
	pt. "Desire" & pt. "Huart" – for h/o George Robins	240
	"Jennings Hope" – for h/o George Robins	718
	"Buckingham" – for self	903
	"Chance" – alleged in "Cooks Manor"; denied	100
Nicholas Goldsborough, Sr.	pt. "Hir Dier Lloyd"	400
	"Grissell"	150
	"Partlett"	100
	"Ottwell"	500
	pt. "Marshy Point"	157
	"Addition" – surveyed for (N) Taylor; arrears paid by John Bozman	80
	"Theagles Request" – will disclaim	125
Jonathan Gibson	⅓ "Edmondton"	100
	⅓ "Champenhams Addition"	16
	pt. "Rebeccas Garden" tbc John Gibson	100
	pt. "Rebeccas Garden" tbc John Gibson	50
	⅓ "Leith"	13⅓
	⅓ "Champenham" & ⅓ "Bendon"	183⅓

Woolman Gibson	⅓ "Edmondton"	100
	⅓ "Champenham Addition"	16⅔
	pt. "Bryans Lott"	12½
	⅓ "Leith"	13⅓
	⅓ "Champenham" & ⅓ "Bendon"	183⅓
49:1756:35 ...		
Richard Grason	"Tanners Hope" a/s "Hely"	50
	"Personage Addition"	50
	pt. "Kings Forrest"	75
	"Roberts Infamy"	65
	pt. "Kings Plains"	79
	"Grassons Discovery"	106½
Mr. Robert Goldsborough	pt. "Cottingham"	150
	pt. "Ashby"	250
	pt. "St. Michals Fresh Run"	50
	pt. "Rich Range"	140
	"Chance" – surveyed for (N) Carter	50
	pt. "Rich Farm Addition" a/s "Rich Range Addition" – for his wife	86
	pt. "Peters Rest"	50
	"Newnams Addition"	50
	"Benjamins Lott"	50
	"Fox Harbour"	148
	pt. "Fragment" – for his wife	6⅓
	"Woodland Neck" – will disclaim	106
w/o Thomas Gully	pt. "Ashby"	150
Greenwood Gaskin	pt. "Middle Spring"	130
John Goldsborough	"Hoggsdon"	100
	"Thief Keep Out"	36
	"Goldsboroughs Tryangle"	45
	pt. "Adventure"	100
	"Cannadays Hazard" a/s "Canadays Hazard"	29
	pt. "Four Square"	650
	"Marshey Peak"	132
	"Peaks Marsh"	318
	"Kannadays Addition"	23

49:1756:36 ...		
Richard Gibson	pt. "Addition" – surveyed for (N) Woolman	50
	pt. "Timber Neck"	60
	pt. "Bryans Lott"	12½
	"Doctors Gift"	100
	pt. "Bettys Dowry"	75
Rev. John Gordon for glebe land	"Forked Neck"	50
	"Holden"	225
	pt. "Bite"	15
Richard Glover	½ "Upper Range"	50
	"Mount Hope"	75
	pt. "Upper Dover"	114¾
John Garey	"Strawberry Field"	100
Nicholas Glinn	pt. "Cookes Hope"	200
William Garey	"Little Brittain"	150
Mary Grace (widow), Sarah Case (widow), William Hutchins for wife, & Peter Hinesly for wife	pt. "Morgans Neglect" & "Morgans Addition"	36
49:1756:37 ...		
Thomas Goldsborough	"Barmiston"	74
	"Coxes Chance"	160
Jacob Gore	"Frampton" – thrice charged	122
	"Dernsmore Heath"	200
	"Frampton" – twice charged	122
Peter Garron	pt. "Dems Range" – for his wife	50
	"Piccadilly" – for his wife	150½
Jeremiah Grisingham	pt. "Lloyd Costin" – for his wife	419
Anthony Gregory	"Turners Chance" tbc Elizabeth Lord (53⅓ a.)	100
	"New Begun"	91½
Joshua Grason – grandson of Edmond Fish	"Fishes Hazard"	18
Nicholas Goldsborough, Jr.	pt. "Halls Neck"	20
	"Conjunction"	279
William Gale (White Haven)	"Fishers Discovery"	1/
49:1756:38 ...		
Roger Grose	pt. "Ashby" – alleged in water; not to be found	9

h/o Jacob Gibson	"Todd Upon Drivin" – will disclaim; in elder surveys	320
h/o John Glover	pt. "Upper Dover" – alleged in His Lordships Manor	344
William Gaskins	"Gaskins Pasture" – escheatable; not to be found	50
h/o George Gary	pt. "Hemsleys Arcadia" – not to be found	249
John Gibson	pt. "Lambeth" & pt. "Brittania"	71½
49:1756:39 ...		
Mr. Jacob Hindman	pt. "Kirkham"	273
	pt. "Kirkham" & pt. "Hampton"	200
Philemon Hamilton	"Martingham"	200
	"Cambridge"	100
	"Middle Neck"	100
	pt. "Mount Misery"	50
	"Sherwoods Island"	20
	pt. "Adventure"	113½
	"Hamiltons Addition"	100
	pt. "Newport Glascow"	36½
	"Huckleberry Garden"	175
William Webb Haddaway	"Mile End"	250
	"Merchants Folly"	150
	pt. "Haddaways Lott"	73
	pt. "Haddaways Lott" – more; denied	27
	"Grafton Manor" a/s pt. "Rich Neck"	150
	"Rich Neck" – alleged in "Grafton Manor"	150
George Haddaway	pt. "Lostock"	102
w/o George Haddaway, Jr.	pt. "Lostock"	70
49:1756:40 ...		
Dr. Michael Hackett for h/o William Sharp (cnp)	pt. "Hir Dier Lloyd" tbc Burket Sharp	100
	"Rattle Snake Point"	150
	"Moorfields" tbc Ann Sharp	100
	"Little Bristoll"	320
	"Adventure" tbc Ann Sharp	100
	"Eassons Neck" tbc William Sharp	100
	pt. "Conjunction"	25
	"Fancy" tbc William Sharp	50

	"Easons Lott" tbc William Sharp	50
	pt. "Inclosure" tbc William Sharp	300
	"Sharps Addition"	24
Mr. Henry Hollyday	"Tilghmans Fortune" – for his wife	445
	pt. "Ratcliffe Manor" – for his wife	150
	pt. "Ratcliffe Manor" – more	100
	pt. "Brittainia"	150
	"Turkey Park"	329
Edward Harding	pt. "Tilghmans Fortune"	19
	pt. "Bite" – resurveyed & called "Hardings Endeavour"; denies	13
	"Hardings Endeavor"	200
John Holmes	pt. "Sutton" – surveyed for (N) Skinner	125
	pt. "Sutton Addition"	25
	pt. "Bick Row"	40
James Hopkins	pt. "Hopkins Point"	100
	pt. "Hopkins Point Addition"	25
	pt. "Partnership"	65
49:1756:41 ...		
Benjamin Hopkins	pt. "Hopkins Point"	133⅓
Richard Hopkins	pt. "Hopkins Point"	142¾
Dennis Hopkins	pt. "Hopkins Point"	90
Samuel Harwood	pt. "Cottingham"	150
Peter Hopkins	pt. "Nominy"	100
Thomas Harrison	pt. "Crooked Intention"	80
	"Josephs Lott"	31
Phillip Horney for his wife	⅔ "Batchelors Hope" tbc Richard Barrow (½)	33⅓
	pt. "Bartram" tbc Richard Barrow (½)	100
	⅔ "Fools Parradise" – tbc Richard Barrow (½)	33⅓
	⅔ "Scotts Lott" – tbc Richard Barrow (½)	66⅔
	"Skeggs Springs" – for himself	50
	"Pattingham" – for himself	100
	pt. "Kinniments Delight" tbc Richard Barrow (½)	112
	⅔ "Hopewell" – for h/o (N) Kinnement; tbc Richard Barrow (½)	53
Edward Hopkins	pt. "Beech & Elliotts Lott"	100

49:1756:42 ...		
Esther w/o John Hughs	pt. "Beech"	12
	"Chance" – surveyed for (N) Emory	100
	pt. "Jones Progress"	35
	"Taylor & James's Discovery"	100
John Hopkins	pt. "Beech, Elliotts Lott, & Elliotts Folly" tbc Petter Blake for the heir	100
	"Cays Neck" a/s "Clays Hope"	102
Jo. Harrisson	pt. "Hop Hazard"	50
	pt. "Crooked Intention"	50
James Harrisson	pt. "Prouse Point", pt. "Haphazard", & pt. "Foresail"	38
	pt. "Poplar Neck"	42
Elizabeth Harrison (bayside)	"Prouss Point" & pt. "Haphazard"	12
	pt. "Poplar Neck"	58
	"Mount Missery Addition" tbc Jos. Harrison	12
Joshua Hopkins	pt. "London Derry"	103
Elizabeth Harrisson	pt. "Mount Missery" tbc Joseph Harrison	25
Thomas Haddaway	"Barken Point"	100
	"Lancashire"	50
	"Haddaways Addition"	75
49:1756:43 ...		
John Holt	pt. "Broad Oak" tbc Thomas Jenkins for h/o (N) Holt	25
Jo. Hopkins	pt. "Enlargement"	50
	"Rays Point"	150
	"Jordans Folly" – denied	100
	"Snellings Delight"	150
William Harrisson (Irish Creek)	pt. "Ashford"	50
	"Long Neglect"	35
Jo. Hix	pt. "Ashford"	50
Henry Harris	"Cornwell" a/s "Cromwell"	100
	"Josephs Lott"	100
Mary w/o John Hunt	pt. "Devine St. Andrew" tbc John Hunt s/o John (⅔)	150
	"Content"	98

h/o Philemon Horney	"Batchelors Branch" tbc Solomon Horney	100
	pt. "Addition to Batchelors Branch" tbc Solomon Horney	94
	"Skinners Swineyard" – for h/o (N) Higgs tbc Philip Horney who married w/o (N) Higgs	200
John Harrington	pt. "Buckby"	150
49:1756:44 ...		
w/o Thomas Huchinson	pt. "Buckby"	200
	"Huchinsons Discovery" – alleged in "Cooks Manor"	300
	pt. "Lords Gift" – alleged in "Pitts Range"	15
	"Beverly" – alleged cannot find bounds	522
	"Beverly Addition" – alleged cannot find bounds	230
	"Huchinsons Point" – cannot find bounds	72
Peter Hunt	"Anketill"	40
	"Larramores Addition" – from (N) Laramore; denies 60 a.	110
	"Larramores Prudence"	87
w/o John Hixon	pt. "Hobsons Choice"	21
	"Poplar Hill"	57
John Harrington (bayside)	"Hatton Garden"	50
William Harris (Miles Creek)	pt. "Hutchinsons Addition"	100
Robert Hunter	"Jacobs Beginning"	110
	pt. "Dudleys Demesne"	40
John Higgens	"Barams Range"	177
	pt. "Lowes Rambles"	28
49:1756:45 ...		
Susanna w/o Rowland Haddaway	"Fishbourns Landing"	104
Robert Harwood	"Newnames Folly"	50
	pt. "Swifts Chance"	23
	pt. "Harwoods Neglect"	27
	pt. "Barwicks Discovery"	123
	"Harwood Hill"	620
	"Rich Farm" – alleged in older survey; denied	150
	"Rich Farm Addition" – alleged in older survey; denied	200

Pere Harrisson	pt. "Bensons Enlargement"	190
	"Feddemans Discovery" – for his wife w/o Richard Feddeman	408
William Hadden	pt. "Rumleys Forrest"	107
Paul Holmes	"Sidenburgh"	100
	"Plansly" – not on Rent Rolls	100
John Hammilton	"Williston"	224
Samuel Hopkins	"Rigbys Discovery"	105
John Hewey	pt. "Carters Inheritance"	100
49:1756:46 ...		
Sarah w/o Robert Hall	pt. "Partnership"	10
	"Halls Range"	353
	"Halls Addition"	12
Henry Henrix	pt. "Discovery"	20
Edward Harrisson	pt. "Timber Neck"	175
William Harrisson (Miles Creek)	"Taylors Ridge"	100
Peter Harwood	"Addition" – dead; tbc: • Robert Harwood – 60 a. • Solomon Harwood – 112¼ a. • Petter Harwood – 112¼ a.	284¼
h/o Dennis Hopkins	pt. "Coventry" – alleged will disclaim; not to be found	50
h/o Thomas Hopkins	"Hopkins Point Addition" – alleged in "Hopkins Point"; not to be found	50
h/o Robert & Thomas Hopkins	pt. "Hopkins Point" – alleged lost in water; not to be found	24
~~Thomas Harwood~~ h/o Thomas Hammond	"Hampton" – alleged in older surveys	62
49:1756:47 ...		
h/o John Homewood	pt. "Home Hill" – alleged in older surveys; not to be found	4
h/o Thomas Hethod	pt. "Mount Misery" – alleged in older surveys	25
	"Plumt Point" – escheatable	100
	"Timber Neck" – escheatable	100
h/o Robert Hall	"Olive Branch" – says would disclaim; not to be found	100
h/o William Hampstead	pt. "Sutton Grange"	45

Samuel Harbert (North Carolina)	pt. "Herbert Choice"	86
	pt. "Mitchels Hermitage"	25
h/o Richard Haward	"Griffiths Adventure" – escheatable	50
h/o Robert Harrisson	pt. "Prouss Point" – alleged in older survey	10
James & John Harrisson	"Dover Marsh"	74
	"Dover Marsh"	150
49:1756:48 ...		
Walter Jenkins	pt. "Patricks Ridge" a/s "Powicks Ridge"	240
Elizabeth Jenkins	pt. "Patricks Ridge" a/s "Powicks Ridge"	560
Thomas Johnson	pt. "Patricks Ridge" a/s "Powicks Ridge"	100
Thomas Jenkins	pt. "Double Ridge"	120
	pt. "Sutton Grange"	120
	"White Gore"	40
w/o Robert Jadwin (QA)	pt. "Parkers Range"	60¾
Jeremiah Jadwin (QA)	pt. "Hampton" & pt. "Parkers Range" – alleged in Tuckahoe & Highfield Creek	223
David Jones	pt. "Knaps Lott"	105
	pt. "Prospect"	106
	"Wilderness"	75
	"Flemmons Freshes"	215
	"Jones's Interest"	40
h/o Vincent Jones – Pooley Jones is tenant	pt. "Nobles Chance"	89
49:1756:49 ...		
Elizabeth Jones (widow)	pt. "Heworth"	17
Dr. John Jackson (QA)	pt. "Waterton"	170
	"Finneys Range"	225
Lewis Jones	pt. "Tryangle"	44
Elizabeth w/o John Jones (tanner)	pt. "Cumberland"	80
h/o William Johnson (ENG)	pt. "Heworth"	133
William Jump (QA)	"William & Margerett"	100
h/o John Jadwin	"Jadwins Choice" – supposed neglected	300
Jeremiah Jadwin (QA)	"Hampton" & pt. "Parkers Range"	223
49:1756:50 ...		
Fran. Kersey (cnp)	"Webbley"	300
	"Sarahs Neck"	5[illegible]

	"Kerseys Good Luck" – denied	37
h/o Matthew Kemp	"Woolsey" or "Chancellors Point" – formerly charged to William Edmondson	1000
Jo. Kinnimont	⅓ "Dundee"	133⅓
Samuel Kinnimont	⅓ "Dundee"	133⅓
William Kemp	"Mabell"	100
	pt. "Kemps Lott"	50
	"Mabells Addition"	50
	"Kemps Lott Addition"	26
w/o Matthew Kirby	"Swamp Hole"	100
Michael Kirby	"Buck Range"	50
	pt. "Duns Range" tbc David Kirby	102
	pt. "Buck Range Addition"	55
	"Bows's Range"	235
John Kinnimont	pt. "Lambeth" tbc: • John Gibson – 71½ a. (f. 34) • William Elbert (QA) – 28½ a.	100
49:1756:51 ...		
James Kemp	pt. "Dudleys Chace"	50
	pt. "Sybland"	121
	pt. "Sybland Addition"	55
	"Boltons Addition" tbc Benjamin Kemp	50
	pt. "Maxfield"	64
	pt. "Cowallyn"	100
John Kemp	"Bolton"	100
Benjamin Kemp	"Woolf Harbour"	62
h/o John King	pt. "Kings Neglect"	8
Sarah Kemp – said Sarah is runaway & no heirs	pt. "Sutton" & "Suttons Addition" tbc Trustram Thomas	7
	pt. "Sutton", pt. "Suttons Addition", & pt. "Hardship" tbc Trustram Thomas	6
Dr. Edward Knott (Dover on Delaware)	pt. "Pooleys Discovery" – denied	116
	"Nobles Addition"	207
	"Pooleys Discovery on Resurvey"	75
Thomas Keetts	pt. "Stevens's Plains"	50
49:1756:52 ...		
Michael Kirby, Jr.	"Kirwicks Addition"	49

w/o David Kirby	"Limrick"	60
	pt. "Turners Range"	40
	"Kirbys Interest"	30
Richard Kirby	"Venture"	37
	"Kirbys Outlett"	47
James Kendrick	pt. "Coventry"	250
Parrott Kirby	"Kirbys Endeavour"	98
Simon Keld	pt. "Keilds Inheritance"	219
Robert Kirby	pt. "Dudleys Demesne"	50
James & Solomon Kenting (QA)	pt. "Bloomsbury" – supposed in older surveys; not to be found	12
h/o John Kinnimont	pt. "Lambeth" – alleged in older surveys, if not in QA; tbc William Elbert	28½
h/o Isaac Kittson	pt. "Upper Dover" – alleged in His Lordships Manor; not to be found	56
49:1756:53 ...		
h/o Dam. Kirvan	pt. "Cuba" – alleged in His Lordships Manor	100
Hon. Edward Lloyd, Esq. (cnp)	"Salter Marsh"	100
	"Scotts Close"	150
	"Lynton"	600
	pt. "Todd upon Dirvan" – should only be 80 a.	160
	"Thrimby Grange"	500
	"Meers Gate"	300
	"Nathaniels Point"	50
	"Crouchle Choice"	150
	pt. "Addition" – surveyed for (N) Woolman	150
	"Sauldiers Delight"	100
	pt. "Timber Neck"	60
	"Abbington"	400
	"Batchelears Delight"	100
	pt. "Wheatstone"	100
	"Advantage"	500
	"Wesbeck" tbc Thomas Lane	100
	"Fortune"	150
	"Grunny"	100
	"Doulys Lott"	50
	"Town Road"	50

	"Bettys Branch"	325
	"Knightlys Addition"	50
	"Garys Delight"	50
	"Falconars Folly"	100
	"Triangle"	55
	"Dirty Weeden"	100
	"Brafferton"	100
	"Henrietta Marias Discovery"	216
	"Fortunes Addition" a/s "Fortune"	52
	pt. "Brittania", pt. "Hillsdon", & pt. "Costins Chance"	300
	"Outlett"	220
	pt. "Kings Forrest"	75
	pt. "Woolmans Hermitage"	55
	"Stock Range" a/s "Bennett Lloyd"	400
	pt. "Bettys Dowry"	75
	"Farm"	348
	pt. "Kings Plains"	79
	"Newtown"	100
	"Sweatnames Hope"	120
49:1756:54 ...		
Hon. Edward Lloyd, Esq. (continued) (cnp)	"Meersgate Addition"	267
	"Long Neglect"	133
	"Inlett"	88
	pt. "Carters Inheritance"	300
	pt. "Roadway"	50
	pt. "Woolmans Inheritance"	104
	"Lotts Crook"	679
	"Bodwells Indian Neck"	913
	"Planters Increase with Turners Ridge"	504
	"Carslaks Content" – overcharged	60
	"Tobacco Pipe Resurveyed" & "Hackers Oldfield"	745
	"Bennetts Kind Caution"	322¾
	"Gareys Security"	124
	"Lloyd Addition to Brerely"	380
	<n/g> – another tract of (N) Woolman	150

	"Lloyds Lott"	141
	"Bennett Lloyd"	348½
	"Daniels Addition" – alleged in older survey; denied	135
	"Huntingtons Addition" – alleged in older survey; denied	150
	"Timber Neck" – alleged in elder surveys	100
Mr. John Leeds	"Wades Point"	400
	"Hatton" tbc w/o John Love & overcharged in "Rackliff Mannor"	500
	"Long Delay"	33
John Lookerman	pt. "Kirkam" & pt. "Harryton"	147
w/o John Lowe	pt. "Rattcliffe Manor"	150
	pt. "Hatton"	63
	pt. "Haddaways Lott"	50
	pt. "Grafton Manor"	245
	"Piney Neck"	107
49:1756:55 ...		
Mr. Robert Lloyd	"Pickbourn"	200
	"Tally Farm"	100
	"Hope"	100
	"Elliotts Discovery"	100
	"Adjunction"	50
	"Widows Chance"	500
	"Scottland"	50
	"Vincents Lott" – for h/o (N) Hemsley; denied	43
	"Lloyds Discovery"	96
	pt. "Partnership"	1200
	"Hemsley Upon Wye" – for h/o (N) Hemsley	1160
	"Hemsley Upon Wye Addition" – for h/o (N) Hemsley	146
	"Graves" – for himself; will disclaim	280
	"James's Folley" – alleged in elder surveys; denied	50
	"Greenland" – alleged bounds lost; will disclaim	50
Mrs. Margaret Lowe (cnp)	pt. "Aderton"	300
	"Adertons Addition"	100
	pt. "Lowes Rambles" – denied by her executor	1068

	pt. "Discovery" – says would disclaim; denied by her executor	127
	"Good Luck" – says would disclaim; denied by her executor	26
	"Devises" – says would disclaim; denied by her executor	440
William Landman or Lambden	"Sumerton"	200
	"Winterton"	50
	pt. "William & Marys Addition"	52
	pt. "Grafton Manor"	100
	"William & Marys Addition" – alleged in "Grafton Manor"	100
49:1756:56 ...		
Thomas Loveday	"Knave Keep Off"	68½
	pt. "Middle Spring"	270
	pt. "Hampton" & pt. "Parkers Range" – from Robert Greenwood	<n/g>
	"Dudly"	200
	pt. "Parkers Farm"	100
	pt. "Swineyard"	88
	pt. "Swineyard" – for h/o (N) Dickinson	<n/g>
	pt. "Hatton"	459
	"Frankford St. Michals"	616
	pt. "Baildon"	30
	pt. "Crooked Lane"	116
	"Bennetts Freshes"	423
Mr. James Lloyd	pt. "Marsh Land"	265
	"Buck Land"	250
	"New Mist"	200
	"Rumley Marsh"	300
	"Addition" – surveyed for (N) Gurling	100
	"Partnership"	310
	"Morrey"	150
	"Grundys Inclosure"	170
	"Buckland Marsh"	50
	pt. "Gurlington"	100
John Lloyd	pt. "Piney Point Advantage"	150

Robert Larramore	"Larramores Neck"	100
	"Bampshire"	50
Thomas Lane for his wife	"Poplar Hill"	200
	pt. "Waterton"	290
	pt. "Normanton"	767
	pt. "Kings Neglect"	107
	pt. "Bettys Dowry"	2
49:1756:57 ...		
Anthony Lecompt	pt. "Cumberland"	50
	pt. "Easoms Addition"	78
	pt. "Lobb Corner"	23
	"Anthonys Inlargement"	108½
h/o Charles Lewis	"Chance" – alleged in elder surveys	79
Robert Lambdon	pt. "Sands Lott"	50
	"Bridges"	176
Rebecca Lynch	"Mullikins Choice"	100
w/o Robert Lowther	pt. "Beaverdam Neck"	70½
	"Forrest & Dike"	116¼
Dennis Larey	pt. "Beaverdam Neck"	70½
	pt. "Partnerships Hazard"	142
Mary Lurty	"Old Womans Folly" – during life	172
John Lookerman, Jr.	"Sekeemers Neglect" – taken by elder survey	44
h/o Nicholas Lurty	"Eastons Hazard" – alleged in "Grafton Manor"; not to be found	52
Vincent Lookerman (Dover on Delaware)	"Harriss Lott" – alleged not patented; denied	111
49:1756:58 ...		
John Leonard guardian to Jogate	pt. "Hopkins Point" – not to be found	50
Timothy Lyndal	"Duxbury" – escheatable; not to be found	250
Jonas Lambert	"Lambert House" – escheatable; not to be found	50
Thomas Martain, Sr.	pt. "Hir Dier Lloyd"	296
	"Attwell"	100
	"New Scottland" – for h/o (N) Giddin tbc William Martin	700
	"Tawney Close"	50
	pt. "Hard Measure"	5

Thomas Martain, Jr.	pt. "Hir Dier Lloyd" a/s "Wilderness"	100
	pt. "Shore Ditch"	25
	"Rich Neck"	300
William Martin	pt. "Hir Dier Lloyd"	75
	"Mitchams Hall"	300
	"Martins Purchase"	3¼
	~~"New Scotland" – for h/o (N) Gidings tbc Thomas Martin~~	~~700~~
James Millard	pt. "Canterbury Manor"	170
Phillip Martin	"Bullins Chance" a/s "Choice"	350
	pt. "Conjunction"	25
49:1756:59 ...		
Daniel Mannadier	pt. "Marsh Land"	70
	pt. "Jamica"	50
	pt. "Goldsborough"	187
	"Timothys Lott"	25
	"Tattechurts"	38
	"Fottrells Discovery"	93
Jane w/o Edm. Marsh	pt. "Studds Point"	50
	pt. "Hulls Neck"	40
John McMahan	pt. "White Phillips"	42
	pt. "Lowes Rambles"	30
William Modesly	pt. "Boones Hope"	40
Charles Morgan	pt. "Chesnutt Bay"	95
	pt. "Dudleys Clift"	133
Ann w/o Patrick Mullikin	pt. "Taylors Ridge" tbc John Cox (⅓)	100
	pt. "Partricks Plains" tbc John Cox (⅓)	210
Sarah Morgan	pt. "Holm Hill"	62
	pt. "Smiths Clifts"	258
Samuel Mullikin	pt. "Partricks Plains"	90
	pt. "Mullikins Delight"	52¾
49:1756:60 ...		
Hezekiah Mackey	pt. "Bullen"	40
	pt. "Broad Oak" & pt. "Bullen"	60
	pt. "Brad Oak"	116⅔
	⅔ "Holmby"	133⅓

Rachell Mackey	pt. "Broad Oak" & pt. "Bullen"	18⅓
	⅓ "Holmby"	66⅔
Richard Mansfield	"Up Holland"	50
Thomas Matthews (Kings Creek)	pt. "Rich Farm Addition" & pt. "Bedworth"	80
Edward McDaniel	pt. "Fishbourns Lott"	100
Patrick McQuey	pt. "Devine St. Andrew"	50
	"Fools Paridise"	38
John Markland	"Morgans Point" a/s "Plinkimmon"	50
h/o Jo. Merrick	pt. "Batchelors Range Addition"	37
Dr. Henry Murray	"Gatterly Moore"	120
John Mears	"White Chappell"	100
49:1756:61 ...		
William Morgan	pt. "Morgans Neglect"	66
	pt. "Rumleys Forrest"	43
William Mulliken	"York"	306
	pt. "Timber Neck"	55
	"Mullicans Chance" a/s pt. "Taylors Ridge"	100
	"Yorks Destruction"	50
	pt. "Timber Neck Addition"	50
Thomas Matthews (Tuckahoe)	pt. "Bloomsberry"	88
Samuel Morgan	pt. "Dudleys Clift" – not to be found	51
Olliver Millington	pt. "Betteys Chance"	100
	"Epson"	100
	"Addition" – denied; get copy of certificate from QA Rent Rolls p. 344; surveyed for Robert Betts in 1681 & said Betts assigned it to John King & his wife in 1724	100
Solomon Marshall	"Kinsale"	126
w/o James Millis	pt. "Advantage"	100
49:1756:62 ...		
James Merrick	"Hazard Addition"	9
	"Powers Hazard"	50
Rev. John Miller (DE) for his wife	pt. "Nobles Meadows"	114½
	pt. "Betts Addition"	103½
Sarah Millington	pt. "Nobles Meadows"	114½
	pt. "Betts Addition"	103½

Henry Martin	"Crooked Ramble"	75½
h/o William Moore	"Chance Rdge" – alleged in "Anderton"	150
	"Moreland" – land to be neglected	100
Walter Malton, John Price, & Robert Bryan	pt. "Hattfield" & pt. "Hattfields Addition"	163
h/o Henry Mitchel (CV)	"Reach Blossom" – alleged in "Jennings Hope"	600
h/o Charles Masters	"Vineyard" – alleged in elder surveys	250
49:1756:63 ...		
Joseph Merchant (QA)	"Fairplay"	50
John Morgan	"Cabbin Neck" – alleged in elder surveys	500
Thomas Manning	"Hopewell" – owner unknown	100
	"Tryangle" – escheatable	50
Thomas Miles	"Miles End" – escheatable	75
Thomas Manning & John Ingram	"Norwich" – escheatable	200
Patrick McDaniel	"Patricks Delight" – escheatable	65
h/o Phillip Massey	"Tilghmans Fortune" – escheatable	215
49:1756:64 ...		
Elizabeth Nicols	pt. "Hopkins Point" – during life	86
Edward Needles	pt. "Rackliffe"	150
	pt. "Pitts's Range"	200
	pt. "Johns Neck"	23⅓
	pt. "Killon" a/s "Killom"	140
Jonathan Neale	pt. "Chestnutt Bay" – for h/o Phi. Jenkins	205
	"Edmondsons Freshes" – for h/o Phi. Jenkins	300
	pt. "Dudleys Clift" – for h/o Phi. Jenkins	16
	pt. "Falconars Square" – for h/o Phi. Jenkins	100
	"Falconars Hazard" – for h/o Phi. Jenkins	60
	"Bannings Hazard" – for h/o Phi. Jenkins	50
	pt. "Hickory Ridge" – for h/o Phi. Jenkins	50
Mrs. Deborah Nicols for h/o Jeremiah Nicols on devises; runaway, tbc w/o Jeremiah Nicols or Dr. Edward Knot	pt. "Planters Delight"	34
	pt. "Stephens Plains"	50
	pt. "Bettyes Chance"	100
	"Richmond"	41
	"Richmonds Addition"	282
	pt. "Nobles Addition"	84

George Noble – runaway; if it should not be charged to Jere Nicols's widow or Dr. Edward Knot	pt. "Planters Delight"	66
	pt. "Nobles Addition"	59
Edward Neale	pt. "Mount Hope"	50
	pt. "Nanticoke Manor"	171
49:1756:65 ...		
Fran. Neale	pt. "Mount Hope"	50
	"Adventure" – alleged in His Lordships Manor; denied	150
Fran. Neale, Jr.	pt. "Heworth" & pt. "Edmondsons Freshes"; denied "Heworth"	100
	pt. "Edmondsons Freshes"	50
	pt. "Hickory Ridge"	284
	"Franch Hazard"	41
	pt. "Dennys Content"	12
Fran. Neale (from above)	"Cuba" – alleged in His Lordships Manor; denied	50
	"Cubas Addition" – alleged in His Lordships Manor; denied	72
Mr. William Nicols	pt. "Galloway"	204
	pt. "Bryans Lott" tbc James Tilghman	12½
	pt. "Mickle More"	230
w/o Edward Needles	pt. "Killam" a/s "Kitton" tbc her son Edward Needles	419
Mr. Jonathan Nicols (QA)	"Partnership" – lies in QA & charged there	500
	pt. "Maiden Point", "Maiden Point Addition", & "Withers Range"	300
Solomon Neale	pt. "Hickory Ridge on Resurvey"	137
Robert Newcomb	"Robert & Margarett"	441½
49:1756:66 ...		
h/o Henry Nicols	pt. "Wethers's Range"– denied by heirs	156
Thomas Nowland (CE) for wife	pt. "Nominy" – alleged in elder surveys	148
h/o Henry Newnam	"Luck Will" – escheatable	179
	"Wittingham" – escheatable	50
h/o John Newnam	"Newingham" – said to be lost	100
Mr. Edward Oldham (cnp)	pt. "Anderton"	100
	pt. "Nether Foster"	50

	"Jacks Point"	100
	"Comsberry"	100
	"Rich Park"	569
	pt. "Judiths Garden"	130
	"Oldhams Discovery"	115½
Maurice Oram	"Waste Land" & pt. "Tryangle" – for post pones	40
	pt. "Fox Hole"	145
	pt. "Fox Harbour"	50
	"Whaterford"	100
	"Foxes Denn"	56
49:1756:67 ...		
William Oxenham (QA)	pt. "Sommerly"	50
	"Moorfield"	280
Richard Oyston	"Bobbs Hill" a/s "Hobbs Hill"	100
	pt. "Discovery"	117
Andrew Oram	pt. "Adventure"	100
John Osmont	"Neglect" tbc Archibald McKinness who married the widow	107
Frances Porter (widow)	pt. "Hemersby"	100
Robert Porter	pt. "Hemersby"	100
Thomas Parsons	pt. "Hammultons Neck"	66
Penelope Parrott	pt. "Canterbury Manor"	56⅔
h/o Robert Pickerin	pt. "Ashby"	100
49:1756:68 ...		
h/o James Parrott tbc John Holmes guardian to the heirs	pt. "Cattline Plains"	10
	pt. "Buckrow"	150
	"Abbington"	100
	"Walnutt Garden"	50
	pt. "Hulls Addition"	100
	pt. "Mullikins Delight"	11
Mr. Grundy Pemberton (QA) (cnp)	"Fentry"	100
	pt. "Smiths Clifts"	232
	pt. "Heworth"	205
	pt. "Cumberland"	30
	"Long Point"	42
	pt. "Lobbs Corner"	14

	"Rome" – denied	56
Thomas Powell	pt. "Beaver Neck" tbc Howell Powell (129 a.)	259
	pt. "Advantage" tbc Howell Powell (21 a.)	42
	"Powells Meadow"	34½
	"Powells Misfortune"	42½
Daniel Powell – William Brooks "Lambeth" to him	"Rigbys Marsh"	300
	pt. "Troths Fortune"	153½
	pt. "Troths Fortune"	246½
John Pritchart	pt. "White Phillips"	75
Thomas Purnall	pt. "Hampton"	8
	pt. "Rich Range" – not allowed	218
49:1756:69 ...		
Abner Parrott	pt. "Jamaica"	100
John Porter	pt. "Friths Neck"	33
John Potts	pt. "Saint Michaells Fresh Run"	75
	"Potts Discovery"	60¼
Aaron Parrott	pt. "John's Neck"	264
	pt. "Kingston"	51½
	pt. "Kingston" – more; said will disclaim	48½
	"Oaken" – said will disclaim	100
h/o William Parrott	pt. "Highfield"	50
	"Marshy Point Addition" – alleged in "Marshy Point": "Marshy Point" not to be found or heirs unknown	100
w/o Thomas Perkins	pt. "Carters Farm"	400
	"Perkins's Discovery"	193½
Lawrence Porter	"York"	100
Francis Pickering	"Sarahs Lott"	50
Edward Perkins	"Newnames Range"	100
49:1756:70 ...		
h/o Benjamin Parrott or h/o Thomas Turner	pt. "Parrotts Reserve" – not to be found	50
George Parrott	pt. "Goughston" – denied	100
	"Abrams Lott", pt. "Millroad 2nd Addition", & pt. "Goalston"	230
John Plowman	"Auston"	200
Fran. Parrott	pt. "Lords Chance"	100

John Poor	pt. "Union"	50
John Porter, Jr.	"Willens Good Luck"	65
Capt. Thomas Porter	"Kimbles Industry"	283
(N) Page (barber) for his wife late Jane Stitchberry	pt. "Boones Hope"	33⅓
	"Studhams Chance"	18
h/o James Perry	pt. "White Marshes" – or h/o (N) Berry	240
h/o John Parr	pt. "Swineyard" – says will disclaim	88
49:1756:71 ...		
h/o Thomas Phillips	"White Philips" – alleged in elder surveys	38
John Paddyson	"Foston" – says will disclaim	100
h/o Fran. Porter	"Hazard" – says will disclaim	70
h/o Benjamin Pemberton	"Security" – alleged not patented; tbc Samuel Dickinson (80 a., f. 23)	406
h/o John Padley (ENG)	"Chestnutt Bay"	600
h/o John Preston (North Carolina)	pt. "Hatton"	78
h/o Robert Philips (SM)	"Little Minores"	200
John Pitts or h/o (N) Willson	pt. "Mill Land" – escheatable	70
John Pitts	"Pitts's Freshes" – escheatable	200
49:1756:72 ...		
Quakers Meeting	pt. "London Derry"	3
Arthur Rigbye	"Anderby"	100
	pt. "Hopkins Point" tbc Sarah Bartlet	100
	pt. "Fox Hole"	65
	"Crawford"	100
	"Lambeths Addition"	150
	"Rigbys Folly"	45
	pt. "William & James"	33
	pt. "Reynolds Point"	100
	pt. "Maxwell Moore"	100
	"Rigbys Choice"	101½
	"Lamberton"	109¼
Thomas Ray	⅓ "Dundee"	133⅓
	pt. "Addition to Batchelors Branch" tbc Solomon Horney	6
Richard Robinson	pt. "Long Point"	100

John Robinson	pt. "Long Point"	150
	pt. "Goldsborough"	87
	pt. "Goldsborough" – denied	13
	"Robinsons Beginning"	17
w/o James Robass	pt. "Newnames Lott"	100
	pt. "Nobles Chance"	100
	pt. "Planters Delight"	100
	"Stevens Lott" – says will disclaim	19
	"Addition"	75
49:1756:73 ...		
Feddeman Rolls	"Hoopers Enfall"	200
	pt. "Grafton Manor"	28
	"Cabbin Neck, Sandy Bitte, & Halls Fortune"	238
	"Doretheys Inlargement"	45
	"Rolls Range"	237
William Ridgeway	pt. "Whaste Land"	100
John Register	pt. "Acton"	5⅜
	pt. "Darlington"	88½
	pt. "Kingsberry Addition"	122¼
William Robins	pt. "Holm Hill"	434
	pt. "Smiths Clifts"	201
	pt. "Rich Farm Addition" a/s "Rich Range Addition"	14
	pt. "Fragment"	13⅔
William Roberts	"Chance" – surveyed for (N) Walker	100
	"Knave Stand Off" – for his wife	50
Bartholomew Roberts	pt. "Friths Neck"	17
	pt. "Ennions Range"	50
	"Roberts Addition"	47
George Rull	pt. "Carters Farm"	100
49:1756:74 ...		
Henry Robson	"James's Lookout" & "Partnership"	93
w/o John Rathel	"Strawberry Hill Addition"	50
	"Rathels Chance"	50
James Rattcliffe (cnp)	pt. "Jacob & Johns Pasture"	170
	pt. "Addition" – for (N) Carter	52

	"Rattcliffe Highway"	113
	"Maple Branch"	40
James Rattcliffe, Jr.	pt. "Jacob & Johns Pasture"	50
	pt. "Goughston"	100
Thomas Roberts	pt. "Moorfields"	84
	"Tall Tales Loss"	125
	"Charlevile & Cork"	250
	"Vickers Lott"	52
Fran. Register	pt. "Parrotts Reserve"	150
	"Francis's Plaines"	64½
	pt. "Stevens's Range" –says will disclaim	14
	"Durham" – says will disclaim	73
Henry Richardson	"Pasly Necke"	24
	"Ponis Lookout"	8½
Thomas Robson	pt. "Partnership"	82
49:1756:75 ...		
Phillip Rigby	"Ealom"	90
Hugh Rice	pt. "Tanners Choice" – for his wife	256⅓
h/o Thomas Read	"Roadly" – alleged in water	20
h/o James Raglass	"Rogue Keep Out" – alleged in His Lordships Manor	50
h/o John Richardson (PA)	pt. "Willenbrough" – alleged in elder surveys	150
	"Jamacia Addition"	50
h/o John Rousby	"Morgans Hope" – alleged lost	300
h/o Edward Russum	"Russums Inclosure" – alleged will disclaim	65
h/o Michael Russel	"Cornelius's Cove" – alleged cannot be found; tbc Cornelius Daily	50
	"Shenp's Fortune" – alleged cannot be found	100
h/o Thomas Richardson	"Addition" – alleged in His Lordships Manor	190
h/o Anthony Rumbal	pt. "Hemsleys Arcadia"	100
49:1756:76 ...		
Elijah Skillington	pt. "Turners Point"	200
	"Skillingtons Hap"	20
Thomas Skinner	pt. "Marshey Point"	100
John Sherwood, Jr. s/o Edward Man Sherwood	pt. "Exchange"	100

Daniel Sherwood, Jr.	pt. "Exchange"	100
	"Allemby's Fields"	124¾
Elizabeth Stevens (widow)	pt. "Cattline Plains"	80
	⅓ "Buck Row"	16⅔
	⅓ "Dawsons Fortune"	16⅔
	pt. "Campton"	6⅔
	pt. "Edmunds Cove"	58
William Stevens	pt. "Cattline Plains"	160
Thomas Stevens	pt. "Cattline Plaines"	150
	⅔ "Buckrow"	33⅓
	⅔ "Dawsons Fortune"	33⅓
	pt. "Dudleys Choice"	100
	pt. "Coxes Addition" tbc Alexander James	70
	pt. "Straw Bridge"	163
	"Williams Lott"	49
	pt. "Edmunds Cove"	116
	"Campton"	108
	pt. "Hampton" – alleged in part that he escheated	14
	"Stevens" – alleged cannot be found	50
49:1756:77 ...		
George Sailes	"Rich Range"	300
	"Delph"	100
Ruth w/o William Skinner	"Clays Hope" tbc James Edge	200
	pt. "Fairplay"	25
	pt. "Mainsaile"	50
Thomas Sherwood, Jr. guardian to h/o Mary Davis	"Batchelors Point"	100
	"Hope Chance"	50
	"Knave Keep Out"	50
	"Parsonage"	100
	"Addition" – surveyed for (N) Davis	350
	pt. "Killam" a/s "Killon" – for himself	229
Thomas Sheriffe	pt. "Smiths Clifts" – for h/o Daniel Bartlett	94
	pt. "Hases Green" – for h/o Daniel Bartlett	50
h/o John Shaw	pt. "Hulls Neck"	150
Edward Sherwood	pt. "Pitts's Range"	200
Peter Shannahane	"Chance" – surveyed for (N) Rowe	100

Fran. Stanton	pt. "Bantry"	100
49:1756:78 ...		
John Damm Saunders	pt. "Hammiltons Park"	137
	"Davis's Outlett"	50
Phi. Skinner	pt. "Enlargement"	50
	"Skinners Point"	50
	"Skinners Addition"	23
	"Skinners Discovery"	70
Robert Spencer	"Fox Harbour" tbc Ann Spencer	50
	pt. "Edwards Hopewell"	45
	pt. "Bensons Enlargement" tbc Ann Spencer (107 a.)	187
	pt. "Matthew Circumvented"	14½
Benjamin Silvester	pt. "Johns Neck" – from (N) Sharp in 1744; not to be found	39
William Shield & James Sanders	pt. "Rich Farm Addition" & pt. "Bedworth" – not to be found	97
Thomas Sherwood	pt. "Fishing Bay"	12
	"Cabbin Neck, Potters Delight, & Potters Lott"	150
	"Daniel & Mary"	375
Charles Spencer	pt. "Fairplay"	25
	pt. "Jones Progress"	35
	pt. "Ennions Range"	96¾
	pt. "Mainsaile"	48
49:1756:79 ...		
John Small	pt. "Sommerly"	250
Daniel Sherwood	pt. "Anketill"	400
George Sprouse	pt. "Cumberland" & pt. "Chance Help"	157
	pt. "Lowes Rambles" – as guardian to William Ardery; tbc George Prouse, Jr.	200
Robert Sands	pt. "Sands Lott"	103
	pt. "Chance" – surveyed for (N) Sands	25
Sarah Spencer	pt. "Bensons Enlargement"	28½
	"Sarahs Garden"	13
	"Chance" – surveyed for (N) Elliott	183
Solomon Sharpe	"Chance"	40
Jo. Spencer	pt. "Ennions Range"	49

Thomas Smith (schoolmaster)	pt. "Grafton Manor" a/s "Goose Neck"	100
49:1756:80 ...		
George Sexton	"Woolf Pitt Ridge" – for his wife	50
	pt. "Turners Discovery" – for his wife	30
Christopher Sprye	pt. "Partnership"	54
	pt. "Maxwell More"	150
w/o Edward Starkey	"Bite the Biter"	35
Hugh Spencer	pt. "Matthew Circumvented"	150
John Silvester	"Horse Point"	21
Robert Stonestreet	"Tilberry"	376
Andrew Skinner	"Tanners Choice"	512⅔
Rebecca Sherwood	pt. "Huntington" tbc James Wrightson	130
h/o John Stevenson	"Acton Addition" – alleged partly in His Lordships Manor	57
	"Troths Addition" – alleged partly in His Lordships Manor	100
	"Hackney Marsh" – alleged in elder surveys	50
	"Troths Securyty" – alleged in elder surveys	109
h/o William & John Shaw	pt. "Cottingham" – alleged in water	73
49:1756:81 ...		
Trustram Thomas	pt. "Roadley"	200
	pt. "Double Ride"	280
	"Killingsworth"	50
	pt. "Sutton", pt. "Suttons Addition", pt. "Hardship", & pt. "Partnership"	278
	pt. "Thief Keep Out"	38
William Thomas	pt. "Anderton"	100
	pt. "Canterbury Manor" – for h/o William Parrott tbc Samuel Mullikin	113⅓
	pt. "Cottingham"	190
	pt. "Cottingham" – more for his wife	125
	pt. "Judeths Garden"	63
William Trippe	⅓ "Edmundton" – for his wife	100
	⅓ "Champenhams Addition" – for his wife	16⅔
	⅓ "Leith" – for his wife	13⅓
	⅓ "Champenham" & ⅓ "Bendon" – for his wife	183⅓

James Tilghman, Esq.	"Fausley"	250
	"Edmonds Range"	400
	"Addition" – surveyed for (N) Edmondson	100
	pt. "Sharpes Chance"	221
	pt. "Abrams Lott"	100
	"Dixons Outlett" a/s pt. "Dixons Lott"	50
William Tayler	pt. "Middle Spring"	25
	pt. "Turkey Neck"	243
	"Turkey Neck Addition"	35
49:1756:82 ...		
John Tomlinson	pt. "Rockliffe"	50
Richard Turbutt	pt. "Bless Land & Baggs Marsh"	460
William Troth	pt. "Acton"	294¼
	pt. "Darlington"	8
	"Bennington"	38
George Thompson	pt. "Smiths Clifts" – not to be found in county	454
	"Smiths Clifts" – more by the name of "Mill Land"	12
Miss Bettsy Trippe	"Harwoods Lyon" tbc Mr. George Maxwell	600
John Thomas	"Winkleton"	185
	"Mitchells Hall"	200
John Tayler	pt. "Kingston"	100
h/o or w/o Jo. Turner	pt. "Johns Hill"	180
	"Turners Discovery"	92¾
Abner Turner	pt. "Johns Hill"	90
	pt. "Hasco Green"	160
49:1756:83 ...		
Mr. Matthew Tilghman	"Wells's Outlett"	50
	pt. "Chance" – surveyed for (N) Sands	25
	"Bradford"	62
	pt. "Union"	611
	pt. "Coopers Lott"	25½
	"Choptank Hundred"	1468
	"Rich Neck"	577
	"Three Necks"	165
Mr. William Tilghman	"Henrietta Marias Purchase"	412
	"Couart Road"	138

h/o John Theobald (bayside) or h/o Peter Caulk	"Theobalds Addition"	20
John Thornton	"Moorfields Addition"	65
Peter Turner s/o Thomas	pt. "Stoppard Moore" – not to be found	67
Thomas Turner s/o Thomas	pt. "Stoppard Moore"	33
MM James & Edward Tilghman	"Elizabeths Venture"	1192½
49:1756:84 ...		
Col. Richard Tilghman (QA)	pt. "Canterbury Manor" – alleged in elder surveys	100
h/o Richard Talbott (AA)	"Parsons" a/s "Pawsons Ridge" – not to be found	500
h/o William Turner (Carolina)	pt. "Turners Range" – not to be found	10
h/o Thomas Taylor	"Addition" – escheatable	172
h/o James Tucker	"Stampforth Point" – escheatable	100
h/o John Thrift or devises	pt. "Hemsleys Arcadia" – not to be found	50
49:1756:85 ...		
Visitors of the County School	pt. "Tilghmans Fortune"	100
Daniel Vinton	pt. "Edwards Hopewell"	55
Vestry of St. Peters Parish	"Tranquelity" – alleged in "Pitts Range"	185
49:1756:86 ...		
Sarah Webb	pt. "Roadley"	150
John Watts	pt. "Hammiltons Neck" – pt. "Hamiltons Park" tbc John Watts, Jr. (66 a.)	234
James Woolcott, Jr.	pt. "Canterbury Manor"	210
James Wrightson	"Lurkey"	250
	pt. "Bryan Lott"	12½
	"Wrightsons Addition"	83
Thomas Winchester	½ "Widows Choice"	320
	"Braintree"	500
	"Braintree" – more by the name of "Bantry"	60
	"Marlings Folly"	50
	"Marlings Chance"	50
	pt. "Braintrees Addition"	10
	"Marlings Neglect"	57
	"Spring Close" — for h/o (N) Marling	100
William Willson	pt. "Middle Spring"	150
	pt. "Kingsberry"	70
	"Willsons Lott"	190

James Willson	pt. "Middle Spring"	50
	"White Oak Swamp"	100
49:1756:87 ...		
John Willis (KE)	pt. "Long Point"	25
	pt. "Long Neck"	90
	pt. "Benjamins Lott"	50
William Warring	pt. "Hampton" tbc Thomas Loveday	200
Phillip Walker	pt. "Upper Range"	112
	"Jordan Hill"	157
William Warner	pt. "Nobles Chance"	82
Jacob Wootters (QA)	pt. "Smiths Clifts" – not to be found	95
John Wootters (QA)	pt. "Smiths Clifts" – not to be found	20
William Whilby (QA)	pt. "Rich Range" – tbc Thomas Frampton (50 a.); not to be found	42
Henry White	"Goldsborough"	113
	pt. "Willenbro" & pt. "Gurlington"	93
	"Gurlington"	75
49:1756:88 ...		
Isaac Williams	pt. "Sybland" tbc George Williams	26
	pt. "Dudleys Choice"	50
	pt. "Maxfield"	88
Jo. Williams	pt. "Sybland"	53
	pt. "Sybland Addition"	55
John Wiles	pt. "Bentley Hay"	33⅓
h/o James Webb (QA)	pt. "York Shire" – not to be found	125
Samuel Wright	"Harriss Range"	400
William White	pt. "Sutton Grange"	280
w/o John Walker	pt. "Jamaica"	92
Peter Webb	"Poor Hill"	37
49:1756:89 ...		
Richard Wootters (QA)	"Richard & Marys Forrest"	80
Thomas Whittington	"Boston Clift" – alleged in His Lordships Manor	130
h/o John Williams	pt. "Enions Range"	24¼
	pt. "Fishbourns Lott"	50
	"Clay Bank"	50
	"Enions Lott"	151

h/o Jo. Winslow (NE)	"Duerbury" – alleged to be lett fall	680
h/o Robert Wolene	"Armstrongs Gift" – alleged in elder surveys	200
John Warner	"Poormans Portion" – escheatable	80
Samuel Winslow	"Delight" – escheatable	250
Fran. Whitefield	"Addition" – escheatable	300
h/o Edward Winkle	"Winkles Ridge" – escheatable	250
John Winfell	"Winfells Trouble" – escheatable	200
John Whittington	"Fishbourns Neglect" – alleged in His Lordships Manor	130
	pt. "Lower Dover" – alleged in His Lordships Manor	200
h/o Rowland White	"Youngs Adventure"	175
49:1756:90 ...		
h/o Thomas Skillington	"Hamiltons Neck" – not to be found	256
Charles Sinklair	pt. "Hoden Range", pt. "Millroad", & pt. "Millroad 2nd Addition" – alleged to be in "Edmonds Range"	120
h/o Thomas Smithson or devises	pt. "Mickle Mire" – alleged in elder surveys	150
	"Gatterly More" tbc Dr. Henry Murray	120
	pt. "Holden Range"	73
	pt. "Holden Addition"	50
	pt. "Millroad", pt. "Millroad Addition", & pt. "Millroad 2nd Addition"	120
h/o William Smith	pt. "Smiths Clifts" – alleged in elder surveys	496
Isaac Sasserson (North Carolina)	"Abrams Hermitage" – doubtful to be found	160
Thomas Sprye (AA)	pt. "Johns Hill" – not to be found	40
John Stewart	"Abrams Choice" – escheatable	50
Anne Stevenson	"Anns Chance" – said to be lost	50
h/o (N) Sing	"Newnames Fortune" – escheatable	100
William Shears	"Rich Neck" – escheatable	50
Jonathan Sybery	"Wickem" – says never made such survey	170

49:1756:91 List of lands charged in Additional Rent Roll		
James Tilghman	"Faulsey Meadow"	50½
Impey Dawson	"Crommell Resurvey"	476¾
Samuel Chamberlaine, Esq.	"Rome"	138½
James Broadaway	"Dudley" tbc Thomas Loveday	200
James Kemp	"Kemps Discovery"	9½
Col. Thomas Chamberlaine	2 lots in Oxford	1½
49:1756:<2 unnumbered> Recapitulation		

49:1757-8:1 ...		**Acres**
Samuel Abbot	pt. "Hutchesons Addition"	50
	"Beaverdams"	100
	"Minors Lott"	100
	pt. "Sutton" – surveyed for (N) Skinner for h/o (N) Holmes	125
	pt. "Sutton Addition" – surveyed for (N) Skinner for h/o (N) Holmes	25
	pt. "Buckrow"	40
Joseph Atkinson	"Cottingham"	100
	⅓ "Skipton"	100
	⅓ "Finneys Hermitage"	66⅔
	"Newnam"	50
	"Atkinsons Chance"	43
Thomas Atkinson	"Cottingham"	37
Henry Alexander	"Wales"	54
	"Irish Freshes"	50
	"Alexanders Chance"	250
	pt. "Good Luck"	100
William Alexander	"Dobsons Advantage"	28
	"Worgans Reserve"	200
Jonathan Airey	pt. "Rockliff"	118
	"Davids Ridge"	125
William Ayres	"Studs Point"	100
	"Ayres's Venture"	96
w/o Richard Aldern	"Yaffords Neck"	300
	"Royston Addition"	150
	"Alderns Island"	41
Thomas Ashcroft	"Beech & Elliots Lott"	18[illegible]
	"Davenport"	114[illegible]
Mary w/o William Adams a/s Eusebius Adams (the heir)	pt. "Hatfield & Hatfield Addition"	75
	"Adams's Right"	7[illegible]
	"Hatfield & Hatfields Addition" – denied	[illegible]
Samuel Atwell	"Bantry"	20[illegible]
49:1757-8:2 ...		

Joseph Arrington	"Adventure"	113
	"Arrington's Delight"	50
	"Pooley Neck"	25
	"Point Look Out"	6½
John Auld, Sr.	"New Port Glasgow"	221½
John Auld, Jr.	"Aulds Security"	47
	"Elliots Folly" – from your father	50
	"Grantham" – for his wife	106
Ann Arrington	⅓ "Middle Neck"	33⅓
Thomas Ayres	"Millar's Hope"	121
49:1757-8:3 ...		
Francis Baker	⅔ "Finneys Hermitage"	133⅓
	⅔ "Skipton"	200
Thomas Browning	"Hier Dier Lloyd"	75
	"Hier Dier Lloyd on Resurvey"	37
Ann Bowdle w/o Loftus	pt. "Hier Dier Lloyd"	61
	pt. "Hard Measure"	37
Lambert Booker	pt. "Tilghmans Fortune"	88
	"Saint Michaels Fresh Run"	100
Phebe Barnett	"Shore Ditch"	75
	"Swamp Tick"	100
Jacob Brommell	"Anderton"	100
	"Cove Hall" – to Robert Brumwell	100
	"Fort Venture" – to Robert Brumwell	50
	"Wintersell" – to John Brumwell	145
John Barnett	pt. "Bullen"	150
	"Catlin Plaines"	100
Joseph Bartlett	pt. "Ractliff Mannor"	270
James Bartlett	pt. "Ractliff Mannor"	250
Union Barwood	"Hopkins's Point"	66⅔
w/o Adam Browne	¼ "Parkers Point"	30
	¼ "Enlargement"	45
Thomas & James Barrow	pt. "Ashby"	93
	pt. "Bettys Cove"	13⅓
George Brinsfield guardian to William Arrington	"Middle Neck"	100

James Brainsfield	"Studs Point"	50
	⅔ "Middle Neck"	66⅔
John Blades	"Mathew Circumvented"	169
John Ball	pt. "Long Point"	25
	pt. "Long Neck"	90
	"Benjamins Lott"	50
49:1757-8:4 ...		
John Bozman	"Cardiff"	100
	pt. "Timber Neck"	150
	"Providence"	7
	pt. "Timber Neck"	64
	"Teats Lott"	459
	"Browns Park"	119
	"Bozman's Addition"	185¾
Anthony Bacon (London)	"Worgans Reserve"	300
	"Turkey Neck"	125
	"Mount Hope"	50
	"Parkers Park"	500
	"Brownes Lott"	200
	"Hasley"	200
	"Mill Land"	20
	"Widows Lott"	85
	pt. "Dobsons Advantage"	7
	pt. "Partnership Hazard"	142
	"Addition"	229
James Benson	"Huntington Grange"	80
	"Neglect"	18¼
	"Mistake"	25½
	"Fishing Bay"	126¼
Richard Barrow	"Batchelors Hope" – for his wife	25
	pt. "Bartram" – for his wife	75
	"Fools Parradise" – for his wife	25
	"Scotts Lott" – for his wife	50
	"Kininmons Delight" – for himself	84
	"Hopewell" – for his wife	40
	"School House Lott" – for his wife	59

Nicholas Benson	pt. "Hog Hole"	50
	"Bensons Enlargement"	42
	"Bensons Chance"	89
Samuel Bowman	pt. "Saint Johns Neck"	350
James Barnwell, Jr.	pt. "Mount Hope"	50
	pt. "Rich Farm Addition"	50
	"Partnership"	42
James Barnwell, Sr.	pt. "Mount Hope"	27
	pt. "Bisworth"	150
	pt. "Rich Farm Addition"	23
Mathew Lewis Barnett	pt. "Kingstown"	133⅓
	"Millingtons Choice" – for his wife	70
	pt. "Hollands Addition"	13⅔
	"Kingstown" – for h/o (N) Conerly	266⅔
	"Holland Addition" – for h/o (N) Conerly	27½
49:1757-8:5 ...		
Sarah Berry & John Berry	"White Marshes" tbc: • John Berry – 380 a. • James Berry – 190 a. • Benjamin Berry – 190 a.	760
	pt. "Rich Farm" tbc John Berry	<unr>
w/o Gilbert Barrow	pt. "Rich Farm"	50
	pt. "Mill Land"	40
	"Oxford"	338
Andrew Bandy	pt. "Kingstown"	100
Thomas Bruff	"Daniells Rest"	38
	"Walkers Tooth"	47
	pt. "Inclosure"	150
	"Daniels Addition"	70
Richard Bruff	"Daniels Rest"	12
	"Walkers Tooth"	100
	"Walkers Corner"	18
	pt. "Partnership"	96
Daniel Bridges	"Blydon"	100
w/o William Bush	pt. "Arcadia"	166
Risdon Bozman (cnp)	pt. "Kemps Lott"	50
	"Watson & Partnership"	150

	"Folly"	100
	"Kemps Lott Addition"	26
	"Sherwoods Neck"	268
	"Hemersly"	273
	"Lewis' Point"	145
	"Gaskins's Point"	50
	"Willsons Addition"	73
	"Neglect"	34
	"Moor & Cassell"	34
Richard Beswick	"Christophers Lott"	100
	"Stevens's Plains"	50
Rev. Thomas Bacon	"Cross Haze"	50
	pt. "Hull" – for Charity School	70
	"Partnership"	34
	"Davids Folly"	50
	"Chance" – for Charity School	23
Samuel Broadaway	"Sam's Fields"	102
	"Ramah"	104
	"Broadaways Medow"	100
49:1757-8:6 ...		
James Benny	"Morgans Neglect"	14
	"Morgans Addition"	46
	"Rumbley Forrest"	78⅓
	"Falconers Square"	100
	"Good Luck"	60
	"Duck Pond"	50
	"Rumbly Forrest"	6⅓
	"Bennys Addition"	32
	"Rumbly Forrest"	36
Abraham Brommell	pt. "Bensons Enlargement"	1
	pt. "Bensons Chance"	1
John Bonnett	"Moorefields Addition" – for his wife	38
	pt. "Moorefield" – for his wife	10
	pt. "Duns Range" – for his wife	100
Sarah Bartlett (cnp)	pt. "Hopkins" pt. "Addition"	25
	pt. "William & James"	25

	pt. "Partnership"	120
	pt. "Reynold's Point"	50
h/o William Bandey	"Adventure"	70
Anthony Booth	pt. "Bloomsbery"	100
Sarah Benny	"Rumbly Forrest" – 6 a.	34
	"Bennys Addition" – 28 a.	
Sarah Beswick	"Stevens's Plains"	50
	"Christophers Lott"	286¼
	"Sarahs Addition"	50
Henry Burgess	"Hopewell"	50
	pt. "Discovery"	10
	"Neighbours Standof"	18¼
John Bracco	"Poplar Ridge"	249
James Barnett for Rachel Barnett	"Patricks Ridge" a/s "Powicks Ridge"	100
	pt. "Discovery"	140⅔
	pt. "Discovery" – from Ann Corkrin	70⅓
49:1757-8:7 ...		
Peter Blake guardian to James Wrightson	"Jordans Folly"	100
	"Clays Neck"	102
Christopher Birckhead	pt. "Lowes Rambles"	100
Daniell Berry	"Chance"	7
	pt. "Bozmans Addition"	108
Robert Bromwell	"Cove Hall"	100
John Bromwell	"Wintersell"	145
John Berry	pt. "White Marshes"	380
	"Rich Farm"	50
Jo. Berry	pt. "White Marshes"	190
Benjamin Berry	pt. "White Marshes"	190
49:1757-8:8 ...		
Samuel Chamberlaine, Esq.	"Hookland"	100
	pt. "Hier Dier Lloyd"	928
	pt. "Halls Neck"	286
	pt. "Hopkins's Point"	7½
	pt. "Four Square"	350
	pt. "Stevens's Range"	186
	pt. "Sheephead Point"	196

	pt. "Braintree Addition"	50
	"Gore"	45
	pt. "Arcadia" & "Abrahams Lott"	100
	"Rest Content"	100
	pt. "Goodwins Addition"	90
	"Enlargement"	71
	pt. "Cumberland"	100
	"Clays Addition"	50
	pt. "Yorkshire"	155
	pt. "Rocky Nook"	75
	pt. "Plain Dealing"	100
	"Endeavour"	50
	"Grundys Lott Resurveyed"	55
	"Cabbin Neck"	50
	"Contention"	100
	"Bishoprick"	100
	pt. "Chance"	40
	"Goose Neck"	50
	"Intention"	50
	pt. "Tilghmans Fortune"	75
	pt. "Abrams Lott" & "Millroad Addition"	33
	pt. "Bartlets Inheritance" & "Bensons Enlargement"	50
	"Marys Dower"	200
	"Morgans Addition"	137
	"Turners Hazard"	100
	"Bullens Addition"	102
	"Resurvey of Rome"	138½
Benjamin Cooper	pt. "Mile End"	65
	pt. "Mile End" – more	10
James Chaplin	pt. "Roadley"	80
	pt. "Broad Oak"	300
	"Enfield"	200
	"Intention"	100
	"Sutton Grange"	33
Capt. John Coward	"Plinkimmon"	600

49:1757-8:9 ...		
John Caulk	pt. "Lostock"	50
	"Caulks Addition"	236
William Cooper	"Harrisons Security"	167
	"Hap Hazard"	100
John Cowley	pt. "Lostock"	184½
Francis Chaplain	⅓ "Parkers Point" & "Enlargement"	50
Peter Cox	"Marshland"	165
	"Lords Gift"	200
	"Newlin"	140
	"Turbots Fields"	168
	"Bullens Discovery"	136
Samuel Cockayne	"St. Michaels Fresh Run"	386
Powell Cox	pt. "Nominy"	302
	"Knaps Lott"	50
	"Boston Clift"	260
	"Chance"	40
	"Hier Dier Lloyd"	392
Henry Corkrin	pt. "Discovery"	147
49:1757-8:10 ...		
h/o John Carslake	⅓ "Bartram"	17
	⅓ "Carslakes Discovery"	39⅓
Rebecca Clark	"Hampton" & pt. "Parkers Range"	200
	pt. "Parkers Range"	58
	pt. "Highfield"	100
	"Highfield Addition"	150
	"Berrys Range"	130
Frances Camperson	pt. "Hampton"	50
	pt. "Rich Range"	50
	"Frances's Delight"	48
William Cooper	"Bently Hay"	16⅔
Peter Commerford	"Saint John's Neck"	350
	"Salop" – for h/o (N) Parot	167
Col. Thomas Chamberlaine (cnp)	"Rock Nook" & "Rocky Nook Addition"	158
	"Ealones Addition"	60
	"Lobs Corner"	23

	2 lots in Oxford	1½
Lemon John Cathorp	"Mount Hope"	61½
	pt. "Buckley"	50
	"Cathorps Security"	192
Joshua Clark	"Johns Neck"	118
	"Clarks Folly"	101
49:1757-8:11 ...		
John Cox	"Spring Close"	50
	"Coxes Venture"	38
	⅔ "Taylors Ridge" & ⅔ "Patricks Plaines"	206⅔
h/o Sarah Cockayne	"Carters Plaines"	294
William Cummings	"Lurkey"	50
w/o John Cuthcart	"Cornelius's Garden"	50
Edward Clark	"Parkers Farm"	350
	"Parrotts Lott"	82
	"Pigg Point"	40
	"Parkers Farm Addition"	42
William Carr	"Millers Chance"	100
	"Lowe's Rambles"	114
James Callahan	pt. "Brittania"	100
~~William Cole (dead)~~	~~pt. "Brittania", pt. "Hellsdown", & pt. "Costins Chance" tbc Col. Edward Lloyd~~	~~142~~
Philemon Lloyd Chew	"Clayburns Island"	700
William Carey	pt. "Sutton" & "Sutton Addition"	100
	"Partnership"	18
49:1757-8:12 ...		
Thomas Cummings	"Knave Keep Out"	75
Nicholas Cummings	"Knave Keep Out"	75
Foster Cunliffe & Sons (Liverpoole)	"Hunt Keep Out"	28
Edward Collisson	pt. "Rehobath Point"	33⅓
William Collisson	pt. "Rehobath Point"	16⅔
James Caulk	"Lewis Point"	145
John Clift	"Clifts Addition" a/s "Taylors Ridge"	100
	"Timber Neck"	89
James Connerly	"Hogg Hole"	142

James Lloyd Chamberlaine	"London Derry"	250
Isaac Cox	pt. "Bedsteads Adventure"	14
49:1757-8:13 ...		
Samuel Dickenson	"Herberts Choice"	14
	"Little Creek"	200
	"Samuels Lott"	600
	"Dickensons Lott"	113
	"Cross Dover"	400
	pt. "Roadly"	132
	pt. "Canterbury Manor"	250
	"Evans's Point"	300
	pt. "Wales"	46
	pt. "Sexton", pt. "Stepney", & pt. "Quillen"	134
	pt. "Nominy"	350
	"White Philips"	150
	pt. "Mount Hope"	250
	pt. "Compton"	13
	"Hobsons Choice"	100
	"Hobsons Choice" – another	129
	pt. "Darlington"	119
	"Dickensons Lott"	216
	"Millers Hope"	11
	"Mitchells Hermitage" – from (N) Thomas	50
	"Mitchells Hermitage" – more from (N) Herbert	75
	pt. "Good Luck" – surveyed for (N) Lowe	54
	"Powells Island"	55
	pt. "Hier Dier Lloyd on Resurvey"	101
	"Millers Chance"	85
Isaac Dixon	pt. "Cottinham"	75
	pt. "Ashby"	60
	"Barnetts Hill"	50
	"Ending of Controversy"	150
	"Dixons Outlet"	150
Impey Dawson	"Crommell Resurveyed"	476¾
Thomas Dawson (cnp)	"Cudlington"	400
	"Cudlingtons Addition"	50

	"Cudlingtons Increase"	50
49:1757-8:14 ...		
Henry Delahay	pt. "Hier Dier Lloyd"	125
James Dickenson	"East Otwell"	400
	pt. "Bullen"	350
	"Piney Point" – for his wife	150
	"Timothys Lott"	300
Joseph Dawson	pt. "Lostock"	150
Elizabeth Davis	"Tilghmans Fortune"	33
	pt. "Ashby"	49
	pt. "Bettys Cover"	6⅔
	"Standfords Hermitage"	250
	"Stanfords Folly"	45
	"Bite the Biter"	33
John Dickenson for h/o William Dickenson	pt. "Rockliff"	170
	"Poplar Level" a/s "Parots Levell"	116
	"Dover Marsh"	348
	"Dover"	771½
	pt. "Lower Dover"	241
	½ "Hamiltons Park"	131½
	"Buckingham & Kelding"	196½
	"Addition" – surveyed for (N) Hemsley	63
Thomas Dudley	pt. "Broad Lane"	103
	"Broad Lane Addition"	41¼
	"Beaver Neck" – for Deborah Dudley	100
	"Advantage" – for h/o (N) Husband	18
	"Beaver Neck" – for h/o (N) Batchelor	141
~~Samuel Downing~~	~~pt. "Beaver Neck"~~	~~100~~
	~~pt. "Broad Lane"~~	~~0~~
49:1757-8:15 ...		
Joseph Durden	"Bless Land"	100
	"Turkery Neck"	116
	pt. "Kingsberry"	130
	"Kings Creek Marsh"	50
	"Kingsberry Addition"	37

Cornelius Dailey	"London Derry"	132
	"Cornelius's Cool Spring"	100
	"Surprise"	40
	pt. "Discovery"	20
	"Cornelius's Cool Spring Addition"	11¾
	pt. "Ashby"	100
~~William Dudley~~	~~pt. "Smiths Clifts"~~	~~100~~
Peter Denny	pt. "Heworth"	23
	"Clifton"	200
	"Hiccory Ridge"	12
	"Denny's Content"	73
William Dawson	pt. "Galloway"	100
	pt. "Batchelors Range Addition"	463
	pt. "Shrigleys Fortune"	270
	"Batchelors Range"	250
	pt. "Huntington" & pt. "Huntingtons Addition"	90
	pt. "Huntington"	150
	pt. "Neglect"	78¾
John Dixon	"Carters Plaines"	206
	pt. "Neglect"	126
49:1757-8:16 ...		
Thomas Dudley	"Dudleys Inclosure"	104
	"Dudleys Addition"	37
Ralph Dawson	"Jones's Lott"	50
	"Grafton Mannor" a/s "Eaton's Hazard"	49
	"Johnes Lott Addition"	50
	"Rest Content"	45
Henrietta Maria Dulany	"Woolmans Hermitage"	109
	"Woolmans Inheritance"	206
Joseph Denny	"Wisbeck"	60
Sarah w/o Robert Dawson	"Dawsons Composition"	282
Thomas Delahay	"Delahays Fortune"	100
	pt. "Taylors Ridge"	50
Peter Davis	pt. "Dover"	123½
Daniel Dickenson	"Boston Clift"	260
George Dobson	"Fork"	250

Abner Dudley	"Cowallyn" tbc William Robins	<n/g>
49:1757-8:17 ...		
William Dickenson	pt. "Roadley"	168¾
	"Dickens Fields"	18¾
George Dawson	"Bailey's Fortune" a/s "Forrest"	113
Pollard Edmondson	pt. "Tilghman's Fortune"	138
	pt. "Enlargement"	50
	pt. "Edmundson's Difficulty"	903
	"Jack's Cove"	50
Elizabeth Elsby	¼ "Parkers Point"	30
	¼ "Enlargement"	45
James Edge	"Yaffords Neck"	100
	"Prevention"	50
	"Whartons Glade"	50
	"Bensons Enlargement"	150
	"Couple Close"	100
	"Addition"	32
	"Skinners Lott"	33
	"Scraps"	60
	"Glades's Addition"	71
49:1757-8:18 ...		
devisees of Philip Emorson	½ "Widows Choice" a/s "Widows Lott" – for Mary Trippe	320
	pt. "Whetstone" – supposed lost	150
	"Hamiltons Park" tbc: • John Dickinson – ½ • Mary Trippe – ½	263
	"Buckingham & Kelding" tbc: • John Dickinson – ½ • Mary Trippe – ½	393
	"Addition" – surveyed for (N) Hemsley tbc: • John Dickinson – ½ • Mary Trippe – ½	63
Elizabeth Edwards	"Huntington"	20
	"Mistake"	25½
	"Huntington"	180
James Evans	pt. "Chesnutt Bay"	100

Elizabeth Eubank	"Mount Hope"	35
	"Hattons Hope"	100
	pt. "Discovery"	84
Richard Eaten	"Fox Hole"	100
	pt. "Fox Harbour"	50
	"Eatons Addition"	112
William Elbert	"Rebeca's Garden"	50
	"Lloyd Costen"	240
	"Lloyd Costen" – that was charged to Jeremiah Grassingham in part	159
Tamson Elston	"Omaleys Range"	150
	"Jacob & Johns Pasture"	120
George Eubank	"Omaleys Range"	50
	"Hardwoods Neglect"	11
49:1757-8:19 ...		
Edward Eubank	"Coxes Hazard" – for this wife	103
Edward Elliott	"Elliot's Purchase"	361
	"Pint & Marsh"	50
	"McCotter & Glover"	83
Loadnam Elbert	pt. "Loyd Costin"	260
Rigby Foster	"Foster's Chance" – originally called "Woolsy Addition"	27¼
Col. William Fitzhugh	"Marrow"	130
	"Hern Island"	75
	"Morgans Saint Michaels"	300
John Fairbank	"Campers Neck"	100
	"Fairly"	100
	"Belfast"	100
	"Jones's Hole"	36
	"Fairbanks Chance"	195
	"Good Hope"	23
	"Tobacco Pipe"	9¾
Thomas Frampton	"Rich Range"	50
49:1757-8:20 ...		
John Ferrell (cnp)	pt. "Mount Hope"	80
	"Hauks Hill"	50

	"Cathorps Security"	13
	"Hawks Hill Addition" – for h/o James Ferrell	100
Michael Fletcher	"Sharps Chance"	79
	"Long Acre"	150
David Fitzpatrick	"Tryangle"	56
	"Dirty Weeden"	100
	"Adventure"	100
Abraham Falconer	"Neighbours Keep Out"	46
	pt. "Falconers Levell" – from Adam Eubank	50
Richard Fairbrother	"Sutton Grange"	167
Thomas Frampton	"Framptons Beggining"	96
	"Catline Pasture"	50
	"Framptons Chance"	34¾
Edmond Ferrell	pt. "Coventry"	100
	"Mickle More"	100
	"Porkimney"	179½
Isaac Falconer	pt. "Falconers Levell" – from Adam Eubank	100
~~Abraham Falconer~~	~~pt. "Falconers Level" – from Adam Eubank~~	~~<n/g>~~
49:1757-8:21 ...		
Col. William Goldsborough	pt. "Hier Dier Lloyd"	342
	pt. "Turners"	200
	"Graves"	100
	"Marshy Point"	300
	"Canterbury Manor"	100
	"Jobs Content"	1000
	"Hulls Neck"	300
	"Cooks Hope"	214
	"First Hazard"	358
	"Discovery"	60
	"Desire" & pt. "Hewart"	200
	"Jennings Hope"	718
	"Buckingham"	903
	pt. "Desire" & pt. "Hewart"	10
Nicholas Goldsborough, Sr. (cnp)	"Hier Dier Lloyd"	400
	"Grissell"	150
	"Partlet"	100

	"Otwell"	500
	"Marshy Point"	157
	"Addition"	50
Jonathan Gibson	⅓ "Edmonton"	100
	⅓ "Champenhams Addition"	16⅔
	⅓ "Leeth"	13⅓
	⅓ "Champenham" & ⅓ "Bendon"	133⅓
	"Tod Upon Dervan" – ⅓ of 220 a. charged to h/o Jacob Gibson	73⅓
Woolman Gibson	⅓ "Edmonton"	100
	⅓ "Champenhams Addition"	16⅔
	⅓ "Leeth"	13⅓
	⅓ "Champenham" & ⅓ "Bendon"	183⅓
	"Tod Upon Dervan" – ⅓ charged to h/o Jacob Gibson	73⅓
Rachell w/o Thomas Gully	pt. "Ashby"	150
49:1757-8:22 ...		
Robert Goldsborough – carried to back of this book	"Cottingham"	150
	pt. "Ashby"	250
	"St. Michaels Fresh Run"	50
	"St. Michaels Fresh Run"	185
	"Rich Range"	140
	"Chance"	50
	"Rich Farm Addition"	86
	"Peters Rest"	50
	"Newnams Addition"	50
	"Fox Harbour"	148
	"Fragment" – for his wife	50
	"Benjamins Lott"	50
	pt. "Carters Preserve"	50
	pt. "Carters Forrest"	75
Richard Grasson (cnp)	"Tanners Hope" a/s "Help"	50
	"Parsonage Addition"	50
	pt. "Kings Forrest"	75
	"Roberts Infancy"	65
	"Kings Plains"	79

	"Grassons Discovery"	106½
Greenwood Gaskin	"Middle Spring"	130
Richard Gibson	pt. "Addition" – surveyed for (N) Woolman	50
	pt. "Timber Neck"	60
	"Doctors Gift"	100
	"Betty's Dowrey"	75
Rev. Mr. John Gordon	"Forked Neck"	50
	"Holdon"	225
	"Bite"	15
	⅔ "Bartram" & "Carslakes Discovery"	106
John Garey	"Strawberry Fields"	100
49:1757-8:23 ...		
Richard Glover	"Upper Range"	50
	"Mount Hope"	75
	pt. "Upper Dover"	114¾
Nicholas Glen	"Cooks Hope"	200
William Garey	"Little Brittain"	150
Thomas Goldsborough	"Barmeston"	74
	"Coxes Chance"	160
Jacob Gore	"Frampton"	122
	"Dunsmore Heath"	200
Peter Garron for his wife	"Duns Range"	50
	"Piccadilly" tbc Edward Vickers	100
~~Anthony Gregory~~	~~"Fishs Hazard"~~	~~13~~
	~~"Fishes Range", "Contention"~~	~~<n/g>~~
Nicholas Goldsborough	"Halls Neck"	200
	"Conjunction"	279
William Gale (Whitehaven)	"Fishes Discovery"	⅓
49:1757-8:24 ...		
John Gibson	pt. "Lambeth" & pt. "Brittania"	71½
	"Rebeccas Garden"	150
John Goldsborough (cnp)	"Hogsdon"	100
	"Thief Keep Out"	36
	"Goldsboroughs Tryangle"	45
	"Adventure"	100
	"Cannadys Hazard"	29

	pt. "Four Square"	650
	"Marshy Peak"	132
	"Peaks Marsh"	318
	"Chambers's Adventure"	118¾
	"Bedsteads Adventure"	64
	pt. "Securely" or "Somerly"	50
	"Kennedays Addition"	23
Joshua Grasson – grandson of Edward Fisher	"Fishes Hazard"	18
	"Fishes Range, Contention, & Stapleton" – formerly charged to Tamson Elston	281
Anthony Gregory	"Turner's Chance"	100
	"New Begun"	91¼
49:1757-8:25 ...		
Philemon Hambleton	"Martingham"	200
	"Cambergeshire"	100
	"Middle Neck"	100
	"Mount Misery"	50
	"Sherwoods Island"	20
	pt. "Adventure" tbc Jos. Hopkins	113½
	"Hamiltons Addition"	100
	"Newport Glasgow"	36
	"Huckleberry Garden"	175
William Webb Haddaway	"Mile End"	250
	"Merchants Folly"	150
	"Haddaways Lott"	73
	"Grafton Manor" a/s "Rich Neck"	150
George Haddaway	pt. "Lostock"	102
w/o George Haddaway, Jr.	pt. "Lostock"	70
Edward Hardin	"Tilghmans Fortune"	19
	"Hardens Endeavour"	200
Henry Hollyday	"Tilghmans Fortune"	445
	pt. "Ractliff Manor"	150
	pt. "Ractliff Manor" – more	100
	pt. "Brittania"	150
	"Turkey Park"	329

James Hopkins	pt. "Hopkins's Point"	100
	"Hopkins's Point Addition"	25
	pt. "Partnership"	65
49:1757-8:26 ...		
John Holmes	pt. "Sutton"	125
	pt. "Sutton Addition" – 130 a. on post pone	25
	"Buckrow"	40
	"Catlin Plaines" – for h/o (N) Parrot	10
	pt. "Buckrow"	150
	"Abington"	100
	"Walnutt Garden"	50
	pt. "Halls Addition"	100
	"Mullikins Delight"	11
Benjamin Hopkins	pt. "Hopkins's Point"	133⅓
Richard Hopkins	pt. "Hopkins's Point"	142¾
Dennis Hopkins	pt. "Hopkins's Point"	90
Samuel Harwood	pt. "Cottingham"	150
Peter Hopkins	"Nominy"	100
Thomas Harrisson	pt. "Crooked Intention"	80
	"Josephs Lott"	31
Easter w/o John Hughe	"Beech"	12
	"Chance" – surveyed for (N) Emory	100
	"Janes Progress"	35
	"Taylor & James's Discovery"	100
49:1757-8:27 ...		
Philip Horney	"Batchelors Hope" – for his wife	25
	"Bartram" – for his wife	75
	"Fools Parradise" – for his wife	25
	"Scotts Lott" – for his wife	50
	"Kininmonts Delight" – for his wife	84
	"Hopewell" – for his wife	40
	"Scags Spring" – for his wife	50
	"Skinners Swineyard" – for his wife	200
	"Pattingham" – for his wife	100
Joshua Hopkins	pt. "London Derry"	103

Joseph Harrison	"Hap Hazard"	50
	"Crooked Intention"	50
	"Mount Misery" – of James Harrisson	25
	"Mount Misery Addition" – of James Harrisson	12
Elizabeth Harrison	"Prouse Point", pt. "Hap Hazard", & pt. "Foresail"	12
	"Poplar Neck"	58
James Harrisson	"Prouse Point", pt. "Hap Hazard", & pt. "Foresail"	38
	"Poplar Neck"	42
Thomas Haddaway	pt. "Barkin"	100
	"Lancashire"	50
	"Haddaways Addition"	75
Joseph Hopkins	"Enlargement"	50
	"Rays Point"	150
	"Snellings Delight"	150
	pt. "Adventure"	113⅓
William Harrison (Irish Creek)	pt. "Ashford"	50
	"Long Neglect"	35
49:1757-8:28 ...		
Joseph Hicks, Sr.	pt. "Ashford"	50
Henry Harris	"Cornwall" – by name of "Crommell"	100
	"Josephs Lott"	100
Peter Hunt (the old man)	"Larremores Prudence"	87
	"Devine Saint Andrew"	150
Peter Hunt s/o John	⅔ "Content"	65½
Solomon Horney	"Batchelors Branch"	100
	"Addition to Batchelors Branch"	94
	pt. "Addition"	6
John Harrington	pt. "Buckley"	150
w/o John Hixon	"Hobsons Choice"	21
	"Poplar Hill"	57
John Harrington (bayside)	"Hatton Garden"	50
William Harrison (Miles Creek)	~~"Hutchinson's Addition" – denied~~	~~300~~
	"Hutchison's Addition" – from (N) Abbott	163
	~~"Taylor's Rige" – denied~~	~~100~~
49:1757-8:29 ...		

Robert Hunter	"Jacobs Beginning"	110
	"Dudleys Diameans"	40
John Higgins	"Barams Range"	177
	"Lowes Rambles"	28
w/o Rowland Haddaway	"Fishbourn's Landing"	104
Robert Harwood	"Newnams Folly"	50
	"Swifts Chance"	23
	"Harwoods Neglect"	27
	"Barwicks Discovery"	120
	pt. "Addition" – from Peter Harwood	60
	"Harwoods Hill"	620
William Hadden	"Rumbly Forrest"	107
	pt. "Rumbly Forrest" – that was charged to James Berry	23¾
Perry Harrison	pt. "Bensons Enlargement"	190
	"Feddemans Discovery"	408
Paul Holmes	"Sidenburgh"	100
	"Plansby"	100
John Hamilton	"Williston"	221
Samuel Hopkins	"Rigbeys Discovery"	105
John Hewey	"Carters Inheritance"	100
49:1757-8:30 ...		
Sarah w/o Robert Hall	"Partnership"	10
	"Halls Range"	353
	"Halls Addition"	12
Henry Henricks	pt. "Discovery"	20
	"Storeys Lott"	56
Edward Harrison	pt. "Timber Neck"	175
Peter Harwood	pt. "Addition" – from your father Petter Harwood	112¼
w/o Thomas Hutcheson	pt. "Busby"	200
Solomon Harwood	pt. "Addition" – from you father Peter Harwood	112¼
Mary Hunt w/o John Hunt	⅔ "Content"	32½
John Hopkins, Jr.	"Beech, Elliots Lott, & Elliots Folly"	100
Edward Hopkins	"Beech & Eliots Lott"	100
John Haddaway	pt. "Grafton Manor" tbc James Lowe	110
	pt. "Haddaways Lott"	50

49:1757-8:31 ...		
Jacob Hindman	pt. "Kirkham"	273
	pt. "Kirkham" & pt. "Harrington"	200
	pt. "Kirkham" & pt. "Harrington"	147
	"Rich Range"	300
	"Delph"	100
William Hanson	"Emondsons Deficulty"	350
49:1757-8:32 ...		
Walter Jenkins	"Patricks Ridge" a/s "Powicks Ridge"	240
Thomas Johnson	"Patricks Ridge" a/s "Powicks Ridge"	100
Thomas Jenkins	"Double Ridge"	120
	"Sutton Grange"	120
	"Whites Gore"	40
	"Broad Oak" – for h/o (N) Holt	25
w/o Robert Jadwin	"Parkers Range"	60¾
h/o David Jones	"Knaps Lott"	105
	pt. "Prospect"	106
h/o Vincent Jones	"Nobles Chance"	89
Dr. John Jackson	pt. "Wallerton"	170
	"Finneys Range"	225
w/o John Jones (tanner)	pt. "Cumberland" & pt. "Heworth"	47
Alexander James	"Coxes Addition"	70
Emanuel Jenkins	"Edmondsons Freshes"	300
49:1757-8:33 ...		
Elizabeth Jenkins	"Patricks Ridge" a/s "Powicks Ridge"	560
Francis Kersey	"Webley"	300
	"Sarah's Neck"	50
h/o Mathew Kemp	"Woolsey" or "Chancelors Point"	1000
Joseph Kininmont	⅓ "Dundee"	133⅓
Samuel Kininmont	⅓ "Dundee"	133⅓
William Kemp (bayside)	"Mable"	100
	"Kemps Lott"	50
	"Mables Addition"	50
	"Kemps Lott Addition"	26
49:1757-8:34 ...		
Mathew Kirby	"Swamp Hole"	100

Michael Kirby	"Buck Range"	50
	"Buck Addition"	55
	"Bowes's Range"	235
John Kemp	"Bolton"	100
James Kemp	pt. "Dudleys Choice"	50
	"Sybland"	121
	pt. "Sybland Addition"	55
	pt. "Maxfield"	64
	pt. "Cowallyn"	100
	"Kemps Discovery"	9½
Benjamin Kemp	"Woolf Harbour"	62
	"Boston Addition"	50
	pt. "Bolton"	17½
	pt. "Miles End"	4½
Michael Kerby	"Kirwicks Addition"	49
w/o David Kerby	"Limerick"	60
	"Turners Range"	40
	"Kerbys Interest"	30
Richard Kerby	"Venture"	37
	"Kerbys Outlett"	47
James Kendrick	pt. "Coventry"	250
49:1757-8:35 ...		
Parott Kerby	"Kerbys Endeavour"	98
Simon Keld	"Kelds Inheritance"	219
Robert Kerby	"Dudleys Demeane"	50
David Kirby s/o Michael	"Duns Range"	100
Thomas Keets	"Stevens's Plains"	50
William Kemp (merchant)	"Nobles Addition"	207
	"Pooleys Discovery"	75
49:1757-8:36 ...		
Col. Edward Lloyd (cnp)	"Salters Marsh"	100
	"Grange"	150
	"Scotts Close"	200
	"Lynton"	600
	"Tod Upon Dervan"	80
	"Thrimby Grange"	500

	"Meersegate"	300
	"Nathaniels Point"	50
	"Crouches Choice"	150
	"Addition" – surveyed for (N) Woolman	150
	"Soldiers Delight"	100
	"Whetstone"	150
	"Advantage"	500
	"Addition" – surveyed for (N) Hawkins	100
	"Fortune"	150
	"Grunny"	100
	"Doublys Lott"	50
	"Town Road"	50
	"Bettys Branch"	325
	"Knightly Addition"	50
	"Gareys Delight"	50
	"Falconers Folly"	100
	"Tryangle"	55
	"Dirty Weeden"	100
	"Brafforton"	100
	"Henrietta Maria's Discovery"	216
	"Fortune Addition"	52
	"Brittania, Hilsdown, & Costens Chance"	300
	"Outlett"	220
	"Kings Forrest"	75
	"Woolmans Hermitage"	55
	"Bettys Dowrey"	75
	"Farm"	348
	"Kings Plaines"	79
	"New Town"	100
	"Sweetmans Hope"	120
	"Meersgate Addition"	267
	"Long Neglect"	133
	"Inlett"	88
	"Carters Inheritance"	300
	"Roadway"	50
	"Timber Neck"	60

	"Abbington"	400
	"Woolmans Inheritance"	104
	"Lobs Crook"	679
	"Bedwells Indian Neck"	913
	"Planters Increase" with "Turners Ridge"	504
49:1757-8:37 ...		
Col. Edward Lloyd (continued)	"Carslakes Content"	60
	"Tobacco Pipe Resurveyed" & "Halken Old Pile"	745
	"Bennetts Kind Caution"	323¾
	"Gareys Security"	124
	"Lloyds Addition to Pherely"	380
	<n/g> – another tract of (N) Woolman	150
	"Lloyds Lott"	141
	"Timber Neck"	100
	"Bennett Lloyd"	384½
	pt. "Lostock"	172
	"Batchelors Delight"	100
	~~"Wisbeck"~~	~~100~~
	pt. "Brittania", pt. "Heldon", & pt. "Costins Chance" – from William Cole	162
John Leeds	"Wades Point"	400
	"Hatton"	500
	"Long Delay"	33
William Landman or Lambden	"Summerton"	200
	"Winterton"	50
	"Grafton Manor"	100
	"William & Marys Addition"	52
Robert Lloyd (cnp)	"Peckburn"	200
	"Tally Farm"	100
	"Hope"	100
	"Elliots Discovery"	100
	"Adjunction"	50
	"Widows Chance"	50
	"Scotland"	50
	"Lloyds Discovery"	96
	"Partnership"	1200

	"Hemsley Upon Wye"	1160
	"Hemsley Upon Wye Addition"	146
John Lloyd	"Piney Point Advantage"	150
49:1757-8:38 ...		
James Lowe for w/o John Lowe	"Ractliff Manor"	150
	"Grafton Manor"	135
	"Piney Neck"	107
Robert Larremore	"Larremores Neck"	100
	"Bampfshire"	50
	"Larremores Addition"	50
Thomas Loveday	"Knave Keep Out"	68½
	"Middle Spring"	270
	"Dudley"	200
	"Parkers Farm"	100
	pt. "Swineyard"	88
	"Hatton" – for h/o (N) Dickenson	459
	"Frankford St. Michaels"	616
	pt. "Baildon"	30
	"Crooked Lane"	116
	"Bennetts Freshes"	423
	"Hampton" – from (N) Warren	200
Capt. James Lloyd	pt. "Marshland"	265
	"Buckland"	250
	"New Mill"	200
	"Rumbly Marsh"	300
	"Addition" – for (N) Gurlin	100
	"Partnership"	310
	"Mirrey"	150
	"Grundys Inclosure"	170
	"Buckland Marsh"	50
	"Gurlington"	100
Thomas Lane	"Poplar Hill"	200
	"Wallerton"	290
	"Normantown"	787
	"Kings Neglect"	107
	"Bettys Dowrey"	2

49:1757-8:39 ...		
Anthony Lecompt	pt. "Cumberland"	50
	"Eatons Addition"	78
	"Lobs Corner"	23
	"Anthonys Enlargement"	108½
Robert Lambden	"Sands's Lott"	50
	"Bridgess"	176
Rebecca Lynch a/s Hugh Lindsay	"Mullikins Choice"	100
w/o Robert Lowther	"Beaver Dam Neck"	70½
	"Forrest & Dike"	116¼
w/o John Love	"Hatton"	63
Dennis Larey	pt. "Beaver Neck Dam"	70½
	"Partnership Hazard"	142
49:1757-8:40 ...		
Thomas Martin	pt. "Hier Dier Lloyd"	296
	"Atwell"	100
	"Tawney Close"	50
	"Hard Measure"	57
Thomas Martin, Jr.	pt. "Hier Dier Lloyd" a/s "Wilderness"	100
	"Shore Ditch"	25
	"Rich Neck"	300
William Martin	pt. "Hier Dier Lloyd"	75
	"Mitchams Hall"	300
	"Martins Purchase"	5¼
	"New Scotland" – for h/o (N) Gedding	700
James Milliard	pt. "Canterbury Manor"	170
Philip Martin	"Bullens Chance" a/s "Choice"	350
	"Conjunction"	25
Daniel Maynadier (cnp)	"Marsh Land"	70
	"Jamaica"	50
	"Goldsborough"	187
	"Timothys Lott"	25
	"Fatterhurst"	38
	"Fotrells Discovery"	93
	"Flemings Freshes"	215

	"Wilderness"	75
	"Jones Interest"	40
w/o Edmond Marsh	"Studs Point"	50
	"Hulls Neck"	40
John McMahan	"White Philips"	42
	"Lowes Rambles"	38
49:1757-8:41 ...		
Charles Morgan	"Chesnutt Bay"	95
	"Dudleys Clift"	133
Ann w/o Patrick Mullikin	"Taylors Ridge"	33½
	⅓ "Patricks Plaines"	70
Samuel Mullikin	"Patricks Plaines"	90
	"Mullikins Delight"	52¾
	"Canterbury Manor" – for h/o William Parot	113⅓
Hezekiah Mackey	pt. "Bullen"	40
	"Broad Oak" & pt. "Bullen"	60
	pt. "Broad Oak"	116⅔
	⅔ "Holmby"	133⅓
Rachell Mackey	pt. "Broad Oak" & pt. "Bullen"	18⅓
	⅓ "Holmby"	66⅔
Thomas Mathews (Kings Creek)	pt. "Rich Farm Addition" & pt. "Bedworth"	83
Richard Mansfield	"Upper Holland"	50
	"Larramores Lot"	50
Edward McDaniel	"Fishbourns Lott"	100
Patrick McQuay	"Devine St. Andrew"	50
	"Fools Parradise"	38
John Markland	pt. "Morgans" a/s "Plinkimmon"	50
	"Jacks Point"	100
h/o Joseph Merrick, Sr.	"Batchelors Range Addition"	37
49:1757-8:42 ...		
Dr. Henry Murray	"Gatterly More Resurvey"	206⅓
John Mears	"White Chaple"	100
William Morgan	pt. "Morgans Neglect"	66
	pt. "Rumbly Forrest"	43

William Mullikin	"York"	306
	"Timber Neck"	55
	"Mullikins Chance"	100
	"Yorks Distruction"	50
	"Timber Neck Addition"	50
Thomas Mathews (Tuckahoe)	pt. "Bloomsbery"	88
Solomon Marshall	"Kingsail"	126
James Merrick	"Hazard Addition"	9
	"Powells Island"	50
Rev. John Miller (Kent on Delaware)	"Nobles Meadows"	114½
	"Betts Addition"	103½
Sarah Millington	"Nobles Meadows"	114½
	"Betts Addition"	103½
William Martin, Jr. guardian to Robert Martin s/o Henry	"Crooked Ramble"	75½
William Modesly	pt. "Boons"	40
49:1757-8:43 ...		
George Maxwell	"Harwoods Lyon"	600
Oliver Millington	"Bettys Chance"	100
	"Epsom"	100
w/o James Millis	"Adventure"	100
Simon Stevens Miller	pt. "Newnames Lott"	32¾
	pt. "Planters Delight"	32¾
	pt. "Nobles Chance"	48
	"Addition"	75
Archibald McCallum	pt. "Desire & Huart"	289
	pt. "Enlargement"	50
h/o Michael McGinery	"Piney Point Advantage" – that was charged to John Bozman	100
49:1757-8:44 ...		
Edward Needles	pt. "Rockliff"	150
	pt. "Pitts's Range"	200
	"Johns Neck"	23½
	"Kilton" a/s "Killam"	140
	"Kellam" a/s "Kiltam"	419

Debora Nicols	"Planters Delight"	34
	"Stebbins's Plains"	50
	"Betts's Chance"	100
	"Richmond"	41
	"Richmond Addition"	282
	"Nobles Addition"	84
	"Nobles Addition" – that was charged to William Kemp	100
Edward Neale	pt. "Mount Hope"	50
	"Nanticoke Manor"	171
Francis Neale	pt. "Edmondsons Freshes" & pt. "Heworth"	110
	"Edmondsons Freshes"	150
	"Hicory Ridge"	254
	"French Hazard"	41
	"Dennys Content"	12
	pt. "Mount Hope"	50
William Nicols	pt. "Galloway"	204
	"Mickle More"	230
Jonathan Nicols	pt. "Maiden", pt. "Maiden Point Addition", & "Withers's Range"	300
Solomon Neale	"Hicory Ridge on Resurvey"	137
Robert Newcomb	"Robert & Margaret"	441½
Elizabeth Nicols	pt. "Hopkins's Point" – during life	86
49:1757-8:45 ...		
Jonathan Neale	"Chesnutt Bay"	205
	"Dudleys Clift"	16
	"Falconers Hazard"	60
	"Neales Advantage"	403
	"Hicory Ridge"	50
Isaac Nix	⅓ "Coventry"	41⅔
	"Ractliff Choice"	79
	pt. "Coventry" – from (N) Brascup	30
David Naylor	"Newnams Lott"	100
	"Nobles Chance"	29
Edward Oldham (cnp)	"Nether Foster"	50
	"Coomsbery"	100

	"Rich Park"	569
	"Judiths Garden"	130
	"Oldhams Discovery"	115½
Maurice Oram	"Wasteland" & pt. "Tryangle"	40
	"Fox Hole"	145
	"Fox Harbour"	50
	"Wallerford"	100
	"Foxes Den"	56
w/o William Oxenham	"Somerly"	50
	"Moorfields"	280
49:1757-8:46 ...		
Andrew Oram	"Adventure"	100
Richard Oysten	"Bobs Hill" – by name of "Hobs Hill"	100
	"Discovery"	117
	pt. "Discovery" – from (N) Henricks	20
w/o John Ozment	"Neglect"	107
w/o Francis Porter	pt. "Hemmersby"	100
Robert Porter	pt. "Hemmersby"	100
Thomas Parsons	"Hamiltons Neck"	66
Penelope Parrot	pt. "Canterbury Manor"	56⅔
h/o Robert Pickering	pt. "Ashby" tbc Cornelius Daily	10½
Thomas Powell	pt. "Beaver Neck"	129½
	pt. "Advantage"	21
	"Powells Meadows"	34
	"Powells Missfortune"	42½
49:1757-8:47 ...		
Grundy Pemberton	"Fentry"	100
	pt. "Smiths Clifts"	232
	pt. "Heworth"	205
	pt. "Cumberland"	30
	pt. "Long"	42
	"Lobs Corner"	14
Daniel Powell (cnp)	"Rigbys Marsh"	300
	pt. "Troths Fortune"	153½
	pt. "Troths Fortune"	246½
	"Dick's Marsh" – for your wife	200

	"Little Bristoll"	400
	"Little Bristoll" – more from h/o (N) Burkhead	580
	"Nominy"	200
	pt. "Discovery"	56
John Prichard	pt. "White Philips"	75
Thomas Purnall	"Hampton"	8
	pt. "Rich Range"	210
Abner Parrott	pt. "Jamaica"	100
John Porter	pt. "Friths Neck"	33
h/o John Potts	"St. Michaels Fresh Run"	75
	"Potts's Discovery"	60¼
Aaron Parrott	"Johns Neck"	264
	"Kingstown"	51½
h/o William Parrot	pt. "Hyfield"	50
49:1757-8:48 ...		
w/o Thomas Perkins	"Carters Farm"	400
	"Perkins's Discovery"	193½
Laurence Porter	"York"	100
Francis Pickering	"Sarahs Lott"	50
Edward Perkins	pt. "Newnames Range"	100
George Parrott	"Abrams Lott", pt. "Milroad 2nd Addition", & pt. "Golston"	230
John Plowman	"Austin"	200
Francis Parrott	"Lords Chance"	100
John Porter, Jr.	"Willsons Good Luck"	65
Capt. Thomas Porter	"Kembles Industry"	283
William Page	"Boones Hope"	33½
	"Studhams Chance"	18
Howell Powell	"Beaver Neck"	129½
	pt. "Advantage"	21
49:1757-8:49 ...		
Quakers Meeting	pt. "London Derry"	3
Thomas Price (cnp)	pt. "Carters Preserve"	50
	pt. "St. Michels Fresh Run"	185
	pt. "Carters Forrest"	75
	pt. "Good Chance"	16⅔

	pt. "Newnams Thickett"	16⅔
	pt. "Gore"	56⅔
Arthur Rigby	"Anderby"	100
	"Hopkins's Point"	100
	pt. "Fox Hole"	65
	pt. "Crawford"	100
	"Lambeth Addition"	150
	"Rigbys Folly"	45
	"William & James"	33
	"Maxwell More"	105
	"Rigbys Choice"	101½
	"Lamberton"	195½
	"Reynolds's Point"	100
	pt. "Bettys Cove" – for h/o (N) Botfield	30
	"Bettys Addition" – as "Bettys Cove" for h/o (N) Botfield	50
	"Addition" – for h/o (N) Botfield	50
Thomas Ray	⅓ "Dundee"	133⅓
Richard Robinson	pt. "Long Point"	100
	pt. "Taylors Ridge" – for h/o John Harrison	50
John Robinson	"Long Point"	150
	"Goldsborough"	87
	"Robinsons Beginning"	17
49:1757-8:50 ...		
w/o James Robas	pt. "Newnams Lott"	67¾
	pt. "Nobles Chance"	52
	"Planters Delight"	67¾
	"Stevens's Lott"	19
Feddeman Rolls	"Hoopers Ensale"	200
	"Grafton Manor"	28
	"Cabin Neck, Sand of Bite, & Halls Fortune"	238
	"Dorothys Enlargement"	45
	"Rolls's Range"	237
William Ridgeway	pt. "Wasteland"	100
John Register (cnp)	pt. "Acton"	5¾
	pt. "Darlington"	88½

	"Kingsbery"	122¼
William Robins	pt. "Holm Hill"	434
	pt. "Smiths Clifts"	201
	"Rich Farm" a/s "Rich Range"	14
	"Fragment"	13⅔
	"Cowallyn"	200
Bartholemew Roberts	"Friths Neck"	17
	"Enions Range"	50
	"Roberts's Addition"	47
George Rule	"Carters Farm"	100
Henry Robson (dead)	"James's Lookout" & "Partnership" tbc w/o Thomas Robson	<n/g>
w/o John Rathell	"Strawberry Hill"	50
	"Rathells Chance"	50
49:1757-8:51 ...		
James Ractliff	"Jacob & Johns Pasture"	170
	pt. "Addition" – part of 68 a. from (N) Carter	52
	"Ractliff High Way"	113
	"Maplle Branch"	40
James Ractleff	"Jacob & Johns"	50
	pt. "Golston"	100
Thomas Roberts	"Moorefields"	84
	"Tell Tale Loss"	125
	"Charlevile & Cork"	250
	"Vickers's Lott"	52
Francis Register	"Parrots Reserve"	150
	"Francis's Plains"	64½
Thomas Robson	pt. "Partnership"	82
	"James's Look Out" & "Partnership"	93
Hugh Rice	"Tanners Choice"	256⅓
James Robinson for h/o Zadock Botfield	⅔ "Coventry"	83⅓
William Roberts	"Chance" – surveyed for (N) Walker	100
	"Knave Stand of"	50
49:1757-8:52 ...		

Elijah Skillington	"Turners Point" tbc Mr. William Trippe	<n/g>
	"Skillingtons Hope" tbc Mr. William Trippe	<n/g>
Thomas Skinner	"Marshy Point"	100
John Sherwood s/o Edward Man Sherwood	"Exchange"	100
	"Pitts's Range"	200
Elizabeth Stevens (widow)	"Catlin Plaines" tbc Thomas Stevens	80
	⅓ "Buckrow" tbc Thomas Stevens	16⅔
	⅓ "Dawsons Fortune" tbc Thomas Stevens	16⅔
	pt. "Compton" tbc Thomas Stevens	6⅓
	pt. "Edmonds Cove" tbc Thomas Stevens	58
William Stevens	"Catline Plaines"	160
	⅔ "Parkers & Enlargement"	100
~~Gabriel Sailes~~	~~"Rich Range"~~	~~300~~
	~~"Delph"~~	~~100~~
Ruth w/o William Skinner	pt. "Fairplay"	25
	"Mainsail"	50
Thomas Stevens	"Catline Plaines"	150
	⅔ "Buckrow"	33⅓
	⅔ "Dawsons Fortune"	33⅓
	pt. "Dudleys Choice"	100
	pt. "Straw Bridge"	163
	"Williams's Lott"	49
	"Edmonds Cove"	116
	"Compton"	108
	"Strawbridge"	100
	"Catlin Plains"	80
	⅓ "Buckrow"	16⅔
	⅓ "Dawsons Fortune"	16⅔
	"Compton"	6⅓
	"Edmonds Cove"	58
49:1757-8:53 ...		
Thomas Sherwood guardian to h/o Mary Davis	"Batchelors Part"	100
	"Hope Chance"	50
	"Knave Keep Out"	50
	"Parsonage"	100
	"Addition" – surveyed for (N) Davis	350

Thomas Sherriff	"Smiths Clifts"	94
	"Hasco Green"	50
Peter Shannahan	"Chance" – surveyed for (N) Rowe	100
Francis Stanton	pt. "Bantry"	100
John Dam Saunders	"Hamiltons Park"	137
Philemon Skinner	"Enlargement"	50
	"Skinners Point"	50
	"Skinners Addition"	23
	"Skinners Discovery"	70
Robert Spencer	"Bensons Enlargement"	80
	"Edwards Hopewell"	45
	"Mathew Circumvented"	14½
	pt. "Mathew Circumvented" – from Hugh Spencer	5
Benjamin Sylvester	"Johns Neck"	39
Thomas Sherwood	pt. "Fishing Bay"	12
	pt. "Cabin Neck, Porters Delight, & Porters Lott"	150
	pt. "Daniel & Mary"	375
	"Anketile"	40
49:1757-8:54 ...		
Charles Spencer	pt. "Fairplay"	25
	pt. "Jones's Progress"	35
	pt. "Enions Range"	96¾
	pt. "Mainsail"	48
Daniel Sherwood	"Anketile"	400
George Sprouse	"Cumberland" & "Chance"	157
	pt. "Heworth" & pt. "Cumberland"	50
Robert Sands	"Sands's Lott"	103
	"Chance" – surveyed for <n/g>	25
Sarah Spencer	"Bensons Enlargement"	28½
	"Sarahs Garden"	13
	"Chance" – surveyed for (N) Eliot	183
George Sprouse, Jr.	"Lowes Rambles" – for h/o (N) Ardery	200
Joseph Spencer	"Enions Range"	49
Thomas Smith (schoolmaster)	"Grafton Manor" a/s "Goose Neck"	100
George Sexton	"Woolf Pitt Ridge"	50
	"Turners Discovery"	30

Christopher Spry	pt. "Partnership"	54
	"Maxwell Moore"	150
49:1757-8:55 ...		
w/o Edward Starkey	"Bite the Biter"	35
Hugh Spencer	"Mathew Circumvented"	145
	pt. "Maidens Point" – from Ann Spencer	5
John Sylvester	"Horse Point"	21
Robert Stonestreet	"Tilberry"	376
Birkhead Sharp	"Hier Dier Lloyd"	100
	"Rattle Snake Point"	150
	"Little Bristol"	320
	pt. "Conjunction"	25
	"Sharps Addition"	24
	pt. "Enclosure", pt. "Eason's Lott", "Eason's Neck" & "Fancy"	250
William Sharpe	pt. "Inclosure", pt. "Eason's Neck", pt. "Eason's Lot", & "Fancy"	250
Ann Sharpe	"Moorefields"	100
	"Adventure"	100
Elizabeth Skinner	"Clay's Hope"	200
49:1757-8:56 ...		
Thomas Sherwood s/o Edward Man Sherwood	"Killam" a/s "Kiltam"	229
Daniel Sherwood, Jr.	pt. "Exchange"	100
	"Alembys Fields"	124¾
	"Alembys Fields Addition"	7½
Nicholas Spencer	"Bensons Enlargement" – for (N) Gorsuch	114½
	pt. "Fox Harbour", pt. "Maiden Point", & pt. "Bensons Enlargement"	157
John Small	"Somerly"	200
Andrew Skinner	"Tanners Choice"	512⅓
49:1757-8:57 ...		
Trustram Thomas (cnp)	pt. "Roadley"	200
	"Double Ridge"	280
	"Killingsworth"	50
	pt. "Sutton" & pt. "Sutton Addition"	278
	"Hardship" & pt. "Partnership"	

	"Thief Keep Out"	38
William Thomas	pt. "Anderton"	500
	"Anderton's Addition"	100
	pt. "Cottingham"	190
	pt. "Cottingham" – for his wife	125
	pt. "Judith's Garden"	63
	pt. "Tilghman's Fortune" – for your wife	386
	pt. "Heworth" & pt. "Desire"	64
James Tilghman	pt. "Fairlough"	250
	"Edmonds Range"	400
	"Addition"	100
	"Sharps Chance"	221
	"Abrams Lott"	100
	"Dixons Outlett"	50
	"Taulsey Meadows"	50½
	"Bryans Lott"	50
	pt. "Finnys Harmitage" – from h/o (N) Carter	66⅓
George Thomson	"Smith's Clifts"	454
	"Smith's Clifts" – more by name of "Mill Land"	12
William Tripp	⅓ "Edmonton"	100
	"Champenhams Addition"	16⅔
	⅓ "Leith"	13⅓
	"Champenham" & ⅓ "Bendon"	183⅓
	"Tod Upon Dervan" – ⅓ of 220 a.	73
	"Turners Point"	204
	"Skillingtons Hope"	20
49:1757-8:58 ...		
John Tomlinson	pt. "Rockliff"	50
Richard Turbett	"Bless Land" & "Bags Marsh"	460
William Troth	pt. "Acton"	294
	pt. "Darlington"	8
	"Bonnington"	38
John Thomas	"Winkleton"	185
	"Mitchells Hall"	200
Jonathan Taylor	pt. "Kingstown"	100

w/o Joseph Turner	"Johns Hill"	180
	"Turners Discovery"	92¾
Abner Turner	"John's Hill"	90
	"Hasco Green"	160
Mathew Tilghman	"Wells's Outlett"	50
	"Chance"	25
	"Bradford"	62
	"Union"	611
	"Coopers Lott"	25½
	"Rich Neck"	577
	"Three Necks"	165
	pt. "Union"	50
	"Choptank Island"	1468
49:1757-8:59 ...		
William Tilghman	"Henrietta Maria's Purchase"	412
	"Cucort Road"	138
Thomas Theobalds	"Theobalds Addition"	20
	"Sheep Head Point"	50
John Thornton	"Moorsfields Addition"	65
James & Edward Tilghman	"Elizabeths Venture"	1192
William Taylor	"Middle Spring"	25
	"Turkey Neck"	243
	"Turkey Neck Addition"	35
Mary Tripp	½ "Widows Choice" a/s "Widows Lott"	320
	"Hamiltons Park"	131½
	"Buckingham & Kelding"	196½
Visitors of the County School	"Tilghmans Fortune"	100
Daniel Vinton	"Edwards Hopewell"	55
49:1757-8:60 ...		
Edward Vickers	"Piccadilly"	150½
49:1757-8:61 ...		
Sarah Webb	"Roadley"	150
John Watts	"Hamiltons Neck"	168
James Woolcoat	pt. "Canterbury Manor"	210
James Wrightson (cnp)	"Lurkey"	250
	"Wrightsons Addition"	83

	"Huntington"	130
Thomas Winchester	½ "Widows Choice"	320
	"Braintree"	500
	"Braintree" – more by the name of "Braintree"	60
	"Marlins Folly"	50
	"Marlins Chance"	50
	"Braintree Addition"	10
	"Marlins Neglect"	57
	"Spring Close"	100
William Willson	"Middle Spring"	150
	"Williams Lott"	190
	pt. "Kinsbery"	70
John Wallace (KE)	"Long Point"	25
	"Long Neck"	90
	~~pt. "Kingsbery"~~ "Benjamins Lott"	50
49:1757-8:62 ...		
William Weaver	"Nobles Chance"	82
Rev. Philip Walker	"Upper Range"	56
	"Jordans Hill"	157
Henry White	"Goldsborough"	113
	pt. "Willenbro" & "Gurlinton"	93
	"Gurlington"	75
John Wiles	"Bently Hay"	33⅓
Samuel Wright	"Harris's Range"	400
William White	pt. "Sutton Grange"	280
w/o John Walker	pt. "Jamaica"	92
Peter Webb	"Poor Hill"	37
John Watts, Jr.	pt. "Hamiltons Neck"	66
49:1757-8:63 ...		
James Willson	"Middle Spring"	50
	"White Oak Swamp"	100
George Willson	pt. "Sybland", pt. "Dudleys Choice", & pt. "Maxwell"	162
	"Sybland" & "Sybland Addition"	108

Mr. Robert Goldsborough	pt. "Good Chance"	16⅔
	pt. "Newnams Thickett"	16⅔
	pt. "Gore"	56⅔
49:1757-8:64 Lands since settlement		
h/o John Shaw	"Halls Neck"	150
James Dudly	pt. "Dudly Demeans"	115
49:1757-8:<unnumbered> Certification		

www.ingramcontent.com/pod-product-compliance
Lightning Source LLC
Chambersburg PA
CBHW060132280326
41932CB00012B/1498